The Politics of Caribbean
Cyberculture

The Politics of Caribbean Cyberculture

Curwen Best

First published in 2008 by
PALGRAVE MACMILLAN™
175 Fifth Avenue, New York, N.Y. 10010 and
Houndmills, Basingstoke, Hampshire, England RG21 6XS.
Companies and representatives throughout the world.
PALGRAVE MACMILLAN is the global academic imprint of the Palgrave Macmillan division of St. Martin's Press, LLC and of Palgrave Macmillan Ltd. Macmillan® is a registered trademark in the United States, United Kingdom and other countries. Palgrave is a registered trademark in the European Union and other countries.

ISBN-13: 978-0-230-60376-9
ISBN-10: 0-230-60376-9

Library of Congress Cataloging-in-Publication Data

Best, Curwen, 1965–
  The politics of Caribbean cyberculture / by Curwen Best.
      p. cm.
  Includes bibliographical references and index.
  ISBN 0-230-60376-9
  1. Caribbean Area—Civilization—21st century. 2. Popular culture—Caribbean Area. 3. Computers—Social aspects—Caribbean Area. 4. Internet—Social aspects—Caribbean Area. I. Title.
  F1408.3.B45 2007
  306.0285'467809729—dc22   2007025112

A catalogue record of the book is available from the British Library.

Design by Scribe Inc.

First edition: February 2008

10 9 8 7 6 5 4 3 2 1

Printed in the United States of America.

Transferred to Digital Printing 2008

To my wife, Charmaine, and to our little son Christopher-Chars

Contents

Acknowledgments

To God for the strength and ability. To my wife, Charmaine, for her unending encouragement and support as we pushed to finish the manuscript before the appointed season. To my family, ever strong. To the publishers at Palgrave for their sensitivity and for believing in this work. To all those practitioners and professionals who contributed and provided insight. To all others who contributed in various ways. Again to my wife, for all her love, determination, inspiration, and spirit no other time more keenly offered as "when the morning dawns."

INTRODUCTION

Caribbean Cyberculture in the Age of the Machines

Clear and Present Virtual Realities

Caribbean culture, as we knew it traditionally, died in the decade of the 1990s. In the late twentieth century, the rise of the machines signaled the progression of a new set of relations within cultural, social, and economic activity. In the Caribbean, there is the tendency among some people, especially of the older generation, to use the term "machine" in reference to any form of leading-edge gadget or technology. My employment of the term draws from that source, but it also echoes the use of the term in western pop culture, in blockbuster film, as in the Schwarzenegger movie, *Terminator 3: Rise of the Machines*. But coterminous with the death of our traditional experiences with the world around us there was a rebirth of our cultural encounters. Caribbean culture has always had to adapt to the rapid changes taking place within the region, but also in the wider global context. Just before the decade of the 1990s the impending rise of the machines signaled the proliferation of robust digital apparatuses. This anticipated new ways of producing culture, for example, new ways of creating songs, videos, movies and new ways of participating in the global information matrix by way of communication devices like personal computers and mobile phones. Of course, in the 1980s digital technology and advanced research in communication and information systems paved the way for many post–twentieth century innovations.

By the late 1990s Caribbean societies could no longer be categorized as discrete cultural entities. While Caribbean politicians and governmental policies continued to vacillate and flounder over issues of Caribbean unification, while nations childishly squabbled over issues of aviation, maritime boundaries, trade, travel, bilateral arrangements and at times over personal matters, Caribbean cultural experience was being molded by a common source. The philosophy and practice of globalization and its technological imperatives encompassed the region in a way never before experienced.

While Caribbean societies experienced marked new ways of relating to each other (across and within national boundaries) and to the wider world, largely due to a changed cultural climate, much of the academic writing on social and cultural activity struggled to keep up.[1]

This is not a condemnation of academics writing about the Caribbean; academic freedom allows for a range of critical approaches, and the more traditional tried and true methods of cultural engagement are still very important. But there was a considerable lag between the lived experience of postdigital Caribbean society and its decidedly low-tech academic criticism. The phenomenal changes that engulfed Caribbean society made the attempts at catching up seem feeble.

In the domain of popular culture arts and expression there were significant shifts. In the domain of sports, the regional cricket team lost its place of prominence during the decade of the 1990s. This loss of place and face came about at a time when global sports were becoming highly commercialized and technologized as well. The field of play was now not only located in the actual arenas or ovals where the regional team played at home and abroad, but also within the media through which games were being relayed. The regional team, its administrators, and support services like journalists and commentators did not realize that the new arena of engagement and struggle was also shifting to other domains, so that new leading technology drove the sporting world. The game was therefore being waged through the international press and a range of other sites.

Leading cricketing and other sporting nations symbolically and actually took greater control of sports administration. But, more significantly here, they took control of the other major mediums by which sports like cricket and its culture was being shaped and disseminated. The West Indies team was powerless for the most part. Part of its powerlessness had to do with a failure of its administrators and its support institutions to bring this reality to the fore and to provide a set of strategies by which the new reality could be confronted. The regional soccer teams also suffered because of financial and strategic weaknesses.

Communications networks and technologies became even more entrenched after 2000. Satellite television and FM radio, as well as digital radio, became more popular. XM (subscription satellite-delivered wireless radio), though only talked about in the region in the mid-2000s,[2] was on the horizon. The presence of streaming audio and video via the World Wide Web gave audiences greater access to other regional stations, but more so to stations in the Western world. By 2005, the Internet had become an extremely popular social and commercial platform within the region. Though some people had resisted the lure of such wonders, it was clear that by the end of the first decade of the twenty-first century there would be relatively few citizens outside the digital matrix.

This book takes all these and other developments into account. It is intended to examine the impact and imprint of new leading technology on a range of popular expressions within the region. But its focus is also outside the region, because it is intended to discover the ways in which some external mediums have gone about projecting, representing, simulating, and creating Caribbean cultural experience. The chapters are therefore focused on some specific issues to do with core expressions, with popular genres and phenomena, music, film, video, sports, and also everyday experience. What therefore connects these expressions is their mediation by technology. Inasmuch as this work contends that Caribbean culture has gone wireless, virtual, and simulated, it is intended to examine this process.

Strategic Space

The computer had entered into Caribbean society with increasing numbers in the early twenty-first century. It was introduced into the culturescape through a number of routes. The computer was, of course, anticipated by other creations and technological monoliths. The calculator and the digital watch were antecedents to the dedicated computer and its later clones like the laptop, the palm top and roving mobile phones. The computer itself rode on a crest of hype carried over from the Walkman, the CD, and the CD player, and before them the portable boom box and portable radio. Caribbean musicians were a special grouping. These were probably at the forefront of the digital and early computer wave. Musicians were some of the first individuals to talk about computers and also to handle and manipulate them. Digital synthesizers and drum machines drove the evolution of Caribbean music culture. The 1980s gave birth and full bloom to new music styles like dancehall and soca fusion. Musicians knew about the early computers like the Commodore 64.

Like people elsewhere, Caribbean society also beheld the power of future technology through the popular media. Television and film played a significant role in projecting the relations that humans can share with technology. A lot has been written about the social and cultural meanings inscribed, treated, and expressed in Hollywood and Western programs and films like *Star Trek, Buck Rodgers, Space 1999, Star Wars,* and other franchises that project and anticipate a world driven by technology. Critics have analyzed these films from a number of perspectives. But there has hardly been a consideration of the meanings and implications of these films for Caribbean society and Caribbean culture.

Whereas many individuals have theorized about technological nonaccess in negative terms (applying such notions as the "digital divide"), another reality might very well be that some subjects have used the lapse in time between when an innovation is created and when it becomes widely available to strategize their response to the technologies. The flip side to the notion of the digital divide is therefore the formation of strategic space. It is this strategic space that opens up an area and arena of knowledge about evolving technologies. If the technological matrix engulfs the entire world by means of overarching technologies, then regions like the Caribbean have a strategic moment of time and space within which they can formulate real and virtual responses.

The Matricks

The Internet has its origin in the military. Its development can be traced back to the desire to construct a network that would decentralize communications in the event of a large-scale attack and nuclear war. The intention of creating such a network led to the formation of research centers within governmental institutions in the West, as well as within education research centers. The Internet as it has evolved today is not the precise creation that the military and political strategists had in mind. By the early 1990s, it had become a technological, commercial, and cultural phenomenon whose impact altered patterns of life and transformed global and cultural relations. Its commercial and cultural evolution was not anticipated in the earlier conceptualizations of the Web. The World Wide Web has continued to mutate in ways unforeseen. At the end of the first decade of the twenty-first century, the digital matrix was no less volatile. It has effectively played tricks with some human expectations.

The digital divide, which has to do with unequal access to technology by less privileged groups, is in fact vital to an understanding of the politics of technological access and techno-cultural dispersal. The digital divide has implications for disadvantaged groupings such as women and racial minorities. It also has implications within such categories as ethnicity, class, social grouping, education, and so on. In this work, though, I am much more concerned with the digital divide as it relates to so-called leading Western nations and less-well-regarded nations. The Caribbean becomes a point of central focus. I am concerned not merely with access to technology but also with control and control of access. I am concerned with the ways in which this state of affairs impacts the region both directly and indirectly. This book does not conceal the view that there are inherent structures and systems at work within the new and emerging sphere of global cultural engineering. By this I refer to the active process of altering and transforming human behaviors by way of popular technologies. Here I also suggest that there are potentially deeper hidden strategies than most politically correct cultural discourses tend to mention. Is it possible that there are deliberate strategies set in motion to insure the continued hierarchical ranking of nations, cultures, and civilizations? Is it also possible that the motive behind the quest to own and govern new technologies reflects the desire to maintain global and individual superiority? Whereas some cultural critics would see power, or economics, or such categories as xenophobia, race, nation, and identity as the driving principle of all human activity, it is possible that deeper underlying motives exist. Some of the above terms have become playful tropes. They are the tools of the trade of current academic discourse, especially relating to the Caribbean. These terms are often encumbered with the pleasures and baggage of intellectualization. Maybe a reading that acknowledges these terms, but that from time to time goes around and behind the jargon of academic theory to discover things about cultural practice, can be equally rewarding. In the final analysis, all readings of culture are important. But each age requires a mix of old and new approaches and a mix of emphases on old and emerging fields of human activity. Because the world that we know is one that increasingly belongs to us, to others, and to our machines, our continued survival requires that explorers of all professions enter the emerging matrix in order to make sense of the future and of the now. In spite of the Caribbean region's relative timidity in the age of the machines, few cultural critics have undertaken the task of peering into the opaque yet transparent realm that is the matrix—or, as I call it here, the matricks. At the cusp of human experience, we cannot ignore issues to do with technology and with life itself, *its* meaning, its beginning, the end, human destiny, and God. Do the end of the real and the battle for technological control anticipate a virtual apocalypse, a cultural end time? Where are peripheral territories situated in this state of affairs?

CHAPTER 1

Discourse on Technology:
Go Search, Go Figure

The evolution of the World Wide Web as a tool for mass consumption by the mid-1990s created a new set of conditions and situations for artists and writers, who prior to then were actively contending for space in other media like newspapers, magazines, journals, radio, and television. The Internet promised to create a harmonization of several of the older mediums of communication. It promised and continues to work at the task of creating and redefining a virtual and real world of experience.

It is often suggested by cultural and political commentators that some peoples of the world are further removed from leading-edge digital technology than others. This is indeed the case. Some nonindustrialized societies are therefore further removed from electronic and new wave gadgetry than their counterparts in the so-called industrialized world. Proponents of the digital divide hypothesis therefore argue for equal access. The question of access is in many respects central to debates about competitiveness in the still-emerging world of real and virtual relations. But to conceptualize the debate concerning cultural power relations, technology, and development only in terms of access to hardware and software is limiting. Were huge stacks of new technological innovations shipped to all the peoples of the world, there would still be many of the problems that we face with respect to interregional and international relations. Questions of know-how, application, and tweaking are important within the dynamic of location, technology, and power relations. But of even greater significance, I believe, are the issues of "proximity to technology," and the meaning of technology for those people who behold it. I will explore "proximity to technology" a little later on in this book, but for now it can be said to refer to the comparative relationship that different sets of people share with what is termed "technology." This work recognizes that there are inequalities among different strata of peoples in all societies concerning the access to new digital technology. That is, in every society there are some people who have greater access due to certain conditions, whether economic wealth, social standing, education, gender, political affiliation, or something else. As the digital and postdigital revolution has evolved, however, certain patterns of control and ownership of technologies and their conceptualization have emerged. For instance, it is a fact that the United States has greater control of the Internet itself (and by extension what the Internet means) than any other single nation. It is this fact that might cause us to contemplate the possibility that the United States wields greater power in fashioning and defining the Internet than does the entire Caribbean region. The United States is therefore in a position of greater control, a position of enhanced proximity to the Internet, with the potential of asserting greater influence than, say, the Caribbean region. The power that the United States holds in this age of the machines has as much to do with the United States's military and economic might as it has to do with the cultural authority that the nation has built up in the Western world regarding itself and what is the stuff of leading edge technology. It is not only the United States's per capita access to technologies like, say, the Internet that helps to locate their proximity to technology, but it is also the system of cultural authority and ownership that positions the nation where it is globally. The United States's entertainment and cultural sectors have helped to reinforce the perception that the nation's claim to ownership and control of robust technologies is justified.

Some societies share a closer more intimate relationship with new electronic and digital technologies than others. Some important questions that arise in this process have to do with how people respond to new technologies. How do they perceive of this? What do they know of the technology's creation, or its components, function, functionalities, use, and potential abuse, its strengths, failings, and flaws, its creators, its built-in codes, rules, and programming, or its attendant and inherent ideology? All in all, these are hard questions. People cannot be expected to know the finest of details about gadgets. We all know that even in industrialized societies many people use technologies without being really close to them in the sense that I mean here. The point I am coming to is that an awareness about, interest in, and inquiry into the meaning of new technologies can also signify the closeness or proximity between that technology and its user. I am here speaking of proximity in terms of physical and non-physical location. Proximity might relate globally to nations in the race for dominance, but it also has microcosmic significance with respect to the individual's relationship to machines. Proximity is also therefore psychological, attitudinal, conceptual, virtual, and real. This is to suggest that a people's experience with new technologies is very often also (and sometimes foremost) that people's experience with *notions* of these new technologies. In the Caribbean, as in other regions of the world, new technological innovations often first exist as creations within or of the popular and other media, and then later as the "real" thing itself, once it is shipped to the user. For example, the palmtop computer and other PDAs (personal digital assistants) first existed in the consciousness of people through popular construction via television and film. Cartoons like *Dick Tracy*, shows like *Star Trek, Space 1999*, and *Star Wars* presented visions of handheld devices that acted as extensions of the body. These shows were popular in the 1970s and 1980s, but their vision came into partial fulfillment only in the first decade of the twenty-first century. Leading communications companies and entertainment franchises have placed increasing efforts into the expansion of handheld workstations that are capable of multiple tasks. Many consumers worldwide have supported this new trend and lifestyle through the purchasing of these gadgets. The salability of these new wares is a sign of the times. It reflects the marketing thrust within digital technology sectors. But the embracing of these new creations is also for some consumers a fulfillment of their own visions about technology. The embracing of sleek new creations is an act of giving substance and presence to lifelong visions. The current and future financial prosperity garnered by entertainment and communications entities is therefore rooted in the past as much as in the present and the future.

Notions of technology therefore often exist prior to and then in tandem with the very technology itself. This might appear to be an obvious point, especially when you think of how prototyping drives some industries like the automotive and military. Many people will know of how the United States and the Soviet Union have fought for military supremacy by way of creating new war machines. But the arms race was also accompanied by a less-well-known phenomenon of battling in the future. When people see such modern wonders as the United States's F22 Raptor fighter aircraft or Russia's Ka-50 Black Shark attack helicopter, they hardly think of these as having a life prior to their physical construction. But submerged beneath the hardware and the software that controls these machines are the ideas, concepts and the prototypes that first emerged. As the real catches up with its earlier vision, they can merge one into the other, or they can remain as distinct experiences. Very often they remain as distinct, because there are always ongoing projections of technology as time passes in the real world. This dynamic relationship characterizes the critical matrix of experience and application that defines the concept of proximity to technology. But the simultaneity of the real and *its* vision is critical to this process. The digital world of the present is often marked by the intersection of real and virtual experience. This is what makes our present lives so exciting.

The 2005 release of the final (?) installment in the *Star Wars* saga encapsulates the kinds of issues that our future societies will always confront. The prequel's release marked the placing of a missing piece in the puzzle of how and why Anakin Skywalker turned to the dark side of the force. The original or first *Star Wars* had begun where this final instalment ends. Though some movie pundits felt the film *Revenge of the Sith* would not do exceptionally well, because its characters had already been predestined since the original *Star Wars* in 1977, the 2005 release shattered many box office records. The box office success hinged on the muscle of the franchise, on the marketing thrust, and on the fact that the U.S. box office was bound to gain resuscitation after some months of sagging sales in 2005. But the box office success of the 2005 *Revenge of the Sith* also had to do with a set of complex factors outside of purely economic forces. The novelty of prefiguring and reconfiguring *Star Wars* some twenty-eight years after the original release must have been a significant contributor to the box office behemoth. Of further significance is the fact that *Sith's* reconnection with the past is rendered by way of a new set of technological processes. The 2005 release does not return to the late 1970s technology to tell the story. If it had done so, that would have been a triumph for sequential linear actuality. But instead, people who flocked to see the film were also flocking to see the new technology at work, to behold how far technology had advanced. They were able to observe the limitations of late-1970s technology and to contemplate what post-twentieth century technology could have brought to the original *Star Wars*. Silently they also wondered about the making of *Revenge of the Sith* using late 1970s technology. All these questions were wrapped up with the box office saga.

Popular foreign media are responsible for constructing perceptions of new technologies like the Internet. Caribbean societies have been introduced to the Internet largely by way of popular media, through entertainment networks and companies. In Western pop culture, technology is represented as a frontier realm preserved for the leading minds and the leading nations as well. Western entertainment has glamorized technology in many respects, thus creating for viewers even further removed from the digital technology–creation hub a substitute image of the real technology. Caribbean societies have therefore had to contend with these substitutes and have come to experience the same technology in a different way in the real world of use and manipulation. Caribbean society up to the present continues to grapple with working out the relationship between the facsimile and the real. It struggles to negotiate the relationship between technologies and notions of these technologies.

In the article "Debunking the Digital Divide,"[1] Robert J. Samuelson questions the assumption that there is a digital divide. He asks if there isn't indeed greater access by all due to the falling price and distribution of computers. The Fundación Acceso (or Access Foundation), through Ricardo Gomez in the article "The Internet Why and What For?" (Gomez, writing for Costa Rica after consultation with partners in Latin America and the Caribbean), calls attention to the digital divide and the deeply rooted inequalities of modern societies.[2] His findings advocate the need for connectivity and equitable access, and he urges that more in-depth research be done at the level of public policy, among other areas. This and similar documents remind us of the political issues that are also at play when we use the World Wide Web. Economic growth, access to technology, and wealth are considered to be related and correlating issues. In his article "Digital Divide, Economic Growth and Poverty Reduction," Lester Henry holds the view that governments in the Caribbean have recognized the importance of information communications technology (ICT).[3] This might be true, but it could also be suggested that this recognition has not translated fast enough into action because regional governments have tended to lag way behind private organizations and individual citizens with respect to technology use, application, and fashioning. Given the enhanced role played by technology in the twenty-first century Caribbean, the question of how technology is perceived, implemented, utilized, applied, and appropriated is crucial to an understanding of how society, culture, and state-of-the-art begin to "reason together" in the digital dispensation.

In his paper "Technologies of the Self: Foucault and Internet Discourse," Alan Aycock calls attention to the dichotomous role and symbolism of the Internet, which both represents a vision of freedom and also presages a state of "global surveillance and personal alienation."[4] These extremes are also reflected through the popular media. The Western mainstream film industry has perpetuated these extremes. Movies like *The Net* and robust cartoons like *Justice League* and *Appleseed* have presented technology as both a modern-day marvel and a duplicitous tool of the apocalypse. The sensationalist hype of popular entertainment has hardly explored the more complex process whereby "technology" and culture navigate a range of intimate and intricate relationships across cultures.

Yes, it is true that blockbuster flicks like *Transformers, I-Robot, Minority Report, The Lord of the Rings*, and *Chronicles of Riddick* provide substance for contemplation, but then again, this vision is filtered through the experiences within a fixed set of cultural and technological realities.

Aycock's article calls attention to self fashioning, reminding the reader that fashions may both be imposed and freely chosen. This is a significant point. But while his article does tend to promote the two extremes, the "true-true" reality might very well be that cultures and behaviors are at one and the same time being freely constructed as they are also being imposed. Because of this reality it is even more difficult to theorize the resultant outcomes concerning the use and impact of the Internet in Caribbean society. It is perhaps too early in the day to determine the relative presence of freedom and surveillance as technology comes into play with Caribbean culture. After all, it can be argued that the experience with virtual media is still evolving in the early stages by the first decade of the twenty-first century.

Another point of importance here is that Caribbean societies have always reacted cautiously to new technologies. I will again return to this issue when I discuss Caribbean representations and simulation in sports and big-budget films in the final two chapters. But the point must be made here that Caribbean society has on the one hand stood in wonder at new technologies like the Internet while also exhibiting suspicions about its inherent, underlying objectives and attendant politics. This technology was created in scientific labs far away. As with other societies, the new technology was imported into the Caribbean region for individual and collective use. Whereas in the early 1990s it was perceived as a futuristic possibility, by the mid-2000s it was being more widely embraced as a developmental necessity.

Over the decades, Caribbean society has constantly had to rely on its own fluidity and dynamism. Caribbean art forms and genres have consistently come under challenge on account of internal and external factors. External factors have occasionally threatened the demise of traditional phenomena, but they have also resulted in the forging of new and renewed phenomena. Caribbean artists have themselves redefined their fields of practice, whether music, drama, fiction, or painting, as a result of, or as a response to, changing conditions. In the 1970s, when the threat to vinyl recordings was posed by the Phillips cassette revolution, Caribbean artists had to reconsider their art forms in light of the mass acquiring of cassette players in homes. This development gave birth to new ways of conceptualizing, performing, constructing, and packaging music. There was therefore every reason to believe that the society would respond creatively to post-2000 innovations. At least some members of the society would; others would not.

Internet and Democracy

The Internet holds out a promise of being a democratic medium of communication. It proposes to be a more liberating medium than radio, television, or film. Aston Cooke makes this point in his short essay "Caribbean Cultural Identity on the Internet."[5] The Internet holds out this hope in spite of the antitrust debates between Microsoft and the U.S. government, and between Microsoft and the European Commission, and the charges that Microsoft has engineered its continued dominance of consumer PC space. This debate has swung to and fro. It is destined to go on into the future. In December of 2004, the European Court of First Instance in Luxembourg ruled that the penalties enforced on Microsoft earlier that year would stay. Regardless of who is right and wrong in this matter, such confrontations alert us to the politics embedded within the very makeup of digital and new-ware technology.

Every act of technology is encoded. We become implicated in the incessant politics of technology with every task we perform through this technology. The act of purchasing the technology itself is loaded with implications. As we use cutting-edge gadgetry, we become further implicated. There are potential attendant politics at play whenever we select one browser over another (Internet Explorer or Netscape or Firefox), one word processor over another (Microsoft Word or Corel Wordperfect), or one audio-video MP3 player over another (RealNetwork's Realplayer, Microsoft's MediaPlayer, or Apple's Quicktime). Most people take this for granted, but the realization that these competing platforms are engaged in ongoing struggle reflects the volatility of the digital arena, as well as the highly contentious realm within which consumers and users conduct their official and unofficial business. But day-to-day transactions by the public on the Internet hardly take notice of the underlying system of confrontation that threatens to both destroy and reinvent the World Wide Web and its attendant technologies. Maybe if they did, we would be less confident about the things we take for granted, such as sending e-mails or sharing photos. Users of new technology have therefore suspended their fear of the underlying complexities of the digital matrix, while others couldn't give a care about all that. Most people are satisfied to make full use of what technology offers for consumption and function at the surface reality, at the final stage of use. They leave the deeper stuff to the geeks and doubters. It is perhaps only when hackers and viruses and pop-ups intervene into and infiltrate the consumer's space that we are forced to behold and scream in anger at these encroachments into our space of imagined comfort. When the technology malfunctions, therefore, we are driven to the underworld of complex thoughts about the machine and how and why and who and wherefore. Caribbean consumers and users, like others worldwide, have already started to live in the problematic space, somewhere between tech heaven and its underworld.

Search Engines

Search engines are set up on the basis of providing streamlined conduits of connectivity to users. Because the number of hyperlinks and interconnected sites is often infinite in cyberspace, there is some degree of open-endedness to them. This technological grandeur presents the possibility of virtual endless navigational play—as when the navigator through inquiry navigates his or her way through, above, below, within, and without interrelated yet distinct pages of information. There is therefore something postmodernist about this pleasurable, and at times leisureable, construction and about the activity that it engenders. But this pleasurable leisure does often mask the hidden codes that lurk somewhere beneath the cursor (cursory?) play of unsuspecting users.

Search engines are generally believed to present us with choices through a more-or-less scientific process of site rankings whenever we enter a request. These are perhaps just as scientific as the kind of ranking that Amazon.com does for many of the books in its stock, where a ranking of one is the best and over 3 million represents stagnation in sales and turnover.[6] But search engines are not without bias. They are, after all, set up on the basis of presenting a hierarchy of sites. The hierarchical ranking of outcomes points to the existence of embedded cyber schemes. These cyber schemes exist on the basis of preexisting truths and myths in the real world. These truths and myths have infected the machines and hence control the ranking of one site over another. Over time the virtual matrix also upholds the truths and myths fed into it by dominant ideologies. But grand cyber schemes can be challenged and altered over time, especially given the instability of the World Wide Web. The knowledge that search engines (especially Web crawlers) base their ranking on algorithms, location, and frequency of key words, and that some Web site creators boost their ranking through "spamming" of key words, is instructive.[7] This reminds us that there are internal processes in operation on the Web and that these processes are linked to external actions and preexisting concerns and debates. Discussion of Caribbean culture on the Internet represents a new sphere of discourse, but it also represents an extension on to a number of extant discussions about culture, technology, representation, projection, and simulation.

Go Search, Go Figure

Search engines are more integral to an analysis of Caribbean culture than we might imagine. It is often to these sites of knowledge that most navigators turn when in need of guidance, information, and closure as well. Such conceptions as "Caribbean culture," therefore, do not necessarily get their major formation through hard copy texts and academic treatises like this book. The Online Writing lab at Purdue University is at pains to remind users that books and other more traditional media are vital for information gathering. The British Council's article of Autumn 2001 draws attention to the increasing importance of the Internet and the World Wide Web as a source of information.[8] It is good and necessary to produce books of this kind that emanate from the "center" of the culture; but where is the new frontier? It is at the new frontier that such phenomena as "Caribbean culture" (and "Caribbean society" and similar notions) are being not only shaped and refashioned, but also altered, changed, upstaged, and reconfigured. A simple yet significant act of asking a harmless question about, say, what the CSME[9] is can begin to tell us some critical things about the CSME itself and about who or what fashions it online, who are the loudest voices in the virtual discursive domain, and what are the emerging distinctive features of the Caribbean Single Market and Economy. But this question can also reveal information about the very instrument that processes the culture that it simulates.

Google is the search engine around which much of the discussion centers here. This is not an examination of this search engine itself. Rather, this engine is chosen primarily because many users employ it. It is known for its speed, functionality, and style. (I imagine readers of this work will themselves discuss my selection of this search engine.) A search (around mid-2004) for "Caribbean culture" presents a list of hierarchical sites headed by Caribe.com, controlled by a world traveler and writer who has actually met former U.S. presidents Clinton and Bush. Other noted controllers are the Smithsonian Institute; an educational institute in Buffalo, New York; and the Southeast Archeological Center in the United States. Similar searches for "Caribbean Music" lead to diffuse sites of ownership and control. These are: Caribbeanmusic.com, which appears to come out of Maryland; Afromix.com, which seems to emanate from Africa;

Caribbeanmusicexpo.com; and the Trinidadian Rhyners.com, an online music store.

A similar search for "reggae" leads to Niceup.com. Operating through sponsors in the United States, its front page displays the photo of its Caucasian owner. Ranked second is Reggaeweb.com, whose searches are driven by Amazon.com. Another leading site, Reggaesource.com proudly displays New York's top thirty singles chart and top fifteen CD chart. All in all, this initial search reveals the extent to which aspects of Caribbean popular culture are driven by market forces and by external agencies, or at least by agencies working outside of the traditional center that has developed the cultural expressions and nurtured them onto the regional and international stage. Perhaps it can be argued that the hierarchical ranking and external control of a music form like reggae are not important concerns, really, because it must be remembered that Caribbean people are now cosmopolitan and transnational, and they have sought new ways of engaging their culture and talents within the global market place. This is a compelling argument. Indeed, it must be acknowledged too that the fact of Web site ownership does not determine how reggae culture operates on the ground and how it is being driven from the bottom. After all, the Internet is not a standalone medium. It exists in tandem with other media and modes of dissemination. Any conceptual or theoretical formulation about Caribbean cyberculture must be cognizant of the fact that the real and virtual spheres are not independent of each other. An understanding of Caribbean cyberculture and cyber reality cannot therefore be formulated independent of knowledge about the society that it simulates.

Some contemporary positions would contend that ownership is not important; they would argue that inasmuch as regional products get out there in the international realm, then Caribbean culture manages to intervene into world culture and thereby responds to the culture-information-communication imbalance that characterizes the relationship between regions like the Caribbean and industrialized metropolises. These are crucial points to remember. But we must also be aware of the ways in which Caribbean labor, culture, and place have been appropriated or exploited in the past, whether through institutionalized slavery or through more recent experiences as with the battle for the patent rights of the steel pan. This history must in some measure influence the way critics continue to approach questions of Caribbean culture in the clear and present context of cyberculture and the digital dispensation.

If there are misgivings about the equitableness of new creations and gadgets, then these feelings of mistrust will continue until, say, searches for culture-specific phenomena located in the industrial centers also justly reflect the impact of other peoples on the creation of those phenomena. Arguably the low ranking of Caribbean based sites on searches relating to nonindigenous Caribbean phenomena might reflect the attention Caribbean sites give to external forms. But it might also partially reflect the imbalance built into contemporary technology. Technology does not begin from a position of innocence or ignorance or neutrality. Technology is always infected with the raw data of cultural experience, location, and power.

Search engines can act as gateways or as gatekeepers, but finally, users of the Internet do not have to go through search engines. Users can go directly to specific sites once they are out there and addresses are known. It is this kind of flexibility built into the Internet that assigns it its fluidity. In many respects, the extent of one's presence on the Internet is largely dependent on one's use of the facility itself. Some Caribbean cultural agencies and users of the Internet are aware of this, and over the past few years they have searched for avenues of circumventing the Web's controlling principles. Whereas large international institutions and agencies are some of the highest-ranking disseminators and controllers of discourse about Caribbean culture, at the micro level of the individual artist there is personalized, constructive, discursive space where the individual artist breathes his or her own virtual life into existence. Many Caribbean popular artists and local institutions now host their own Web sites, but many more of them are being fashioned on the Internet through subsidiary sources. These subsidiary sources are diverse and varied, and they thrive on the need to become popular and to make money through the sale of products, whether directly online, or through more traditional retail outlets.

It would be impossible to examine most of the sites that present and represent Caribbean cultural expression. It is, however, possible to examine features of selected sites that represent, construct, and simulate aspects of Caribbean society. Through this examination we can begin to describe the features that are attendant to cultural construction and simulation in the matrix of global digital culture. In this way, we begin to better understand how the World Wide Web interfaces with culture and what are the set of practices that come into play as Caribbean society gets up on the Internet.

CHAPTER 2

Internet and the Culture Wars: Caribbean Literary/Cultural Studies in Cyberspace

Literary-Cultural Studies

Caribbean cultural studies is a vast area of investigation. Arguably, it is defined by the body of work in a range of disciplines such as history, sociology, literature, linguistics, politics, and economics, but also in law and pure and applied science. Caribbean academics, as well as foreign academics writing about the Caribbean, have for a long time concerned themselves with the role that culture plays in the formation of Caribbean place and space. Cultural studies as an institutional practice was a much later phenomenon. When the Birmingham cultural studies program was being put to rest in the 1990s, the University of the West Indies' Cultural Studies Initiative was being set up. Of course, Caribbean academics were already participating in the global debates that define cultural studies. Caribbean studies scholars conducted discourses and published texts on a range of subjects, including folklore, customs and traditions, sports, communication and communications, literature and writing, music, leisure, politics, subcultures, deviance, the environment, built environment, religion, and more. Although there might be the temptation to suggest that Caribbean cultural studies developed in the shadow of Anglo-American cultural studies, a more careful examination might suggest that not all Caribbean thinkers were influenced heavily by the formal cultural studies movement in the West. Some people might indeed want to trace the lineage of Caribbean cultural studies through the work and influence of Stuart Hall and his involvement in the most celebrated case of institutionalized cultural studies, at the University of Birmingham's Center for Contemporary Cultural Studies. This is a significant tributary of Caribbean cultural studies, but most others would acknowledge that Caribbean commentators and academics were doing cultural studies even before the Birmingham center began to make its mark. Interdisciplinarity has been the hallmark of leading Caribbean cultural critics. Many of them were drawing from Euro-American thought, but they also drew freely from non-Western thinking and methodologies. The strength of Caribbean cultural studies is the practice by Caribbean critics of adapting theories, methodologies, and practices to suit the specific context of the region and its culture. The literary and related fields represent vital sites of expression within the arena of Caribbean cultural display.

Caribbean literature has long developed into an identifiable phenomenon and commercial product. The history of this phenomenon is an intriguing one, defined by a series of debates and confrontations between different players and stakeholders. Of course, Caribbean literature or West Indian literature, as it is also called, was not always seen as a legitimate entity. It has variously been subsumed under the banner of Commonwealth, third world, and, more recently, postcolonial literature. Each of these terms contains the seeds of contention, which have germinated within debates about autonomy and creative control of Caribbean art and culture. The Caribbean's literature is widely considered to have come into its own during the middle years of the twentieth century. Although many histories of Caribbean literature, especially its scribal traditions, trace its roots back to historiographic texts of expatriates in the region, to earlier writings in Africa and India, and to the writings of native peoples of the region, most participants in this tradition of Caribbean literature associate it with the rapid developments that took place leading up to the 1950s. Caribbean literature has always had to deal with a number of questions relating to its very identification and identity. Caribbean literature has struggled with questions of its relationship to other literary and cultural traditions. It has had to deal with questions of its relationship to the British tradition. It has had to deal with the relationship of authors to their native country and to foreign audiences. Caribbean literature has always preoccupied itself with publishing and publishers and marketing, and with the very mediums by which the works are disseminated.

Literary magazines throughout the region gave impetus to aspiring writers in the 1930s and 1940s. Many of the canonical writers of the Caribbean came to national recognition through journals like *Kyk-over-al*, *Focus*, *Bim*, *The Beacon*, and *The Outlook*. But even more significant than this phenomenon is the role that extra-regional publishing played in popularizing Caribbean writers and their works in the wider international market. Many of the leading figures of Caribbean literature were elevated to wider acclaim on account of migrating to metropolitan centers in Europe especially, but also in North America. Many of these writers went abroad to gain easier access to publishing houses and to the wider reading public that was abroad. But whereas there is a tendency to focus on the rewards earned by Caribbean writers, it must also be acknowledged that publishing interests also benefited from this movement. Currently the long list of classic Caribbean titles that still remain with major publishing houses attests to the ongoing benefits brought to these commercial houses by their involvement with Caribbean writers. Although cultural criticism has tended to foreground the role of major corporations in the development and exploitation of aspects of Caribbean popular culture, not as much attention has been paid to the nature of the relationship between Caribbean literature and major commercial interests. What must be considered in this era of technological advancement is the range of forces (old and new) that interplay within the arena of discourse inhabited by "literary" culture. Within the arena of the Internet there are numerous factors, forces, and issues at work. These critical hypertextual concerns are discernable to different degrees. A closer examination of the Internet in consort with a scrutiny of sites and links relating to Caribbean literature and culture can reveal many truths about the state and status of this very important area of Caribbean expression.

There are, of course, alternative ways of reading the development of Caribbean literature, other than by route of the literary tradition. The oral tradition is also a pathway of development in Caribbean literature. If the scribal tradition has gathered much of its impetus from the European tradition, then the oral tradition in the Caribbean has drawn heavily from Africa in particularly, but also from the cultures of descendents of indentured laborers from the East Indies. These oral and music traditions are now regarded as major strains in the creation of Caribbean literature. In fact, the oral tradition is regarded as both an autonomous movement and a contributing strand within Caribbean literature. While I am aware of all that, I do not, however, concern myself with exploring the extended parameters of the scribal-oral dialectic. I am rather more concerned with the "literary-literary tradition" (as Kamau Brathwaite calls it) and with *its* intersection with oral artists who acknowledge and celebrate their association with the literary-literary tradition. This does not, however, exclude some discussion of others, but it does not go much further than the performance poets and creative artists like the Trinidadian Paul Keens-Douglas. In any case, other sections of this book deal more closely with more popular practitioners who operate largely outside the parameters that this chapter sets up.

The labeling of the Caribbean's output in literary culture studies is an important part of its historical development. In the 1960s, Caribbean literature was hardly widely acknowledged to be an autonomous category. Indeed, some of the earlier critical works that signaled the coming forth of an autonomous category were *The Islands In Between*, by Louis James (University of Kent at Canterbury), and *The West Indian Novel and its Background*, by Kenneth Ramchand's (University of West Indies St. Augustine).[1] But even throughout the 1970s the label of Commonwealth literature embraced the writings from the Anglophone Caribbean. Writings by Walcott, Lamming, Mais, and Mittelholzer, and company were referred to as West Indian, but larger umbrellas were still imposed. The Commonwealth grouping and its political influence perpetuated this label until the early 1980s, when the category of postcolonial literature and studies replaced the label of Commonwealth. Whereas the Commonwealth label was regarded as outmoded and politically incorrect by the end of the 1980s, its replacement at least was believed to contain a much more dynamic and engaging set of issues and politics. Whereas the Commonwealth banner suggested a harmonious state of affairs, postcolonial studies foregrounded matters to do with cultural difference, contestation, race, identity, power, nation, history, and language, among other concerns. Widely seen as a new set of approaches, postcolonial studies is regarded along with postmodernism and its accompanying poststructuralist methods to have helped save English studies. But if the Commonwealth label was an evident vestige of European expansionist politics, then the postcolonial banner contained covert first-world politics as well. Postcolonial studies still focused heavily on the European and colonial powers and their systems. Many of the so-called leading critics in postcolonial studies were attached to big Western institutions. The contribution of regional critics and writers in the trenches of experience has been subordinated to that of the heavyweights of the postcolonial canon. Caribbean critics, though visible in postcolonial debates, were still in real terms the support cast for other academics. Publishing houses like Routledge and influential wealthy university presses worked in consort with well-placed authors to produce edited works, essay collections, and anthologies that helped to establish the hierarchy within the critical and creative arms of postcolonial literature and postcolonial studies.

By the mid-2000s postcolonial studies had not translated itself into an actual active movement with stated and practiced political, economic, and cultural activities. It remained largely, at its center, a set of intellectual discourses, specialist language, and jargon celebrated by academics who in some instances were less concerned with the primary stuff of the book or the living text or performance than they were with the pleasures of language and debate. Caribbean literary studies certainly entered into the postcolonial arena, though not all academics celebrated its presence. For some academics the jargon was off putting, while some others felt that postcolonial studies was a distraction from the attention needed to be paid to other ways of confronting reality in the late-twentieth-century and early-twenty-first-century Caribbean.

Now that the energy has gone out of postcolonial studies, a wider showing of critics and critical debates is anticipated. Caribbean and anti-colonial cultural studies has set out in search of some new avenue or arena. Publishers are very aware of this and are more open to new debates (even if it was harder to get academic books on Caribbean studies published in the late 2000s). Publishers have been more discriminating partly because they know that when the new trend within literary and cultural studies breaks again, they will be major beneficiaries. Caribbean creative and critical writing has therefore always operated in an arena of conflict and competition. Although this point is not widely espoused within the realm of academic debate, the living reality is that there are numerous players who are actively jostling for position within the arena of Caribbean literary and cultural studies. The advent of the Internet brings this to the fore in a much more stark way.

Caribbean literary scholarship has from time to time grappled with the importance of Caribbean place and space in the formation of Caribbean sensibilities and aesthetics. The identification of Caribbean works and artists has been contested on the grounds that a Caribbean work should reflect some awareness or foundation within its geographical place. Caribbean creative artists have therefore traditionally been considered to be those artists who were born or actively shared in the culture of the region while on actual location. Of course, there are relative components within this debate. Some critics have argued for even higher requirements, while others have defined "Caribbean work" more loosely over the decades. Developments in global economic and international relations sought to encourage the fluid movement of skills and ideas. Because of the philosophical and cultural underpinnings of this set of relations, it was much trendier to traverse traditional boundaries of place, geography, and space and to celebrate this movement. Because of the prevalence of this process it was increasingly more difficult, especially for less-powerful countries, to claim authorship or control or ownership of resources that might have been nurtured and protected by them in past political and cultural global dispensations.

This chapter is concerned with Caribbean culture and Caribbean literature, with writers and the culture that supports their activity, and with how they relate to each other in a new arena of cultural creation, production, consumption, marketing, and dissemination. It is therefore concerned with selected writers and their various works. But it is even more concerned with the set of cultural activities that support and in turn are supported by Caribbean literature. It considers with varying weight such areas as educational and related institutions, publishers and publishing, academic programs, and related issues like piracy and copyright. All these are explored in the context of a fast-changing cultural arena of real and virtual transactions.

Writers in the Net—Pleasures of Virtual Exile, Virtual Pleasure of Exile

Caribbean scribal authors are found on a wide range of sites. The question of access to and dissemination of Caribbean authors and the level of control they have in the virtual realm is something that is better understood with repeated scrutiny of what continues to happen on the Internet. A minority of "traditional" scribal-based authors actually hosts their own Web site. Caribbean creative writers are heavily rotated on Web sites of publishers, academic and learning institutions, and governmental organizations, and so they owe their ongoing visibility on the Internet—as well as their status, image, and personas—to these organizations.

Given the fact that most established writers have delegated the publishing and marketing and distribution of their work to publishing houses, there is the understanding that other forms of promotion come naturally from this process. You cannot expect to come across many of these long-established writers who have official home pages. A random search comes up with very little. When one enters the name of leading Caribbean authors, there are some intriguing and some obvious discoveries. You might come across one page that masquerades as the Derek Walcott Site.[2] The page belongs to a gentleman who has written a book on Walcott and who uses the site to let the world know. Some writers like Lovelace do not appear on a dedicated site of their own, but they can be accessed easily through any search engine.[3] Austin Clarke is much more visible. He has been especially featured through Northwest Passages: Canadian Literature Online, the booksellers. The Barbados-born author has a strong Canadian stamp about his persona, as the Canadian flag flutters visibly at the head of selected major sites where he is found.[4] But, for the most part, Caribbean canonical writers are devoid of an indigenous orchestrated presence on the Internet. The "silver surfers" phenomenon of the late 1990s should have given those averse to technology and the Internet an entry point or excuse for appearing trendy, but by and large, established writers were content to retreat from newer ways of making their voices heard by a wider audience. Given the level of disinterest by individual writers, many other entities and institutions jumped into the arena to grab what they could by way of projecting, promoting, and exploiting the name and persona and iconography of regional literary and cultural creative voices.

But there were some exceptions. One notable case is that of Caryl Phillips, whose official site comes with splash page and gives information on "education and publication, awards, tours, agents," among other things.[5] Given his well-presented and carefully produced site it is possible to position him as closer to the cyber model defined by Caribbean pop and performance-oriented artists than to the more conventional location of other literary artists. But perhaps this has to do with Phillips's multi-disciplinary approach to the arts. His career has developed on a number of fronts. He has written fiction and nonfiction, plays, but he has also produced radio programs. The extent of his diverse approach to the arts is reflected in his writing the screenplay for the Merchant Ivory production of Naipaul's *The Mystic Masseur*. Unlike some other writers, Phillips seems very conscious of his image, his work, and the realities of virtual marketing politics. The hosting of and exerting of control over one's own dedicated site does not, of course, represent a gaining of total control over one's image and being in cyberspace. As is the case with Phillips, his personal information and his work can be accessed at other nonofficial or nondedicated sites like Contemporarywriters.com and Postcolonialweb.org, where several writers are bundled. But it certainly represents a statement of interest in the molding of one's virtual identity. Phillips's site does not represent the frontier domain at which Caribbean artists are located, but it is a model for other literary artists.

Many writers of the previous generation have resigned themselves to working within the safety of longstanding, tried-and-true facilities. They have remained passively connected to traditional sites of presence in the publication catalog of established publishing houses. What better way to remind people of their past exploits? But whereas these writers have held on to this traditional arrangement, and to the legacy of their contribution to Caribbean literature and culture, the publishing houses have long moved on. Unlike some Caribbean writers, many publishing houses are determined to get on with history and to actively reconstruct and reconfigure the future.

Caryl Phillips's reputation as a Caribbean writer who has spent many years abroad also supplements his presence on the Internet. Or rather, his presence on the Net supplements his identification as a writer. Caribbean critics and students have long debated the meaning of a "Caribbean writer." For some, a Caribbean writer should be someone who is born and resides in the region; for others, a Caribbean writer can reside anywhere; he or she can be of any race, color, and ethnicity; they need not have any binding relationship to the hard reality of the region. Many writers considered to be "Caribbean writers" have resided outside the region for substantial periods, working, writing, and earning a living. Their inhabiting the space beyond the physical location on the ground and their professed umbilical relation to a notion of home establishes their status as transient. The creation of the Internet has helped to bridge the gap between home and away. It has also raised further questions about real and virtual communities and the nation. New technologies have caught up with anxieties about distance, location, space, and identity, so does a writer have at all to have actually visited a location to be considered a writer of that location? Digital technology allows people to travel virtually to most locations, so can't creative artists stake claims to having created from those very virtual locations? The future will no doubt open up even newer categories of creative artists. There are already writers who might be termed "virtual Caribbean authors." You begin to imagine that this category will supplant those artists whom we now categorize as being "in between" cultures. The transnation is therefore already an aging concept.[6] The cyber state has superseded it as a frontier category.

Whereas writers of the past generation were in physical exile, the newer emerging generation of Caribbean writers living mostly abroad might claim a different status. They might declare themselves as being in a virtual free state, and as experiencing the pleasures of virtual exile. Because authors now have facilities for connecting and interfacing instantaneously with others and their co-nationals, they are now only virtually exiled. Relatively few Caribbean critics have come around to exploring the virtual pleasures that being exiled in the digital domain can evoke. The new technologies create a space of contact that bridges earlier notions of fracture such as distance and time. Here is a fertile area for future analysis, for reflection and projection.

Writers in real exile, because of their multiple homes and identities, have endeared themselves to critics and thinkers at the end of the twentieth century. There has been an intellectual and cultural movement that has apotheosized creative artists who claim multiple identities and who are said to be difficult to place. The further diffusion of "the real" by new technologies like the Internet provides rich fodder for cultural critics who go in search of endless "pleasure."

Phillips's site is not the most experimental in its employment of the multiplicity of functionalities and processes within the Internet. Colin Channer's official site is less formal. It is also professionally done, but it is more intimate and expressive than many others. Here Channer shares his delight about his children (Americans of West Indian parents) celebrating the Chinese New Year at school, where they learn English and Mandarin. He says, "In their minds the world is not divided into halves of black and white, but in halves of English and Chinese."[7] Such are the differences that many creative writers who have migrated far and wide embrace. On the Internet, Channer proudly declares the absence of "black and white" in his children's world because he, like everyone else, has heard and understands that the Internet is a medium that facilitates transcultural-ism, cyberculturalism, and gestures to a way of life that embraces all experience, no matter how diverse, perverse, crude, experimental, holy, or evil. Whereas in the past ethnicity, race, identity, origin, and place have served as entry points for the assessment of Caribbean literary artists, in the new digital culture of the twenty-first century, "technicity" also presents itself as an index of cultural fashioning. I do not suggest here that Channer might not also make the above comments in another forum, or through another medium; rather, my point is that there seems no better place to declare one's freedom from "black and white" politics than through a medium that contains the seeds of the future, a medium that purports to purge itself of the burdens of history, a medium that is possessed by technology and so discards conventional human biases in favor of openness. When Channer's statement is assessed within a more conventional context, it might be read as a naïve desire for a world free of racial bigotry. When you do a techno-reading, however, the foregrounded presence of the digital challenges the critic to behold more so a world of only virtual infestation and of virtual racial nonidentification. A technologically motivated reading might very well lead you to consider how Caribbean society can borrow from the matrix, how it might reconfigure itself without excessive emphasis on decidedly human categories and markers. For after all, aren't machines more objective than people, devoid of prejudice, bias, and culture?

It must be said that the more contemporary writers just mentioned are not the first set of Caribbean-derived writers who have set up home and shop abroad. These writers are therefore not pioneers in that regard. They are the continuation of a process that has characterized the politics of place within Caribbean literary and cultural arts. Caribbean literature as it developed around the 1950s was characterized by a similar type of migration. Many of the leading pioneer writers traveled to places like London and New York in order to improve their livelihood through greater access to publishing houses and the network of literary, social, and economic activity. Those writers used whatever technology there was in order to fulfil their ambitions and to disseminate their ideas. The Caribbean exiles in Britain therefore used print media, literary journals, and even radio (BBC[8] Caribbean Voices) as part of their well-defined project. But while it might be argued that many of these writers were driven by a sense of nationalism and inspired by the independence movements in the Caribbean and Africa, more contemporary writers do not appear to share the same vision.

It is clear that with the end of the cold war and the emergence of globalization, many Caribbean writers abroad have embraced the pleasures of assimilation and difference. There is now greater weight to the claim of ownership over these artists by extra-Caribbean entities and nations. As a result, the writer, his or her country of origination, and the Caribbean literary and cultural critic have embraced the prospect of a fluid nationality. Everyone is therefore asked to celebrate the multiple nationalities and identities of writers. You must be happy that a writer like Naipaul cannot be placed squarely anywhere in terms of true nationality. The world is a much better place if Barbados and St. Kitts can give in to the rhetoric that Austin Clark and Caryl Phillips belong to them as well as belonging to the world. Everyone gets a slice. Democracy is at work.

What set apart these newer virtually exiled writers from those of the past are not only the issues of age but also the realities of postmodernist existence. The newer writers cannot be located and fixed to a place, identity, and culture, and they do not exude essence in the same way as the older generation. The Internet is aware of this reality and therefore it streamlines and represents these two groupings differently. This statement does seem to assign to the Internet some sort of unilateral capacity to formulate, shape, and disseminate content by itself. Some would remind me that the Internet's democracy means that greater emphasis should be put on the sum of its parts, rather than on its systemic function. And that is a truth. But what my statement above implies is that the system called the Net produces patterns of behaviors. There are some basic scientific principles that undergird the Web, but there are also practical and political practices that have evolved and that now influence the use of the Web. Many users of the Net prefer to fit into preassigned categories, where they share with similarly located souls. In the same way that blog communities attract and harness like subjects, literary artists produce identifiable behaviors online, based on a number of factors, including age, identity, attitude to technology, and so on.

Liminal writers of the current generation share more in common with an earlier exiled writer like Jean Rhys than with earlier writers who have affixed themselves to their nation of birth. You might expect the Web presence of Rhys, a Caribbean British writer of the earlier generation, to be moderated. But given her divided sensibility and nationality, Rhys' status has taken on larger proportions via the Internet. She has appeared in cyberspace in slightly different ways than her dedicated Caribbean contemporaries. Her diffuse personality and indeterminate location seem to provide points of contact at which a diverse range of sites construct themselves. For instance, the Web site of Fu Jen University's English Language and Literature Department provides informative materials concerning Caribbean literature. It is intrigued by Jean Rhys' ambivalence to being fixed in any one nationality, and so this becomes a point at which the site establishes an unstated legitimate partial right to Rhys and thereafter to Caribbean culture and society.[9] The establishment of rights to various authors is a subtext of some Web sites on the Net. One important compendium of electronic resources prides itself as having an "exclusive" to their site: an open page dedicated to the Belizean writer Zee Edgell.[10] It comes with a biography, a bibliography, essays, interviews, and links to her associated virtual locations at Kent State University's English Department, Butterworth-Heinemann her publishers, and Amazon, where her books are displayed.

More traditional authors of Caribbean literature are not to be located on dedicated home pages set up or even officially sanctioned by them. Because of this, there is even fiercer competition to set up de facto "official" homepages for many of these. The race to gain preeminence, to control the iconography and virtual presence of some of these writers via the Internet, is fought by a number of entities. Among those who are directly, indirectly, really, or virtually engaged in this struggle are (as said before) educational institutions; publishers and publishing houses; book retailers; national interests, such as departments of culture and tourism, or other cultural agencies; individual connoisseurs; individual academics; search engines in general; and specialist search engines, which are also in some respects involved in the race to have association with and ultimately control the presence of artists on the Net.

An examination of the ways that some of the above corporations situate themselves in relation to selected canonical Caribbean writers might reveal the nature of this virtual race. Derek Walcott is closely associated with Sweet Briar College regarding a seminar on September 16, 1999. Up to mid-2005, this institution's affiliation with Walcott was still prime among other potential owners of Walcott's hyper-existence. Other Web sites also assert a strong association, offering information on his 1992 Nobel Prize Speech, as well as his selected books, which are also on sale.[11] Like Walcott, George Lamming also belongs first to Emory University, but he also belongs to the BBC, the National University of Singapore, and the innovative Trinidadian company called Banyan. It is instructive that many of these prime sites have not been updated in some cases for eight years. But their pride of place has to do with the kind of basic biographical and other relevant information they provide. Wilson Harris is situated closely with University of Liège. Edgar Mittelholzer, the Guyanese writer who died back in 1965, is found mostly through book dealers. His prolific output of creative works accounts for the frequency with which he is associated with dealers and retailers on the Internet. His virtual existence therefore hinges largely on this fact. The Internet is, after all, a medium of economic activity. In the world of real existence authors rely on publishing houses and book trade to keep up their presence in social and cultural circles, and in the context of virtual reality this is just as much the case. In fact, had it not been for the production of his books, the Internet might carry considerably fewer links to someone like Mittelholzer.

The Grenadian author and scholar Merle Collins appears at a dedicated page.[12] Given her dual role as writer and academic, her presence is projected on two fronts. She appears through her affiliation with the University of Maryland, where she reads from her creative work via Apple's Quicktime platform.[13] She is also featured on Web streams at Research Channel, a consortium of research universities and corporate research divisions dedicated to broadening the access to and appreciation of knowledge by using "program content creation and manipulation processes as testing medium for analogue and digital broadcast and on-demand multimedia offerings."[14] Caribbean writers are therefore often bundled with other colleagues from the region and abroad as part of larger project interests. Caribbean creative artists are therefore part of a larger global process whereby agencies and institutions promote them and in turn derive maximum returns through a system of exposure and exploitation. This practice has hardly been discussed in Caribbean criticism since the mid-1990s, when the Internet began to present, represent, and recast Caribbean icons. By the mid-2000s, Caribbean academics, connoisseurs and researchers in literary and cultural studies have made polite reference to robust innovations but have stopped short of confronting these creations. They have embraced new technologies for accessing information and entertainment but have for the most part fear-fully avoided tampering with the hardware and software belonging to other peoples. They have by the same token fearfully avoided the prospect of intervening into the matrix of ideas and confronting the "intelliware" around which technological innovation surfaces. It is these very ideas that are at the center of production of hardware and software but also at the center of production of knowledge.

Virtually Actually Alive

My analysis recognizes the dynamics of Internet culture. That is why it engages in reading individual sites; but part of its imperative is also to examine the strategies, underlying politics, and real and hyper-real sys-tems of operation within Web culture. The recognition that there are indeed systems of preplay, display, and postplay on the Net makes it pos-sible to actively engage with some of the systemic politics. Because humans appear to have grown lethargic with their "actual experiences" and are investing less effort in "the real," they have devoted much more effort in constructing versions of "the real." Given the near death of the real, the Internet comes alive as a system of technological and cultural and political practices. The existence and perpetuation of these codes reflects the active role of streamlining and control exerted by Net culture. To make this point more simply, each category of Web sites has now estab-lished its set of principles, whether stated or implicit. Web sites within a given category or field or genre often share many similar features. This has to do with the gradual and systematic building in of motifs and features into Web architecture. By the early twenty-first century, many of the pat-terns were known. For example, many news network sites have bundled text, photo galleries, and video streams, having borrowed from their expe-rience with television. But by the early 2000s Net style and architecture was leading the way and setting the trends by which more traditional media streamlined *their* offerings. By the late 2000s, all other mediums of cultural dissemination seemed to turn to the Net for renewed energy and life. The immense web of protocol, articulation, and interconnectivity within cyber systems meant that (indirectly at least) the Internet had established itself as an active medium. It was virtually actually alive.

Performance-Oriented

If Caribbean literary-literary artists have appeared passive to the use and manipulation of robust technologies, then Caribbean artists who are much closer to the oral, music, and performance spheres have been much more active in employing and engaging the Internet creatively. Given their closer association to pop, they have found the trendy functions and facilities of the Internet much more appealing and applicable to their artistic calling. But even so, not all performance-based writers and artists sought for enhanced presence on the Internet. Not all Web sites that put up performance poets and literary-pop hybrids were alike.

An ambitious and informative Web site like 57productions.com provides data on about fifty writers and performers in the UK.[15] This kind of bundling arrangement is effective for writers and performers, but it also locks the writer into closed arrangements and representational formats. Each artist must be satisfied to appear in grey stone and with a terse bibliography. There are few embedded hyperlinks. But happily, the site provides at least one link to another source of information. Sites of this kind have served as important resource locations. Although they do not give in-depth pages on each artist, they nonetheless give a sense of community and association among artists who share at least the same virtual space. In the mid-2000s, 57 Productions unveiled a new Web site. Although its individual artist pages provided little more than on the old Web site, the new page versions seemed fresh due to a significant reworking of graphics, page layout and cleaner, crisper images. The new Web site also promoted its poetry jukebox that featured audio performances by a range of older and new poets. It also invested more in other media, particularly video clips.

Bremen University's site map for dub poetry features fewer dub poets, but gives more information about the culture that has supported leading dub poets. Because it is a noncommercial site, the broader cultural issues it features are understood.[16] It therefore is concerned to give its constituents samples of the performance poems as literary text. It hosts links to what it calls the "reading room." A critical comparison of these two sites (57 Productions and Bremen University) reveals subtle differences that are rooted in their particular orientation. One of the sites is more commercial, while the other has education as a prime objective. Given this general reading of their orientation, it might be suggested that more commercial sites (like 57 Productions) are defined by the presence of specific features and functionalities, as mentioned above, while education-driven sites also have their specific characteristics. These are real points that this book will return to from time to time. But at this stage it is necessary to acknowledge that the two sites also reflect the multilayered nature of performance poetry. On the one hand, performance poets have a history that connects to the literary tradition, but they also evolve and participate within the dedicated realm of pop culture. This is the point therefore at which Web culture wrestles with the very facilities available in cyberspace in order to represent and produce the structures and raw material of complex phenomena like performance poetry. In the final analysis, despite the Web's flexibility, even Web pages of different orientation cannot avoid the reproduction of similar features, information, and similar modes of delivering their divergent visions of a single artistic practice.

Caribbean performance-oriented poets and versifiers make much greater creative use of the Internet than their counterparts of the literary-literary tradition. Artists like Linton Kwesi Johnson (LKJ), Mutabaruka, Binta Breeze, Adisa, and other Rapso poets like Brother Resistance, Kindred, and 3Canal make more concerted efforts to employ leading-edge tools than their counterparts. Caribbean creative writers who are situated in the mainstream—those who have shared a longstanding relationship with publishers, audiences and established media—have not themselves vigorously contested and sought the control of their presence on the Internet. Caribbean performance-oriented artists are different partly for historical, aesthetic, and economic factors, which this book will discuss throughout. Whereas many of the more traditional writers rely on sites to host them, the performance poets are more aggressive in maintaining, managing, and disseminating their iconography. This does have implications for authorship, ownership, control, and power. Although I might seem to be saying that performance poets have much more control over the Internet, that is not necessarily the case, because for every site an artist is able to monitor and seek to influence, there are that many more that are not within his or her grasp, other sites that anyway disseminate their own discursive slant on the artist. But there is something to be said for the establishment of an official homepage and the provision of one's version of "the self" along with other trendy accompaniments, hypertext and hypermedia.

Benjamin Zephaniah promotes his works, but he also provides a space for other creative artists to get up their work through a gateway on his main page that he calls "Outernet."[17] Like those of his contemporaries, Zephaniah's site places great emphasis on text and on the word. Indeed, his site appears to sacrifice other expressive hyperlinks for solid, message-oriented dialog. Mutabaruka's dedicated site comes with audio and video links.[18] Navigation is not the easiest. The contemporary navigator is fooled by a link that says "Videos," which leads not to streaming clips but rather to a listing of his selected video and film appearances. On the contrary, there is much healthier posting of his lyrics from successive albums. It is perhaps disappointing for the contemporary navigator that the site does not provide sample video clips of his performance, given the fact that most Web sites of leading performance-based artists come with a mixed array of media functionalities. But Mutabaruka has arguably always been even more conscious of his impact and lyrics than most. He is a message-based poet above all else. It is therefore not surprising that his use of technological resources has privileged the word above any other single medium of display. He however attempts to make up for this imbalance by providing a substantial number of still photos to give his presence in cyberspace some sense of vitality. But in the final analysis you feel that he would be equally happy if there were only words.

The Web site consisted of a single page.[19] Around 2002 the Barbadian performance poet Adisa showcased his latest CD. Its information was barely sufficient. It provided only a handful of audio clips. Overall the presentation was spare. At the time, the Web site was clearly put up to provide access to his popular work *Doing it Säf*. By mid-2004, the site had been upgraded and reworked. The artist was now more widely known as Aja. Some tweaking had been done to the site. Like the artist himself, who has constantly been tweaking his image, experimenting with different genres, and changing his nomenclature, the new Web site revealed some editing. It contained concise information about his post-2000 releases. It carried his curt philosophizing, and limited samples of his literary and performance-based work. All in all, the Web site was self-contained, surprisingly providing no external links for an artist who has a substantial history outside the secluded virtual space of his domain name.

It is surprising that Jean Binta Breeze, a heavyweight in this genre, does not have a dedicated site but falls back on references via LKJ Records and Bloodaxe books. The pioneering performer Louise Bennett appears at many sites, but the one that carries her name was still under construction around the mid-2000s, when it only displayed two photographs of Ms. Lou. Given the significant effort expended by women to assert their equality, there are grounds for even further investigation of the gender politics at work in several spheres of virtual representation.

Brother Resistance and fellow rapso performance poets largely share an orientation to that of their dub-based colleagues. Not all rapso poets are featured on the Internet. The pioneers Karega Mandela and Lancelot Layne are found on archive-type sites, and more contemporary outfits like Kindred and Ataklan are diffuse in representation, not having a focal location. The similarities between dub and rapso poets have to do with their relationship to the scribal and popular oral and music traditions. While traditional dub poets were influenced by reggae culture, and more contemporary performers by dancehall and post-dancehall culture, rapso poets have significant influence from calypso, soca, and post-soca culture. But their strands of performance poetry have impacted one another. While it was easier in the 1980s to talk of these as distinct movements given their geographical, philosophical, aesthetic and stylistic traits, by the mid-2000s they had evolved, borrowed, and transformed. A unifying influence in their evolution over the decades has been the significant impact of the global entertainment industry and the contribution of Western pop culture. But in spite of the substantial weight exerted by commercial pressures, not all artists reflected the same tendencies and outlook in their use of the Web.

Brother Resistance, who had been around since the 1970s, still fought to locate his tradition in old time carnival talkers and figures like the "midnite robber."[20] By the post-2004 period Web culture also embraced this kind of performer. Likewise, Brother Resistance carefully embraced cyberculture, attempting to fashion his image and message, but all the while tweaking, fixing the technology so that it conveyed his iconography. Like many other performance poets on home pages like Mutabaruka.com and Benjaminzephaniah.com, Brother Resistance tried to provide selected access to his material and philosophy by way of various functions of the technology. Biography, discography, photo gallery, and sales were all categories and links provided. He also provided MP3 downloads. The visual layout of the site was characterized by a collage of cuts from different photos. These were pasted onto and below what appeared to be a motley aluminum barrier with traces of graffiti. All in all this gave the Web site and the artist a rough edge. The measure of his acknowledgement of rapso's link to reggae culture was symbolized in the Web page's showing of a hanging medallion with the word RAPSO pasted onto a background of red, yellow and green.

Another outfit, 3Canal, is variously accessible through carnival and soca sites. Curiously, around 2004 their Web site 3canal.com, promoted what they called the 3 Canal Show, and it could only be accessed with a user name and password.[21] This facility was both a barrier and a marketing tool. The Web site's only other function was to advertise the rapso group's T-shirt line. This site reflected the height of new commercialism but also the realities of direct product marketing. 3Canal has never seemed to conform to normative standards. They have always seemed to be "out there somewhere." One feels that such an outfit might be better placed within the realm of Caribbean rapso or Caribbean alternative performance. Because information about the group could be gleaned from elsewhere, their new dedicated site seemed clearly focused on a few limited goals. One therefore suspected that the site was intended to be a transient construction. Its objective revolved around a set of specific goals. This method was recognition that the Internet itself is hardly stable. Sites are constructed and they die. The 3 Canal experiment seemed a self-consciously constructed space or moment that paid homage to this very fact of cyber reality. As the first decade of the twenty-first century was coming to a close, more and more Caribbean artists of all disciplines sought pathways by which they could enhance their standing. While the more established performers were more cautions about their use of traditional and emerging technologies, it was clear that even younger creators would be more aggressive.

Presses, the Net, and Caribbean Studies

Because most literary artists are best known for their creative work, it is only logical that the Internet reflects their close association with publishing houses as well as with book retail sources. Many of the leading publishers of Caribbean writers act as de facto hosts of Web pages for authors. In the absence of dedicated Web pages for authors, the publishers stand in as surrogates. Some publishing houses have spent considerable effort to project not only the books on sale but also the authors. Heinemann is a leading publisher of Caribbean material. In the mid-2000s, their Web site listed the names of all their authors. It is an impressive showing. But the sheer number of writers on the roster seemed to have affected the company's ability to get up and maintain any kind of credible biography for even one of their own writers. These were not given the courtesy of a face on the site, neither did the cover of their books appear. This could, of course, be a reflection of a Web site in transition. One feels that the publishers will look to enhance this in the future. But it is also possible that the company is satisfied with its place in the market and relies on its traditional standing, as well as on other support means of attracting viewers and purchasers for their books. In spite of these shortcomings, their Web site was visually captivating. What it lacked in substance it provided in appearance. On the Internet, it is possible to get away with such tradeoffs and transactions.

There are few publishers and sites devoted to Caribbean studies that are better presented and conceptualized than that of Macmillan Caribbean. On the Net, they parade their healthy catalog devoted to primary, secondary, and tertiary studies. Macmillan/Palgrave built their catalog through a series of strategic associations between itself and university departments, but also through longstanding association with key educational institutions, distributors, bookshops, and authors. Its University of

Warwick Caribbean Studies series spawned a number of groundbreaking and seminal works in Caribbean cultural studies. Their Macmillan-Caribbean Web site boasts of being "the world's leading publisher for the Caribbean."[22] Its Web site is colorful without being ostentatious. Its bright color motifs and actual shots of the Caribbean support its user interface, which is quite easy to navigate.

Peepal Tree Press also supported a number of important publications about and from the region. Although it does not possess the financial might of Macmillan, Peepal Tree Press was driven by the vision and passion for literary studies by its publisher Jeremy Poynting. The intimacy and personalized treatment given to authors and books within its catalog is captured on the press' Web pages.[23] Their home page, for example, foregrounds the face of authors and their work. Macmillan Caribbean, by contrast, does not display its authors so intimately, so upfront, on its main pages. Peepal Tree's Web site also reflects its attention to quality. Its sales pitch declares that it publishes "some of the best in contemporary Caribbean, Black British and South Asian fiction, poetry and academic studies." While people in the industry have made mention of the absence of marketing muscle in small presses, this press, like others its size, has sought to confront this limitation by providing two dedicated links to subscriptions and online shopping at their home page. Another prestigious publisher with a Caribbean catalog is Faber and Faber. In 1998, they launched their Caribbean catalog. It included names like Antonio Benítez Rojo, Edwige Danticat, Robert Antoni, Wilson Harris, and Earl Lovelace. A few years later it was still nearly impossible to identify their Caribbean affiliation on their Web site.[24] This was a strange occurrence.

In the United States publishing houses like Africa World Press and Greenwood Press were some of the presses being approached by authors to publish their critical writings on Caribbean literature and culture. University publishers like Duke University Press and University of Michigan Press paraded their Caribbean studies texts, although many potential authors felt that university presses outside the Caribbean were redirecting them to Caribbean-based publishers. Throughout the 2000s there has definitely been a drying up of publishing options for Caribbean Studies material among the more traditional academic publishers.

Routledge, which published a number of works on Caribbean and postcolonial studies, continues to be a powerful publishing outfit worldwide. By the late 1990s, it was acquired by the even more powerful Taylor and Francis group. In the mid-2000s, this group boasted of being able to publish more than one thousand journals and around one thousand eight hundred new books each year, with a books backlist in excess of twenty thousand specialist titles. In the annual report of 2004 for the year ending December 2003, they reported good profits. In their corporate strategy, they spoke of "strengthening the portfolio" and "widening the customer base."[25] Prior to its acquisition for about 90 million British pounds, Routledge had, however, already published works related to Caribbean studies. It had produced the student's postcolonial bible titled *The Empire Writes Back* in 1989. It also carried *The Routledge Reader in Caribbean Literature*, their "Research in Postcolonial Literatures Series," and *The Post-Colonial Studies Reader*, which one reviewer quipped was "boring academic jargon at its worst."[26] Routledge has therefore been a major force in facilitating the expansion of postcolonial studies, if not Caribbean studies specifically. It has given priority to the postcolonial project, particularly as articulated from the new centers of postcolonial studies in specific academic institutions, in certain parts of the world. Routledge cannot claim to be a radical publisher. It has played it safe, upholding the status quo. The truly radical thinkers at the fringes of post-colonial and related studies could not hope to gain full access to discourse through this publisher. Its agenda was clearly set. It invested ideologically in the present while looking through financial eyes into the future. While some other less well organized and financed publishers tried to come to terms with the Internet, the Taylor and Francis group also reported healthy returns with downloads of its research articles increasing by more than 35 percent in the year 2003. Its commercial sites therefore reflected heavy investment in digital information.

E-books, though growing in popularity, were not widely embraced by Caribbean readers by 2005. These books came in HTML editions, which meant that they could be read either using the Web browser or offline. One of the preferred formats for digital reading was the Acrobat PDF format, because most computer systems, old or new, have it installed. The newer Microsoft Reader claimed to make the reading exercise less stressful on the eyes by allowing for tweaking of the appearance, texture, and size of the text. Accompanying software like Microsoft's text-to-speech package also promised to enhance the process.

Ian Randle Publishers started around 1991. By the mid-1990s, they were a leading name in the publishing industry in the Caribbean region. Their emphasis has grown to cover many aspects of Caribbean literary and culture studies, but their forte has seemed to be in history, politics, and sociology. Their interest in Caribbean literature has been relatively muted. In the period of the late 1990s and early 2000s, they seemed to be more open to publication of creative poetry, prose, and drama. Their interest in culture has tended to privilege authors and works that come to culture by route of the social sciences. Their catalog therefore reflected works on culture that were filtered through the prism of more traditional methodologies. Caribbean literary and cultural researchers from outside their captive group of authors sought publishing options elsewhere. As a robust unit, this company managed to help transform publishing culture in the region. They have also worked hard to change the attitude of Caribbean institution toward works published within the region. In the mid-1990s, some regional institutions debated (informally) the quality, value, and standing of regional publishing houses like Ian Randle and the weighting that should be given to academic works under its imprint. By the mid-2000s, there was much greater recognition and wider acceptance of works coming out of independent publishing houses. Other regional publishers like Arawak Publications and House of Nehesi continued to wrestle with questions of quality, standards, commercial viability of productions, and academic weighting. Writers like Lamming lent support to these institutions.

Ian Randle's Web presence (throughout most of the years) reflected the ambitions of a small, well-focused outfit with dreams of grander feats. Its home page sought to present and interest you in a range of products and services available through the company. It therefore emphasized content-driven pages while treating the aesthetics of layout as secondary. In the past, their home page has therefore come over as being cluttered and too busy. This is not necessarily a bad strategy, because some navigators are turned on by the presence of copious information and material. One of Ian Randle's most distinctive links at their home page has been the link they subsequently provided to what they call "Caribbean Integration Studies."[27] This category reflected a new vision of the publishers in keeping with the region's own struggle with the perpetual question of integration.

The University of the West Indies Press started in 1992. Like Ian Randle, it too has fought to establish book publishing as an exercise in cultural promotion and regional empowerment. In ten years, it published over one hundred and sixty titles in twelve subject areas. By the mid-2000s, its Web site proudly displayed some of its ware. One of its leading subject areas was Caribbean cultural studies, an area in which the University itself had invested substantial energies and resources as a future growth area.[28] Whereas the link to literature only shows some ten titles, the cultural studies category produced thirty, and history displayed a whopping sixty titles. The listing of books published under headings on the University press' Web site reveals an imbalance, where disciplines like Education, Medical Science and Legal Studies only produced five titles each over a twelve year period. The Web site does not explain or addresses this imbalance, but the reasons might be varied. Many University Presses have clearly expressed their greater publishing interest in some areas. Because the UWI Press is a relatively young outfit it was still by the mid-2000s trying to establish its niche within the regional and the wider world of intellectual discourse. Its words of welcome by the Managing Editor and the Chairman of the board seem to request that supporters of the Press and navigators of its Web site bear this in mind when sampling its ware, whether online or elsewhere.

Educational Institutions, the Net, and Caribbean Studies

The University of the West Indies (UWI) took to the Internet in a noticeable way by the mid-to-late 1990s. Its presence within the domain of Caribbean literary and cultural studies was enhanced by the mid-1990s cultural studies initiative. This UWI initiative was fighting to get running when the most celebrated case of institutionalized cultural studies, at Birmingham, was acrimoniously ending. The UWI initiative had its hub in the Humanities. UWI's literary programs embraced postcolonial studies to some degree. Across the University there were contrasting views about the global postcolonial agenda. On the University's Web sites, staff interests have reflected a myriad of interests within cultural studies. The accessing of UWI's programs and personnel via the Internet also came about around the time of the launch of the cultural studies initiative. There was no causal relationship here, except that maybe the end of the twentieth century brought about a series of recognitions within the institution. The deepening of the process of globalization, the entrenchment of the digital revolution, and the imminent advent of both the Caribbean Single Market and Economy and the Free Trade Area of the Americas forced regional institutions as a whole to reevaluate their mission statements and renew their efforts. Because the education market in the region would some day soon be liberalized, it was imperative that the regional university take more seriously to the Internet as a sign of change and embracing the challenge.

Whereas in the mid-1990s information about the University had to be sought primarily through hard copy handouts, by the mid-2000s there were attempts to harmonize the layout and presentation of UWI Web sites across all the campuses. Like other institutions of this kind, which are part of the emerging techno-driven culture, the university has been challenged to offer even much more information online. Universities worldwide have since the early-1990s grappled with questions of offering face-to-face as well as online distance programs. Most international universities have instituted procedures to facilitate dual mode delivery of programs. The areas of literary and cultural studies have challenged academies and their departments to come to terms with the technologies, which are essential components in mediating the space and distance between the teacher and students. Because Caribbean studies has been such a contested area in the traditional spaces of debate—books, conferences, and journals—the additional challenge of negotiating technology, in addition to clarifying the longstanding debates about Caribbean culture, represented the hard task presented to institutions in the new era of digitization.

Of course, Caribbean literary and culture studies were being offered as viable programs outside the region as well. These were offered with increasing frequency throughout the period of global and regional transformation. The embryonic World Wide Web contributed significantly to and benefited from this process. Traditionally people have felt they had to go on location in the region to do a course of study in Caribbean society or culture, but the advent of virtual technology made the thought of that requirement even more redundant. Since the 1960s Universities in the United Kingdom, like Kent at Canterbury and Leeds (and institutions in the United States and Canada) were producing a number of PhDs who would go on to become leaders in Caribbean cultural and literary studies. These regional minds were being shaped abroad, primarily through programs in Commonwealth and ethnic and related studies. By the 2000s, it was impossible to identify all the institutions worldwide that were offering programs and courses in Caribbean and related culture.

For some of these programs, universities made full use of the facilities of the Internet. They launched text, sound, and video programs to attract students and other interests, but such electronic facilities were also a launching pad for increased harnessing of resource material and databases about regions like the Caribbean. The University of Miami mounted one of the most innovative initiatives involving the Internet and online access. Their Caribbean Writers Summer Institute Digital Archives was a virtual database of performances and moments featuring Caribbean literary and cultural figures.[29] This facility has provided students, teachers, and all other navigators access to selected Caribbean writers and critics reading or discussing their work. Its extensive subject archive has featured artists from St. Lucian Kendel Hippolyte reading "Poem In a Manger" to other streams under the heading of "Carnival," "Intimidation Fiction," "AIDS Drama" and "Women Authors (Guyana)." The video streams are mostly taken from the proceedings of their Summer Workshop Initiative conducted throughout the 1990s and are of varying lengths. Their Web site also gives access to the keynote address delivered in 2003 at the 22nd Annual Conference on West Indian Literature, by Kamau Brathwaite.

From the late 1990s and beyond, Caribbean institutions of learning were faced with the task of keeping pace with developments worldwide in the area of distance learning. Institutions within the region were forced to consider the challenges posed to their longtime dominance of the post-secondary school market by offshore universities, which were either actually relocating in the region or establishing a virtual presence. Units like Skidmore College's University Without Walls (UWW) marketed themselves and their programs throughout the region. Part of their marketing thrust was based on the assumption that traditional Caribbean learning institutions were deficient in catering to the demands of a range of people in the new world of education demand: "If you live in the Caribbean, you may be frustrated by the limited options you have for earning a bachelor's degree without leaving your island. UWW can offer you the option to do just that!" [30] Inherent in this kind of marketing thrust and jargon is not only a competitive attitude, but also a carefully orchestrated practice that weaves the possibility of doing with or without more tradition-bound institutions. UWW (with playful nearness to the more traditional and longstanding UWI) therefore declared that they had "developed models for evaluating transfer credit for Caribbean students."

Distance education and electronic media transfer raised a number of issues to do with ownership, copyright, and integrity. Responding to the Clinton administration's Nation Information Infrastructure Initiative interested people from all over the world met in 1994 to discuss the parameters of fair use in five main areas of educational use: distance; multimedia; electronic reserves; interlibrary loans and image collections. Over the years that followed, talks and agreements on guidelines were difficult to hold together. By 2004, university libraries and educational technology facility centers sought to educate their users and also to protect their boundaries by providing on-site and virtual users of their material with information concerning copyright and fair use. Given the many cases of litigation worldwide between course lecturers and their sponsoring institutions, Caribbean personnel were cautious about how to go forward into the domain of fluid experience and litigious possibility.[31]

While more and more universities and lecturers worldwide now place course material and packages online, this material is at times limited to individuals who share in a set of arrangements set up by the course tutor or controlled by an institution's Web master (though students have circumvented these barriers). But there are also increasing trends towards providing greater access to the public. In this way, students from across the world have shared in the knowledge base created and re-presented by varying sources. This has brought about a bigger and richer pool of resources for access by students, scholars, and all others. For example, there has been an increase in the number of sites devoted to cultural studies, to postcolonial studies, to Caribbean studies.

But not all information put up on the Web is what it claims to be. Course tutors have therefore continued to discriminate and have guided learners to specific sites, some of which are much more valued than others. The presence of freeware has also raised the question of ownership of material, its access, and its use and distribution. Caribbean students, as others, have not only locked into relevant sites (at other institutions) related to their chosen field but have immersed themselves in the growing culture of net discourse. By the mid-2000s, many, if not most, students were beginning to employ the computer and its functionalities and connectivities for producing their work. The promise of the computer to seize all other more traditional tools and media and to render them obsolete led to this attitude among people in search of formal and informal education. Anticipatory education practices therefore led to a category of students who were overly dependent on the Web. This dependence at times bordered on addiction. Teachers and lecturers were themselves forced to keep up with trends because students were prone to use and abuse the facilities of the Internet. While some people resisted this practice, the overpowering preserve of digital culture compelled even the most unwilling to enter the matrix of possibility.

Some sites offered access to reviews, personal essays, and synopses by login membership only.[32] Some sites offered students the prospect of paying to have essays and assignments written for them. Plagiarism and creative deception have become real features of the Caribbean and world intellectual system of knowledge processing. In some cases, students did not read some of the more classic texts from cover to cover but read their synopses. Some others downloaded free copies of books online without going to dedicated bookshops and libraries. All in all, the domain and climate of knowledge gathering was transformed throughout the region and throughout the world. Caribbean literary and cultural studies were particularly challenged because on the one hand, there was a scarcity of material in some areas, but on the other, versions of Caribbean society were being fashioned, constructed, and re-created by way of the very new technology and machines that were taking over the world.

In the online book *The Will to Technology and the Culture of Nihilism: Heidegger, Nietzsche and Marx*, Arthur Kroker declares and explores nihilism as the destiny of technology.[33] Within the region this was hardly the belief held by most. If some viewed technology as a potential danger, they did not see it firstly in terms of Western philosophy. They rather saw certain types of technology as the tool and preserve of interest groups, of Western institutions, and of profit-driven associations that hardly have the interest of Caribbean societies at heart. While Caribbean culture was being re-created in cyberspace, on the ground of experience some people were imbibing the sweets of digitization, while others were a bit more cautious, resisting and even hacking into the processes set in motion to valorize the power of digital culture creation. There has therefore been a mixed reaction to the potential of new technologies.

There has hardly been a uniform process of movement on to the Internet by Caribbean cultural journals. Arguably, larger, better-financed journals from abroad have made the transition more briskly. The paradigm shift towards online access was not an easy moment. It did not just entail the digitizing of hard-copy text and uploading it to the Internet; there were other issues. Because some journals were traditionally accessed as hard text, any shift in their mode of access and distribution entailed a reworking of the structures and procedures of editorial boards and journal marketing. Many Caribbean journals like *Journal of Eastern Caribbean Studies, Caribbean Quarterly, Journal of West Indian History, Journal of West Indian Literature, West Indian Medical Journal, Small Axe,* and *Caribbean Education Research Journal* had to confront the question of finance and marketing. Because some of these University of the West Indies–affiliated journals had to wrestle with challenges of marketing and reconstituting themselves in light of the new dispensation of knowledge dissemination, this effort played some part in diminishing their visibility in the wider world. Not that the question of visibility always has to do with financing, for the true reality might very well be that Caribbean publishing and knowledge dissemination have always been assigned third world status even within the predigital dispensation. Caribbean-based journals have produced high quality work over the years, but these journals have always seemed to judge their own worth based on external categories, rather than assessing the potential of their work to empower the region in the first instance and then to affect the wider global sphere. Caribbean journals have therefore suffered from bouts of regional and institutional inferiority.

The University of Central Arkansas launched its *Journal of Caribbean Literatures* (*JCL*) in the spring of 1997. In the introduction of the hard and soft text of the journal, the publication sets out its difference from the UWI *Journal of West Indian Literature* (*JWIL*), as reflected in the

"Caribbean" in its title. The editor makes it clear that his use of "Caribbean" means that his journal will cover a wider region and that its use of the plural "Literatures" gives his journal wider scope. This technical debate was not alien to *JWIL*, which also published material on the wider region, but the emphatic mentioning of this point on the *JCL's* Web site highlights both an acknowledgement of the contentious nature of the terms highlighted, as well as the marketing imperatives at play in the domain of Caribbean literary and cultural studies.[34] There were many other journals devoted to the study of Caribbean, West Indian, and related culture.

The editorial and advisory boards of some journals reflected the reality that controllers of discourses about the Caribbean and African cultures were not located in Africa or the Caribbean. Around mid-2004, for example, the collective controllers of a journal like *Wasafiri* (then celebrating its twentieth year) were thirty-one academics, twenty-six from universities in the UK, four from the United States, and one from Canada. There were no academics that were either in the Caribbean or working at an institution in the Caribbean. The journal *Interventions*, subtitled "a journal of postcolonial studies," was a little better, being a newer publication. By 2004, it boasted of regional editors. It had nine consultant editors from the United States, four from the UK, one from France, and one from India. There were none from the Caribbean. Being a Routledge publication, by then a subsidiary of the Taylor and Francis group, its supposedly high profile seemed to require managerial and editorial direction from carefully selected locations. The Caribbean just didn't cut it. Routledge launched a new journal for Latin American and Caribbean studies in 2006. The listing of editors and advisors on its Web site seemed concerned with promoting the predominantly metropolitan universities on show more than the actual scholars and their central location at the heart of Latin America and the Caribbean.[35] These were not the only publications that were founded and maintained with specific kinds of controllers; indeed, many works focusing on the region excluded regional institutions and their personnel. This was not exclusive to the domain of literary studies, but in that field the underlying strategy was most blatantly evident.

Many of the well-financed and commercially driven publishers made strategic moves to take full advantage of new facilities offered by the Internet. Whereas some journals like *Caribbean Quarterly*, *JWIL*, and *Sargasso* out of the University of Puerto Rico were subscribed to by the diehard and core researchers concerned with the inner workings of Caribbean culture and criticism on the ground, some other journals noticeably took to the Internet in a big way. *The Caribbean Writer*, a literary anthology out of the University of the Virgin Islands has had a visible presence in cyberspace for some time now. With more than seventeen volumes in publication, their Web site offered navigators and researchers a clear sense of their contribution since 1987.³⁶ *The Caribbean Writer's* impressive showing hinged on the nearly seamless connection of its online material to its hard copy publications. It gave online access to some personal essays by leading writers and critics and to some interviews with seminal authors. This marketing tease on the Internet represented a sizable quantity of what the hard copy provided. The reader was therefore sufficiently stimulated to seek out the hard copy. *The Caribbean Writer* was also careful to establish its visual iconographies in the hard and online versions. The virtual and the hard cover publication therefore shared the same dedicated Verdana and Arial fonts, as well as the journal's brightly colored outstanding borders. They were quite similar to *Wadabagei* therefore in this regard. *The Caribbean Writer's* Web pages were much more intimate and involved than those of other online publications. They were not defined by the almost cold and detached marketing of Routledge's *Postcolonial Studies*.³⁷

Small Axe was first attached to the University of the West Indies Press but then moved on to be published and marketed through Indiana University Press in the United States. *Small Axe* set out in the mid-1990s to revive "the practices of intellectual criticism in the Caribbean." Its move to Indiana University secured a place among other leading international journals. It was therefore present on the Internet on show with other cultural studies journals. As with many other publications of this type, only few selected articles were made available for free download online. But there was ample facility to purchase single articles or issues via the Internet. By the mid-2000s, few publications of this kind ignored the new frontier of knowledge sharing. *Small Axe* was unique in its undying devotion to maintain an agenda that was driven by Caribbean intellectuals and Caribbean intellectual debate. It was very conscious of wider discourses, but its editor, David Scott, seemed to be motivated by the priority of centering Caribbean imperatives foremost.

Editors of *The Atlantic Literary Review*, originating in New Delhi, India, and launched in 2000, mandated that submissions by scholars be done electronically. Whereas many publishers still insisted on traditional submission of hard copies along with a disc in some cases, the reality was that academics and students were demanding a much more fluid and timely process of transferring and disseminating knowledge. *Jouvert*, a journal devoted to postcolonial studies launched around 1996 out of

North Carolina State University, made the bold intervention of publishing its articles online. In their inaugural release, the editors wrestled with the pleasures, complexities, and politics associated with the World Wide Web, discourse, and communication.[38] Its recognition that the very medium of communication it had chosen to employ represented part of the challenge of colonialism, signaled the burdensome task of freeing academic and all other debate from their mediums of dissemination.

Video Style

The later 2003 online free access journal *Anthurium*, out of the University of Miami, also celebrated the liberating potential of the Internet, but its inaugural edition also wrestled with the challenges of digital technology and its implications for individual, public, and practical use. The editors declared that it was easy to reproduce the words of its lead article, which was by Kamau Brathwaite. But they further added that it was challenging to harmonize the quotations in the other essays that quote from it: "The task of synchronizing the variety of fonts used to reproduce and approximate Brathwaite's work [was a] . . . challenge. After careful thought . . . it was decided [to] . . . use only variations of . . . standard fonts in bold, italics, and capitals. . . . Since all attempts to approximate Brathwaite's Sycorax video style would be a misrepresentation of the original, this approach . . . gave us the advantage of uniformity and coherence."[39]

Like traditional publishing, electronic publishing has its attendant rewards and challenges. The self-conscious reflection by the editors on the actual process of publication exposes the teething problems that characterize electronic publishing generally. The dilemma faced by the editors turns on the prospect of providing content and quality with reasonable production effort. The digital process can produce as much disappointment as it can pleasure. The editors' disclosure reflects a measure of professional courtesy; the open declaration is to be commended for its gracious candor. But the declaration is also a result of the tensions that accompany this new enterprise; it is a kind of therapeutic confession. The statements made do not set out to unravel the finer workings of digital writing; that is too grand an undertaking for an editorial preface. Digital writing encompasses the facile everyday activity of scribing e-mail and forming instant messages. But there are always underlying codes and protocols that undergird the simple act of writing in cyberspace. These systems are always present, whether submerged or compressed. There are always other issues in attendance when one enters the domain of digital deployment. There are always hidden codes and hyperlinks within, connected to, and outside the field of immediate critical navigation. While the editors succeed in the task of representing Brathwaite's speech-essay "Namsetoura & the Companion Stranger" by simply employing portable document format, the result is that this version of the Brathwaite script is a little hard on the eyes, and the variation in font and point size forces the reader to tweak the program functions from page to page to compensate for the delivery of the document in this format. This is not a criticism of the publication itself; rather, it is a reminder that technology's power is still relative to the range of situations and conditions under which it is used. Technology in itself is not infallible, and neither are the human subjects who enlist and employ the wonders of leading-edge machinery.

Kamau Brathwaite has, of course, posed some challenges to publishers of hard-copy texts. Oxford University Press, which published some of his earlier work, did not undertake to do his later works. Beginning with *The Arrivants*, his experiments with nation language and page layout were evident. This was continued through books like *Zea Mexican Diary*. His new direction and work with the computer was clearly signaled in *Barabajan Poem*. The latter collection was published under his own imprint of Savacou North. He was making full use of letter size pages for his elaborate experiments with fonts and large point sizes. The appearance of Brathwaite's speech/essay in the groundbreaking *Anthurium* reflects the ways in which the challenges faced in more traditional domains and media also plague the realm of virtual expression. It reflects the potential for surmounting these challenges and the possibility that there are varying degrees of success to be gained over the challenges that arise in the real and virtual worlds of cultural expression.

Our Machines, Our Companions

While the Internet facilitated easier access to information, this ease of access also stood the danger of erasing the attendant politics encoded in the very process and medium of relay. That is to say, the ease of function and use of technology masked the underlying tensions that define cultural and practical relations. This erasing of attendant politics was especially possible in cases where both navigators and the new technology worked in seamless harmony. In the twenty-first century, creators of computer technology have tended to market their creations less as machines and more so as companions. The standard definition of a computer refers to it as a "machine" or "electronic device." But in the world of use, marketing, and instrument aesthetics jargon, these creations have distinct and distinguishing names. Thus the user does not merely purchase a computer, but she or he acquires a special type. Each computer has its own brand of character. It is branded and named and carries its distinct set of characteristics. This is indeed an obvious point, but deeper thought must be given to the ways in which marketers and consumers have entered into an arrangement wherein they accept that some features distinguish one make from another and one category from another. The extent to which users have come to think of computers less as machines and more as companions is reflected in the ease of name calling within the world of desktops, notebooks, and peripherals. Indeed, even the names of producers are part of our tech culture vocabulary and are referred to with terms of endearment. We therefore speak intimately of our "Satellite," "Inspiron," "Powerbook," "Vaio," and "Armada," or our "Moto," "RazR," and so on. These creations are defined by their power, speed, and functionality. But their ability to work and perform tasks as machines is subordinated beneath their sleek, fashionable, appealing exterior. The exterior appearance conceals the gadgetry that dwells inside. The user therefore does not see or think of the mechanical or electronic processes that are at work and at play within the technology when using it. The exterior appearance therefore has the effect of making the world conjured up on the screen appear less forged and more natural in its simulation.

CHAPTER 3

Cyber Reach: Caribbean Gospel (and Religious) Culture (Version 5.0)

Part 1: Gospel without the Net

Gospel and Popular Discourse

Caribbean gospel culture is arguably one of the fasting growing areas of expression within the region. Throughout the 2000s, for instance, a number of religious shows and staged festivals sprang up throughout the region. Many islands of the region held major events that featured leading Caribbean and international religious performers. Religious activities like gospel festivals, conferences, crusades, and seminars appealed to a cross section of the populace. Young people continued to refashion religious activities as the first decade of the twenty-first century came to a close. But in spite of these kinds of advances, gospel culture still remains an underexplored area of cultural debate. Part of the reason for this is that gospel culture is not traditionally regarded as a legitimate site of popular expression. Critics of Caribbean and global culture are much more inclined to discuss "the popular" in the context of what they would call secular cultural expression. This is ironic, because even more mainstream secular agencies like news networks have foregrounded debates about religion, prophecy, and the current social and political reality. Additionally, global and regional (secular) developments have helped to transform religious phenomena. It is therefore possible to talk of a Caribbean popular gospel culture as an identifiable set of traits and phenomena existing by the 1980s and 1990s. A major fillip for the evolution of this cultural grouping and activity has been the wider cultural changes taking place within Caribbean society, global changes within religious worship, the intersecting and interplay between religious and secular institutions, and certainly the influence of technology and communications phenomena, to name some of the major factors.

In an earlier work, *Culture @ the Cutting Edge*, I explored a range of issues relating to popular gospel culture.[1] In that work I attempted to touch on many issues at the cusp of gospel culture. My intention in this work is to advance that discussion in some areas. This work returns to gospel culture because I consider this arena to be one of the most neglected though crucial areas within the development of Caribbean, diasporic, and digital or cyberculture. All in all, however, this chapter represents a renewed undertaking, because it grapples with areas of Caribbean cultural expression that still remain underassessed even though the region has lived for more than ten years in the shadows of a global digital and technological revolution. Even religious activity has been faced with the challenges posed to society since the advent of the computer.

For one thing, I want to examine the music video. I want to dissect selected pivotal gospel videos. This represents an important undertaking, because the music or entertainment video form itself has hardly been understood within the Caribbean context. The Caribbean gospel video and music video format is even more remote. A major concern of this chapter is with the use of technologies and mediums of dissemination within gospel culture. Inasmuch as gospel expression represents the "other" side of Caribbean expressive culture, it is instructive to observe the use of technologies in this segment of the society.

The chapter is also concerned with aspects of the relationship between Caribbean and North American and Western gospel expression. Caribbean gospel culture has always borrowed heavily from Western gospel and popular culture. In the twenty-first century, the influence from North America in particular is staggering. Part of the reason for this increased influence has to do with wider economic, political, religious, and cultural developments. At the heart of this process of influence are the technologies that help transmit cultural data. Although this book considers cyberculture and other emerging spheres of experience as major sites of activity, it should be understood that extant technologies such as television are coextensive mediums of display. This chapter in the final section devotes some time to a description and discussion of the intersection of gospel culture and new media such as the Internet. It for instance examines the uses of the Internet by Caribbean gospel radio networks, by Caribbean denominations, gospel publishing houses, and record companies, as well as individual performers. All in all, it considers some of the popular mediums that have helped to transform Caribbean gospel culture within the first decade of the twenty-first century. What this chapter also raises is the significant question of the place and stance of gospel culture in a world that is becoming increasingly technologized. How does gospel culture respond to the threat posed by technology to old systems of knowledge and to more traditional beliefs about humankind, the future, the machines and "the real"? How does religious activity appropriate technology to construct the message of salvation, while at the same time confronting the belief that technology's power also foreshadows the end of life as we know of and perceive it? How does religious culture negotiate a path at the "end of the real"?

The Caribbean music video has evolved in tandem with the development of Caribbean entertainment culture. The music video is in many respects a medium by which the state of entertainment culture can be gauged. The time, energies, and ideologies that Caribbean performers and others have placed in such phenomena as music and Web videos make these important sources of information. Our failure in the region to explore the wealth of these materials reflects one of the greatest deficiencies in contemporary Caribbean criticism.

I would like to propose that the emergence of new systems of cultural transaction and display marks a critical moment in the passage of Caribbean cultural expression. As the older modes and systems of expression and production pass away, the rise of the machines signals the birth of new practices that are driven by technological innovation. These newer tracks of data represent legitimate actions. These are no less vital tracks of data than what traditionally was displayed via less technologically encoded mediums. These new tracks of data have started to register some time ago, but the digital revolution of the early twenty-first century escalated the production of technologized/digitized culture. At the end of culture (as we once knew it), Caribbean society still contemplates the options available to it in a world fast driven by key industrial, commercial, and political forces. As the global phenomena that seek to streamline and process world culture continue to forge their ideologies, it is striking that Caribbean and associated cultures have not recognized the virtual domain as being a crucial site for the infiltration of future global agendas. There is no better place to begin to trace the strands of control on regional culture than within the arena of religious practice and popular gospel culture. I do not preoccupy myself with that task throughout, because I feel that some groundwork must also be laid, prior to such an intense discussion. But it does manage to provide the context within which further debate can and will be undertaken.

In *Culture @ the Cutting Edge* I discussed the role of gospel in Caribbean society. I also accounted for the development of and limitation placed on gospel acts. Before the late 1990s gospel and religious culture was not perceived as an important category within the wider arena of

Caribbean cultural expression. In the twenty-first century, this has changed somewhat, yet gospel culture still represents an arena that is little understood. By the early twenty-first century, expressions within gospel culture were more visible and better received by the secular arena due to enhanced professionalism within several areas of religious culture. The movement by secular entertainers into the gospel arena also meant that there was greater lateral interplay of skills. There had always been this lateral movement from one domain to the other, but the early 2000s witnessed a heightening of this phenomenon. In spite of the transformations being wrought with regional entertainment culture, gospel still held firmly to its roots in some respects and so continued to wrestle with its very existence.

By the mid-2000s there were still relatively few financially successful gospel professional acts throughout the region. Gospel acts in the region have not generally recorded with the level of frequency of their counterparts in other genres. Because the purchasing market for gospel is not perceived to be very large, this has affected the general desire to produce recordings. Whereas musicians in other categories have secured their upkeep and livelihood through audience patronage, this is not widely the case with gospel. Gospel acts have had to battle against the perception that the work of God should not be offered for sale, as obtains in the secular arena. Gospel acts have therefore had to negotiate payment for performance with some care. Many attempts to operate as professionals have been met with strict condemnation by more conservative factions within Christendom. Groups and individuals who have sought to advance their standing, who have challenged the status quo, have come under severe criticism. Jerry Lloyd, the Grace Thrillers, Promise, Tribal Roots, Shine the Light, Sherwin Garner, Papa San, Royal Priesthood, Stitchie, Sean Daniel, Horella Goodwin, Marcia Griffiths, Monty G, Judah Development, the New Life Ambassadors, and Bro Stephenson "Lil Man" Collymore, are some of these acts.

Globalized Gospel

In the first decade of the twenty-first century, Caribbean religious bodies and their members came under the influences that were affecting the wider society. In many cases, individual participants within gospel culture were affected as participants within global secular culture, as members of their respective denominations, and as members of the local community. By the twenty-first century, even the church operated with a full view of all that was taking place within global culture. Relatively free access to technologies made this process possible.

Caribbean gospel acts and their churches became increasingly aware of the changed arena in which ideological and spiritual battles were taking place. Denominations therefore consciously sought to get up their messages through sponsoring and hosting their own services, complete with their musical acts on television and on radio. In many cases throughout the region, this has been the church's response to the global advent and expansion of digitized gospel.

Throughout the 1980s televangelism impacted the gospel ministry in the Caribbean. Jimmy Swaggart's ministry was immensely popular up until the late 1980s, when the scandal concerning his sexual misconduct broke. In the 1990s, the growing popularity of satellite television and the appeal of gospel networks like Trinity Broadcast Network continued to influence the format of some Caribbean gospel broadcasts. Satellite technology gave Caribbean viewers full access to international gospel networks. In the same way that other sectors of Caribbean society tuned in to Western secular popular culture, so too Caribbean Christian viewers tuned in to American gospel television. Many found leadership and entertainment through these emerging centers of doctrine, habits, and ideology. Trinity Broadcasting Network (TBN), started in 1973 as the dream of Paul and Jan Crouch, has become the world's leading Christian broadcasting network. Its influence and ambition have seen it diversify its product. It has produced one-on-one interviews with major celebrities, has inspired new progressive music videos and also entered into the domain of feature films; *The Omega Code* (1999) represents its commitment to offering an alternative to Hollywood fare. In 2003, as part of the Network's Memorial Day programming, it released the Stephen Baldwin—starred *Fly Boys*. In 2004, it promoted the new end-times thriller *Six: The Mark Unleashed*. The TBN formula revolved around the broadcast of programs featuring established preachers, teachers, singers, and selected celebrities. Its roster included T. D. Jakes, Creflo Dollar, Rod Parsley, Benny Hinn, and Gerald Osteen, and it also showed converts like MC Hammer and Stephen Baldwin.

Many Caribbean believers (and gospel pop culture generally) were influenced by the "Word of Faith" and prosperity teachings of Jakes, Dollar, and Parsley in particular. But TBN and gospel entertainment networks also spawned the immense interest in what the Western Christian entertainment industry called the praise and worship movement. This movement was driven by a spiritual imperative of reassessing the role of traditional Biblical worship habits and appropriating them within contemporary contexts. This was one part of the praise and worship phenomenon. Another arm of the movement was commercially inspired and sought to maximize the returns that could be had from careful branding of products. Praise and worship music in particular led the way in confirming the popularity of people like Michael W Smith and Avalon, as well as enriching the catalog of established record labels like Integrity, who through its corporate values Web page spoke of "encouraging an innovative culture." On its "Company History" Web page it boasts of being "the undisputed leader in praise and worship music, the fastest growing segment of the Christian music industry. Integrity ended 2000 with a remarkable 56 percent market share of the praise and worship music products being sold in Christian retail outlets."[2]

Institutions of this kind were not only confined to music recordings, but they also supported video, print, software, direct mail, and electronic media as part of the drive to capture market share. Caribbean believers were active consumers in this process. Relatively few Caribbean performers participated actively in this international movement as creators. Leading singers and preachers were invited to the region to conduct services, workshops, and outreach activity. They were paid well. This process of dependence and near servitude was reflective of the entrenchment of the hierarchical relationship between Caribbean and North American (leading-world) personnel. There was little reciprocation on the part of North American interests. Caribbean preachers and other performers were hardly accorded the respect or opportunity that they themselves paid to their Western colleagues. All in all, however, Caribbean gospel popular culture developed with two main veins of emphasis. There was the spiritual arm that valorized the ushering in of God's power on an advanced social order, and there was also the commercial wing, which sought new ways of exploring and exploiting the transformations in gospel culture for greater economic returns. But yet, these driving principles were not distinct and separate. They were at times interlocked. There are performers who fit into the two categories, who are at once inspired by "the move of the Spirit" to help usher in the new working of God, but who are also conscious of the need for financial upkeep and rewards.

Although Caribbean gospel broadcasts on television did not exhibit the same grandeur as that frequently projected on TBN, they nonetheless borrowed motifs and style from that network on occasion. Caribbean broadcasts also established their own visual language and style. Many broadcasts by Caribbean denominations have tended to center on the spoken word. The major emphasis has tended to be on "the man of the hour." Generally these broadcasts are free-flowing productions. That is, they reflect the work of one or two camera positions, with little evidence of significant postproduction editing. Many productions tended to be of fifteen-minute or thirty-minute duration, of which at least five minutes are given to special singing and performing by dedicated gospel acts. Various television stations have produced programs devoted to promoting national gospel acts. But even most of these programs are "live" in terms of the feed that is screened. They are not screened as vigorously postproduced segments. Because of this format therefore we cannot talk of these shows as possessing the tight production values that we associate with the music and entertainment video, although it might be argued that the trend of excerpting segments of these free-flowing videos as program fillers on Caribbean television has reconstituted these fillers as virtual entertainment or music videos. These excerpts are introduced without scheduling, and they also disappeared without warning. It is this moment of unexpected flicker that conjures up the music video genre.

It is important to understand that Caribbean religious bodies, especially Evangelicals, vested much interest in traditional and emerging media in the new decade of the 2000s. While preachers and denominations spread the word through open air and actual visits into public spaces, they also used the medium of radio and television. Although the computer and newer technologies were fast becoming mediums of choice, many Caribbean religious bodies had not as yet found those facilities as rewarding as working through more traditional mediums. As had transpired in the arena of secular, non-religious activity, Caribbean religious bodies also delayed their active participation in cyberspace.

Gospel Videos

Traditionally, the music video was regarded as a supporting promotional tool and hardly an end within itself.[33] In spite of its traditional function, entertainment companies have invested substantial energy into this market over the years of its popularization, especially since the early 1980s. By the mid-1990s, music entertainment television and video were serving an even more significant function as part of marketing initiatives, and by the mid-2000s evolving technologies like the Internet, mobile phones, and other peripherals were changing the way that people produced and consumed videos. The international gospel industry has also devoted substantial attention to this genre. In the Caribbean, gospel music videos have not been widely produced by its artists. Many more groups dreamed of producing videos than those that actually did do so. The closest some groups came to having a music video was when their appearance on a longer program was edited and excerpted and replayed on national or regional television. Given the cost associated with traditional video production and the traditionally conservative outlook of Caribbean gospel culture, there have therefore been relatively few groups or artists that have consistently produced music videos throughout the decades of the 1980s, 1990s, and 2000s. But there has nonetheless been a significant dissemination of gospel entertainment videos. Indeed, I would argue that Caribbean gospel culture cannot be properly conceptualized without some understanding of the role, function, and structuring of music and entertainment "television" (including the computer), in recent years.

On the way toward embracing the Internet, Caribbean gospel culture first came up against, explored, and exploited the older technology of television. Caribbean gospel employed television in a number of different ways: through live programming, re-telecasts, discussion forums, and packaged postproduced programs. Significantly, one of the better-known entertainment or music video programs within the region has been a Caribbeanized offshoot of the thirty-minute program called *Fastforward*. This program is devoted to the airing of dedicated music videos. The VJ (video jockey) segment of the program, as shown in the region, has been produced by Grenada's Lighthouse Television Station.

The structural or sequential format of the program sees it being hosted by a local presenter. The presenter stands between the audience and the actual music videos that are to be aired. The presenter talks to the audience about some common youth theme (such as love or lust), while interspersing music videos at selected points of the talk. The presenter mediates the relationship between audience and the video material to be aired. In the earlier series of the program *Fastforward*, there was an attempt to include regional music videos, but over time there have been fewer and fewer regional videos. This might say more about the preference of the producers for middle-of-the-road "international" gospel rock than about the low output of Caribbean gospel.

Despite the relative absence of Caribbean videos, *Fastforward* has been able to get significant distribution within the region. Because most of the music videos on that program tend to be of leading gospel acts in the United States, there is always therefore a recurring situation of distancing. The videos aired are removed from the presenter because they are from a culture extrinsic to the region. The difference and distance between these entities is also evident in the disparate production aesthetics built into the two contexts (the actual music video and the studio feed).

The production quality of the music videos appears more professional and grittier than the broadcast quality that supports the local host in the studio. Arguably, music video always has a heightened production value and impact, but this notwithstanding, the production dynamics between the live studio and packaged videos does not work very well. This has mostly to do with the attempt of the regional studio producers to try to approximate the quality of the pop rock video while filming in a sparsely furnished sound set. The regional producers of *Fastforward*, being conscious of the distance between the regional and nonregional filmic segment, opted for a host in order to mediate these spaces within the telecast. This is but one of several other strategies employed within the program.

On *Fastforward*, the videos are not aired sequentially, wall to wall. This could be disruptive to the viewing habits of Caribbean gospel audiences. Many gospel viewers in the Caribbean, as elsewhere, do feel that music ministry must always employ the literal scriptural verse. The presenter therefore always has a theme that she or he introduces every week when the program kicks off, so that, in a sense, there are two levels of discourse that are in operation. There is the discourse that is convened by the presenter when she or he introduces the theme that will be talked about between music video clips. For example, on a late 1999 episode the young female presenter introduces the theme of "relationships." She talks about the central role that relationships play in young people's lives. She zeros in on love relationships, and then she introduces Jesus as being the best partner anyone can have. All of this is done within a four-minute time span before she introduces the first music video from the group DC Talk. There is a strained attempt to link the discourse that she is conducting with the three or four music videos that are to be aired in the approximately twenty-five-minute program. She marks the first bridge between the discourses by introducing important questions that she poses and leaves with you while the music video begins, this hopefully playing its part in helping to convict viewers on the questions posed: "Hey, you. Are you looking for commitment? I am telling you, search no more. Jesus is the man you been looking for. Do you have a relationship with Jesus? You know, well if not, then that is one reason for you to sit back, relax while we kick it off with DC Talk. (The video plays.)"[4]

Paradoxically, there is no direct relationship between the music video and the discourse that precedes and claims to introduce it. The DC Talk video deals with a series of instances of wrecked lives. Although it is possible to force a connection between this and the initial discourse, the video does not directly reinforce the message being presented by the host. The scriptwriters and producers have had a difficult time bridging the gap between the two discourses.

But there is also some disjointedness at the level of filmic quality. Because the images created by the music videos are bound to be unstable and flickering, the producers of the studio segment have attempted to mesh the two segments of music video and live studio feed by employing an "unstable camera" for the in-house filming of the host. There is some measure of success in this strategy. Successive broadcasts have therefore put the young hosts at the center of three camera shots. The studio for the in-house production is a warm, well-enclosed, and effectively decorated makeshift area. The host stands and pirouettes just in front of two or three tall carefully angled billboards coated with posters of gospel artists, T-shirts, and caps. The three camera positions appear to be one to the left, another to the right, and a third that transmits a blue-coated picture to the viewing audience. Sometimes a camera is positioned above, so that the host looks up to locate it. The camera shots are carefully directed so that no single camera position controls the point of view. Each shot is assigned no more than five seconds. But even the five-second angles given are not stable. Each camera pivots on a central axis dipping to the left and right, and while also slowly zooming in and out with hypnotic possibilities. This camera manipulation attempts to compensate for the fast-paced action of the music videos that fuel the program *Fastforward*. The critical point to make about this program is that it demonstrates how even gospel culture is prone to tension revolving around issues of cultural distance and technology. The message of the gospel can be shared across cultures, but the timbre of this message gains varying definitions across different cultures. Where technology has the capacity to mend the real and apparent differences across gospel cultures, its presence can also serve to emphasize these differences.

Music Video Models

In spite of the inherent differences within gospel culture, there have always been attempts within the region to match the standards and features of leading edge gospel acts from outside the region. Many gospel music videos that are seen by Caribbean audiences are predominantly those screened from the United States. Those emanating from the United States are either filmed excerpts edited from longer "live" performances (such as I have referred to above) or other bona fide packaged music videos. The bona fide music video from North America has been the model for many regional videos in the religious as well as the secular domain. The divide between what is called white and black gospel significantly tends to throw up two types of music video. There is always, for me, some difficulty when such categories are created and used loosely, because anyone who knows the history of Western popular music is aware that the musics labeled black or white are themselves inspired and developed by a range of people. But this notwithstanding, it is still possible to talk of musical genres and subgenres as having dominant filmic aesthetics that help to fashion the evolution of that category of music. There is indeed some difference among the various categories of "international" gospel videos that Caribbean people have come to know. Because these different videos have inspired regional videos, it might be useful to examine at least one "international" video from each of the two groups by way of describing some of the conventions that regional acts and viewers have experienced, if not internalized. Ultimately, we will be better placed to assess the nature of Caribbean gospel video in light of the relative presence and absence of external and internal influences. Because the assumption is that Caribbean gospel borrows freely from global and international spheres, it is reasonable to assume that Caribbean gospel video is not radically different. But how heavily do leading Caribbean gospel acts invest in local, regional, and international conventions? The objective here is not to look for specific traces of North American video aesthetics in specific Caribbean videos, but rather to suggest how, like North American video, Caribbean video also straddles a number of categories.

There is a difference between the music videos of acts like the Newsboys and Kirk Franklin. Acts like the Newsboys, Michael W Smith, and Steven Curtis Chapman tend to approximate the music video styling of secular acts like R.E.M, Smashing Pumpkins, and other alternative performers. But then again, these gospel performers are also performing their messages to the musical styling of alternative and pop rock. The sound and image texts are constructed in a particular way. They share a tight relationship. In the sound mix of Newsboys' "Everybody Gets a Shot," the vocals are immersed within the musical mix of drums, bass guitar, lead guitar, and synthesizers. In the video domain, the high-powered sound clash of instruments is sequenced with an equally charged, cataclysmic projection of images. The music video is set exclusively in a "live" performance context. But the video is the result of much postproduction work. The images are cast from camera shot to camera shot, from angle to angle. The cameras, even when they zero in on the lead vocalist, are hardly stable. They are constantly in motion. Most other shots, other than those of the lead vocalist, only remain one and a half seconds on screen. Lighting effects are heavy. Red and orange give way to gray and blue light projections. But the cameras also seem to project and encode their own light.

Shots of the audience are interspersed with those of the performance on stage. The camera finds a middle-aged mother in the audience. By locating her, the producer seems to be saying that it is OK for older grownups to listen to this youth-oriented music. The camera also finds a young boy who seems to know the words of the song, although they are not easily decipherable to the ears: [5]

> wonder if there's someone up there
> Sums it off with don't know don't care
> O God he doesn't exist . . .

During the song's chorus, guitars take over the music, leading it to a crescendo of noises. The images follow suit. As is customary in other alternative music videos, the images flicker with greater rapidity when the music amplifies.[6] All in all, the music video might appear to some audiences and to some film theorists as being chaotic and postmodernist. But although there is much flickering of images and some lyrical incoherence, on a deeper level of analysis, it is evident that there is some logic to the construction and production of this type of gospel music video.[7]

Caribbean gospel acts are conscious of the types of videos that project groups at the cutting edge of alternative gospel internationally. Although most Caribbean gospel groups don't perform or produce alternative-type gospel videos, they sit in awe of such video productions. As they sit in awe, they think of two things. They think of the finance required to produce this VH1-type production. Most denominational centers that provide the support base for Caribbean gospel artists would react negatively to this type of music video production—that is, with its accompanying sound track of overactive electronic gadgets. Admittedly, by the mid-2000s, some gospel acts have taken the chance at producing comparatively "noisy" and fast-paced music videos, but most of these acts are self-supporting and semi-autonomous of institutional conservatism. Contemporary post-soca and post-dancehall gospel has drawn quite significantly from the conventions that define alternative gospel.

The music video model provided by black gospel acts has proven to be more palatable to Caribbean gospel consumers and performers. Kirk Franklin's "You Are the Only One" and similar videos are admired by the majority of youths and by progressive popular gospel acts in the Caribbean. To the extent that Kirk Franklin's music can be said to have had the biggest impact on popular gospel acts in the Caribbean between 1998 and 2003, many of these artists have also valorized his music video productions.

His "You Are the Only One" contains a number of features that differentiate it from the method of the Newsboys. The most striking difference is the tendency not to "hide" behind the shadows or remain inhibited by instruments. Whereas the Newsboys video is built on heavy simultaneous lighting and film editing, the Kirk Franklin video seems to free itself from the claustrophobia of that gospel video genre. The Franklin video claims to take place in an open American street. There is a lot of choreographed dancing, and the wearing of matching outfits by many of the people in the video. The clothing color motifs are yellow, red, and blue. Franklin sports a bright yellow and green sweater-type shirt in some shots.

The video's narrative unfolds around a stalled convoy of believers who open up the hood of their broken-down sport-utility vehicle. While they await its repair, they proceed to hold a dance worship session in the middle of the street. They anger a group of street thugs. But they don't care. Instead, the song's lyrical track invites all, especially the young:[8]

> What yah saying now . . .
> All the young people driving down town in them jeeps
> I want you to pump this up so loud so the neighbors can hear you . . .

The remainder of the video is a defiant celebration of religious freedom. The musical score in this video is not gritty street hip hop; rather, it is much closer to new jack swing or hip hop soul. Nonetheless, it is gospel with an attitude. It represents the left wing styling of black contemporary gospel. For Franklin's music has tended to revolve on strong funk motifs, and the lyrics have openly proclaimed the Savior, while struggling to employ street jargon. But arguably it is his performance, representing Kirk Franklin at his most daring best. In terms of production quality, it is in the same or approximate league with any other secular video produced for international consumption. The video's main setting is in the open street, but it also moves into an enclosed studio, where colored backgrounds and close-up shots call attention to the rap chant that carries the song's main verse, before returning to the open spaces to capture the infectious revelry of the brethren in the streets. This is carefully worked out, as is Kirk Franklin's audacious manner and the camera's uncomfortably close proximity to his gesticulating hands. Whereas the alternative gospel video is self-consciously reliant on editing, sound, and postproduction features to constitute its presence and impact, the funkified gospel of Kirk Franklin foregrounds the performing subjects and their choreographed routines as critical to the message that they deliver: "You are the only one."

In the Caribbean there is a noticeable gospel culture. Young people make up the majority of this movement, or body. Some of these are singers themselves, but mostly they are concertgoers and supporters of religious and associated events. This body of people is pretty much attuned to the happenings within gospel outside of the Caribbean. They are familiar with the leading gospel acts outside of the region and most would claim to like Kirk Franklin, Donnie McClurkin, Michael W. Smith and Yolanda Adams. Most performing popular gospel acts are also au fait with the cutting edge of international gospel and so aspire to become international acts. But much of this admiration and ambition is tempered by the recognition that American gospel operates within a different setup to the extent that American gospel in its many styles can find legitimizing forces from some quarter; in the Caribbean, gospel does not have an array of multifarious support bases. As I have been saying for some time, it is the relationship between gospel acts and denominational centers that has kept many Caribbean gospel acts in line, so to speak. By the late 1990s, a number of secular performers within the Caribbean began to perform gospel, changing their lyrics but maintaining many of the musical traits that made them familiar stars. Some of these were King Obstinate, King Short Shirt of Antigua and Barbuda, Carlene Davis, Papa San of Jamaica, and Tambu of Trinidad, among others. But in terms of visibility, these had not replaced the more longstanding gospel acts by the end of the twentieth century. Caribbean gospel acts have therefore striven to keep up with trends taking place abroad. Still, there is the feeling that most gospel acts are indifferent to the new strides developed in message dissemination after the early 1980s. The vigorously postproduced Caribbean gospel music video is still not a visible commodity. There are relatively few groups that make consistent use of their own packaged music videos for distribution or even promotion nationally and regionally.

Packaged Gospel Video—The Grace Thrillers

The music video collection *Make Us One*, by the Jamaican vocal and musical group the Grace Thrillers, represented a major effort by this Caribbean act when it was released. The Grace Thrillers was at the peak of their popularity between the mid-1990s and early 2000s. Whereas Promise of Barbados's videos have reflected a number of tensions that have to do with their negotiation of the liminal space between showmanship, entertainment, and ministry, the Grace Thrillers seemed to have faced none of this in the conceptualization and production of their popular video collection *Make Us One*. But perhaps I should make the point that the Grace Thrillers collection released in 2000 represented a commodified, packaged production. It was not their first such production: *Crown Him* had appeared before. *Make Us One* was done for sale, whereas the Promise videos were produced primarily for distribution to television stations as promotional support for their audio recordings.

The Grace Thrillers have built their popularity around a very tightly spun formula. They have tended to rework familiar gospel standards and Negro spirituals. They have repopularized these to mento, reggae, and soul-oriented styling. Audiences have come to expect certain formulaic performances from this core vocal group and their band of musicians. Their tightly structured vocal harmonies, steady musical accompaniments, and clear delivery of the gospel message define the Grace Thrillers' method of ministry. It is therefore not surprising that their videos try to capture and reproduce this very formula in the arena of multimedia display. But having made these choices, the group must still have confronted and wrestled with the processes and practicalities that constitute and define the music video genre. For instance, what might appear as forthright ministering of a song in the audio domain, as on CD or in the live performance setting, can come over as dry, noncommercial, and trite in the music video sphere.

Overall, the Grace Thrillers' performance on their music videos has not gone beyond their well-established parameters. They have delivered what is expected. It is a success. The production's first video is the title track "Make Us One." It begins with the screen blacked out. Sound takes over. The first sound is the words spoken by the male lead vocalist. This primary inscription serves to establish the rootedness of the entire production in the spoken word, in the Word of God. As the male vocalist introduces the song, the camera, beginning from below the shoulder slowly but predictably zooms in on his face, close-up. He declares,

"The word of God says that we should serve the Lord our God with all our hearts, all our souls, all our strength, minds, and we should love our neighbors as ourselves. There is many divisions in the world today, and because of this we would like to dedicate this song to the nations of this earth."[9]

This introduction serves as a reminder to audiences that this packaged video performance is rooted in the evangelical Christian experience, which the performers feel can easily be lost to the glitz and glamour of the music video and its attendant technology. So the words of invocation are a reminder to the audience and to the performers themselves, who set about to proclaim the Word of God by employing the technological tools that the world has manipulated for monetary and other gains.

The centrality of the Word is again reinforced in this video after the second verse, when in the song's open spaces (where the vocals stop and the electronic instruments come to the fore), there is a spoken segment that introduces the voiceover of a female. The words of her sermon come up on the screen, scrolling upwards to reinforce the message of the gospel. Of note also is the fact that the speaking voice is not attributed to any of the performers on screen. The production makes it abundantly clear that this is not the voice of any one of them: by clearly positioning all of the members in a wide shot, the director allows us to recognize that their mouths do not move. This method therefore calls attention to the centrality of the spoken word. It also ascribes to the spoken voice an existence beyond the camera's all-embracing politics.

Whereas the camera claims power of fashioning, fixing, and controlling the discursive space in film and in the music video format, the Grace Thrillers video seems to challenge the camera's and technology's claims to authority and control. In a video like Kirk Franklin's "Revolution," for example, the camera's power of control compresses Franklin and his other performers into a series of contorted and genie-like spheres of representation. One therefore leaves the Franklin video with a sense of gratification on having experienced the full controlling power of the camera's embrace. But in the Thrillers video, the voice remains outside of the camera's (and video's) range of control and construction. This is not a case of a badly edited video that inadvertently fails to sequence sound and image and hence creates the impression of sound and image hermeneutical displacement. Rather, here is a clearly established directorial practice/ideology. In the absence of the camera's ability to locate the source of the sound, the words and their voice take control. They gain focus. They assume power—an awesome power:[10]

> Oh Lord God
> Father of the Universe,
> Creator of Heaven and Earth,
> . . . .
> Make us one . . .

The spoken words here reconnect to those spoken initially before the cameras rolled to begin to capture video images. This reference to the earlier verbalization not only establishes a cyclic pattern of interconnecting tropes within the production but also suggests another kind of connectivity. Given the confidence exuded by the performers, the video posits that they have made an even more profound connection. Whereas the camera cannot always locate the voice, its source, the director, situates the group as having found the Source. Whereas some viewers are positioned as being outside of this possibility at the given moment, the production's intention is to heighten this sense of distance and difference between the Thrillers and some of their viewers in order to impress the necessity to reestablish a link between those who are "torn" and the Creator. This is one way of reading the music video. Another perspective might certainly conclude that far from any such deep meaning and inscription, the music video simply strings together a set of recurring images, shots, and tropes. Given the attention paid to realist presentation, some would even argue that this Grace Thrillers video is most effective when read at the surface level.

The entire *Make Us One* music video production is filmed on location at what appears to be an events complex. Much of the filming takes place in a semi-outdoor location with plants, flowers, arches, and a smoothly cemented floor. The setting is carefully embellished with strategically positioned floral decorations. The ambience is one of serene solitude. This setting tends to locate the singers as in harmony with nature and the even larger world.

The camera shots for the entire production are clearly defined in the opening video. The first shot is of the speaker, the second focuses on two singers, from the waist upwards, the third shot locates three singers from the waist up. The fourth shot is a wider shot that shows all of the chorale members in harmony at the end of the a cappella chorus section of the song. This widening of the camera's visual reference locks home the song's imperative of advocating total Caribbean and global harmony and unity.

Shots fade in and out of one another, but not in a disconcerting way, not to detract from the sound and the words. The soundtrack therefore maintains a clear sense of importance throughout. There appear to be two cameras in operation. These two cameras interplay between close-up shots and wide shots, or set-left and set-right angles. They therefore help to maintain the video's interest at the visual level without overpowering the other constituents of the production. There is every indication that postproduction was minimized. Indeed, there appears to have been a decided objective to limit the appearance of excessive technological intervention.

The singers change their costumes throughout. They dress alike in the first song of unity but diversify as the video production continues. In "I Am the Way," they engage in a choreographed dance routine that represents one of the more expressive music video performances by the group. But even so, the choreography is tame by mid-1990s standards when also compared to the street dance references in videos by acts like Gospel Gangstaz and Kirk Franklin. The group makes use of shoulder and hand movements while the camera seems timid in its showing of movements below the waist. This timidity is compensated by an interplay between close-up and wider shots in the song's call and response section of the chorus. Here the shifting camera angles correspond with the shifts between the call and the response sections of the chorus.

But this is the exception on Grace Thrillers videos. This type of visual pleasure is subsumed beneath the production's major imperatives. The most popular visual process is without doubt the fading in and out of frames. This is especially utilized in performances of slower songs like "Jesus is the One" and "I Love Him." The possible intention of this method is to convey an aura of wonder, transience, and the supernatural. Therefore in many instances the production situates three realities on the same screen at the same time and holds them, until they dissolve into one shot.

This predictable, noncomplex, but effective production reflects a clearly worked-out strategy on the part of the director and executive producers. They have clearly discussed their objectives and have not sought to conceal their politics within these music videos. Viewers are able to see through the production techniques after just a few viewings of a video. In this way, the attention is drawn away from the music video and from the genre itself and redirected to other more important issues. When one compares many of these Grace Thrillers videos with contemporary videos within the Western music industry, there is therefore a deliberate attempt by the Thrillers to subvert the growing trend among leading gospel acts. Where leading acts like Kirk Franklin and the Newsboys related to technology as a source of inspiration and wonder, the Caribbean's leading vocal group showed how it was possible to use technology in limited doses for the effect of asserting the need for humankind to come to terms with their salvation; yet without the encumbrance of human technological excess.

In the earlier works *Roots to Popular Culture*[11] and *Culture @ the Cutting Edge*, I discussed the nature of Caribbean gospel's conservative alignment to denomination and institutional controllers. Although the Caribbean gospel music video reveals traces of this denominational controlling politics, it is evident that gospel acts have contemplated their location between denominational and wider market interests, and so they have strategized accordingly. Not all groups over the past fifteen years have been as conservative as the Grace Thrillers. But most of them have had to negotiate the fragile terrain that constitutes Caribbean gospel. Some videos have revealed cleverly crafted productions that reinforce vocal performance. For some of these, the video is not meant to supplant but to buttress their audio recordings. Therefore, the perceived conservatism in the video domain can be explained as a deliberate attempt to remain true to their primary format, which is still the audio CD. The Grace Thrillers video successfully supports their sound recordings.

The primacy of the audio over the video is established by the tendency among some groups to perform their visuals for the video "live" but retain the vocal track from the original audio CD recording. This is an economic decision as well, because it is less costly to do so than to do a raw live audio performance along with the live visual enactment. A live audio recording also necessitates the employment of excessive amounts of technological gadgets in order to capture the kind of refined compressed and "effected" sound that characterizes music like that of the Grace Thrillers. Thus, although the Grace Thrillers' music video performance claims some degree of forthrightness on account of employing few technological feats, it still comes to viewers loaded with a number of intricate technological processes. In retaining the audio tracks from another studio recording, the video's visual performance creates a distance between that original oral rendition and the music video performance that claims to be authentic in its delivery. One does not doubt the intention of sincerity on the part of the performers, but the splicing of video and audio tracks, when it is examined through a close multi-tracked reading of the production, begins to reveal the extent to which all contemporary performances are servants of technological guile. This is not a statement that is meant to cast judgment on groups like the Grace Thrillers and Promise and all those that have done videos; rather, I want to suggest that most, if not all employment and dispersal of sound and video brings into play the presence of technology.

The Grace Thrillers are therefore very much agents of technological exploration. The verbal exhortation that comes before the first song, and the actual commencement of the first song, represents the initial moment of this splicing of audio and video, of present and past, of reality and perception. In the final analysis, it is on this technology that they depend in the grand construction of their music videos. The entire production is founded on technology's sleight of hand. It is founded on technology's creating the impression of live audio sound. Technology therefore acts as ventriloquist manipulating the singers, creating the impression that their moving lips are producing the audio output that one hears. But perhaps the Grace Thrillers have claim to a voice, on account of the fact that the vocal track to which they lip-synch is indeed their own voices, only removed in time and space.

The Grace Thrillers' "I Will Follow King Jesus" is without doubt their most dynamic music video of the late twentieth century. It is an up-tempo song. It is gospel in the soca idiom. The camera is less stable than in most other Thrillers videos. Its movements are mainly lateral ones, as it scrolls across the faces of the singers who stand and dance in line. The shots fade in and out and cut sharply against each other unsystematically. At times, the visual shots captured are more natural than in other videos. The group must have deliberated over some shots, such as: those of the male vocalist with mouth wide, wide open in exaltation; those where the camera at knee-level captures the bodies of the female singers as they turn backwards onto the short gaze. This video marks one of the most radical Grace Thrillers performances, and in a sense, it is the best music video performance and production done by the group on the *Make Us One* VHS production.

The decade of the 2000s saw the revamping of the group. When the new group was launched, the group members were a new crop of young performers. The lead singer was the son of the group's managing director. If the founding Grace Thrillers appeared on the Internet primarily via music retail outlets, the new generation of Thrillers seemed intent on asserting even greater control of their image. Their dedicated site Thegracethrillers.com featured "Bio, members, products, events contact." The older generation was tentative in the presence of new technology; the new Grace Thrillers took their confidence to MySpace. Their live video performance there is less self conscious than that of their elders. The official Web site that proclaims the launch of the new group does not reveal the circumstances surrounding the new constitution, but the period of transition is defined by marked changes in gospel and tech culture. Age and other natural factors are often determinants in the reconstitution of groups, but external factors are also critical. There are times when the changes in culture brought on by newer innovations precipitate the reevolution of cultural and iconic institutions.

Gospel Band on Video and Television—Promise

If the Grace Thrillers has consistently been the leading chorale group within the Caribbean, then a group like Promise reflects some of the advances undertaken by music and technology-driven outfits. It is possible to theorize that Caribbean gospel is not only polarized in terms of musical styles—that is, the traditional style versus the more innovative—but there is also a sharp contrast between vocal groups and other groups that are constituted on the strength of musical instrument use. If the Grace Thrillers founded their ministry on the power of vocal performance, then Promise reflected a shift of emphasis towards the musical accompaniment and the kinds of technologies that create it.

Promise, the leading band from Barbados (for some twenty years beginning from the mid-1980s), has done more videos than most other groups in the Eastern Caribbean. As with some other groups, their videos have tended to be set in the television studio. This has had to do with minimizing the cost of producing the music video. But also, their videos have largely served as marketing tools for their audiocassette releases. They therefore shared this similarity with Grace Thrillers.

Their video to the song "It's Not Raining" reflects the group's strong musical showing.[12] Indeed, whereas another group like Shine the Light has built its fame around vocal harmonies and strong references to traditional gospel songs, Promise's path has been characterized by the steady modernization of the gospel song. They have therefore performed covers of contemporary gospel by the likes of Dallas Holm, Al Green, and the Imperials, but mostly they have composed their own songs. With James Leacock as their main songwriter (up until his departure in 2004), and also occasionally utilizing the talent of Vasco Greaves, their major contribution to Caribbean gospel must be their own brand of progressive Caribbean religious song. They have made use of contemporary pop rock and technologized reggae and soca. The song "It's Not Raining" is an original hard-edged pop rock work that deals with the liberation of the Christian from the murky quagmire of sin when the sun (the Son) appears: "Praise the Lord, it's not raining anymore."

At various stages of their development, they have proved themselves closer to alternative-gospel music styling than most other Caribbean gospel groups. They have drawn from such outfits as the Imperials, Petra, and the Newsboys, as well as black outfits like Commissioned and Fred Hammond and Radical for Christ. Promise is above all a serious band. Their forte is the competent employment of technology, mastery of their instruments, and a tight, disciplined sound. Their videos seek to reinforce this image. They are never away from their instruments. The locating of these instruments in their videos is all about their upholding of an image. But the centering of their instruments and the technology represents their celebratory mastery of the technology.

In the video "It's Not Raining," the stage set is laid out in the traditional way as for a classic rock band. It is blatantly positioned so. The drum set sits as the centerpiece of the stage layout. It is a mixture of acoustic skins and electronic sets, the latter left over from the 1980s Simmons SDS 8 craze. The bassist stands with his new five-string stage left, next to the drummer. This is conventional in band setups, inasmuch as the drums and bass interact as timekeeping and groove-forming constituents. Next to the bassist is the lead guitarist. The keyboardist is situated on the opposite side of the stage. In full display are his two powerful synthesizers. They are the 1980s Yamaha DX7, and the Kork M1, a major polyphonic synthesizer workstation of the early and mid-1990s.

So concentrated is the band on instruments and technology that their video does not make use of elaborate costuming to complement the almost bare embellishments of the studio setting. This is the classic instrument-driven band. The vocalist is up-front in this group. There is resonance of the Newsboys, as discussed earlier, but minus the fireworks, shifting camera angles, and postproduction editing. Unlike the Grace Thrillers, Promise does not aim for the soft background of the open sky and the well-flowered garden, but instead. they perform on a sparse stage with psychedelically colored rear projections. Like the Grace Thrillers, Promise in their videos does not valorize the technological excess that characterizes much of Western leading-edge gospel video.

The Promise video presents the band performing over a re-playing sound track. The lead and background vocalists lip-synchs. This is done to capture the quality and feel of the primary audio recording. The average viewer is not conscious of this fact. But one's attention is drawn to the distance between video and audio performance due to the absence of connecting instrument line cables from the synthesizers and the hybrid acoustic and electronic drum set. But this is not a major area of emphasis here, because the music video form is constructed upon this anomaly. The alternative-music video is especially characterized by the many contradictions that it presents between seeing and hearing and between the real and the fabricated (world of the music video). Although in orientation, Promise is closer to alternative-music aesthetics than most other Caribbean gospel groups, it has not invested consistently and heavily enough in institutionalizing music video practices from the alternative-music tradition. Like the Grace Thrillers, they have sought to reflect the influences and pressures and realities of Caribbean religious culture as encountered by them at home in the region throughout the decades up to the 2000s.

In the Promise video "Love Letters," a number of the set motifs referred to above are repeated. But there are some changes that are worthy of note, inasmuch as they help to create a sense of the filmic practices that are attendant to progressive gospel signification in the late twentieth century. The major distinction between these two videos is that whereas "It's

Not Raining" is classic slow gospel rock, "Love Letters" is a bouncing reggae original. Its lyrics build an engaging narrative around the speaking voice that agonizes over Jesus' departure from the earth and waxes lyrical about the "love letters" that Jesus leaves for humankind within the Bible. The song is therefore constructed around the metaphor of love and falling in love. It centers the comfort brought to humankind through the written "letters" of God:[13]

> You wrote love letters
> Straight into my window my heart
> Love letters
> You see I'm so proud to read Your holy Word

The filmic directorial angles are quite similar to the earlier video. The marked difference between them is the use of stage lighting to create an orange-red background in "Love Letters." This gives the set an altered appearance from the natural, invisible lighting employed before. This Promise performance alludes to the rock genre in its employment of altered visual appearance, creating a surrealistic atmosphere. The Newsboys video, though, utilizes many more camera angles and so is much more eclectic. The Promise video also wants to create the transfixed reality, as in keeping with the theme of the supernatural connection between God and Man. It does so without distracting audiences from fixing on the messenger and the message. The video seems a bit inhibited by its own careful construction, where the director does not want to present the band as overly radical, so a sense of balance is sought after by offsetting the loud color backdrop with somewhat stable, almost predictable camera angles.

But although I make these comments, it must be understood that this type of video still represented leading video performance in the 1990s. When one understands the fragile nature of the relationship between many Caribbean gospel acts and their denominational centers, then one understands how many bands felt they had to walk the thin line between conservatism and radical performance. After I have said this as well, a fundamental point that should also be stated is that the Promise videos discussed here represented major financial and promotional undertakings. Much more financial input would have been needed to produce and post-produce a more technologically daring sequence of these approximately five videos that support the album *Love Letters*. When considering their budget, Promise would have concluded that it was more productive to film five relatively inexpensive music videos than just one or two technologically elaborate and potentially alienating music videos. Such are the choices that gospel and religious groups have faced when they sought to take Caribbean religious expression to the frontier of music and entertainment television just before the Internet came into prominence. Like the Grace Thrillers, Promise still continued performing way into the 2000s. Also like the Thrillers, they have undergone changes in personnel. Unlike the Thrillers, they have transitioned smoothly. It is surprising, though, that a group that represented the cutting edge of Caribbean gospel in the 1980s and 1990s has not secured a dedicated Web presence.

Part 2: Gospel Within the Net

This assessment of the relationship between leading groups, television, video, and audiences really reflects the tensions at work within Caribbean gospel just before even newer technologies infiltrated the region en masse after the early 2000s. Before the popularization and expansion of the Internet and newer mobile technologies, Caribbean religious culture treated television as the leading-edge frontier for the expression and dissemination of the message of Christ. The explorations by groups like the Grace Thrillers and Promise, though relatively conservative, still represented major excursions into the realm of possibility. Many other groups beheld the work of these two outfits with admiration and some envy. While television still remains a major conduit for disseminating the gospel, it is no longer seen as the leading frontier. The entertainment and hardware and software industries have already predicted the death of the dedicated television set.

With the popularization of the World Wide Web, groups and establishments within the region found it easier to enter the domain of technological display and to mount the same platform as leading Western religious and secular institutions. Where the televised music video represented the forefront of gospel expression for many years in the region, the birth of the Internet and the expansion of virtual technologies rendered this medium of expression relatively obsolete. Yes, it was still expensive to do a music video, and it was still desirable to have a packaged religious production for television and radio, but these did not carry the same trendy appeal as having a Web presence, regardless of the kind of presence mounted online. Caribbean gospel and religious popular culture can therefore be conceptualized with respect to their technological preoccupation. The set of experiments with the packaged performance (by musical groups) is but one component of the system of engaging and dispensing with new technologies in regional societies. Within this system of relations, Caribbean societies have stopped short of immersing themselves wholesale into the frontier arena of technological deification. This has been the case partly because a full emersion of Caribbean society can signal a loss of power in the face of leading industrialized nations that have placed a hedge about their ownership and control of new technologies. Given the current entrenchment of real and virtual domination, regional entities have thought it most strategically prudent to engage and dispense with new technologies. This strategy allows for the possibility of some leverage and autonomy in the future, as the world system of domination constructs itself in preparation for the end of the culture wars.

Pope John Paul, Web Parishes: The Real-Virtual Struggle Abroad and in the Region

If participants in Caribbean gospel culture encountered its major exponents locally and abroad via radio and television throughout the 1970s and up to the 1990s, then by the turn of the new millennium they were also accessing these acts via the Internet. For instance, Caribbean gospel radio was accessible on the Internet in the same way that secular radio programming had moved to cyber wave throughout the late 1990s. Caribbean Gospel Network was a leading site that provided access to information and facilitated the purchase of music CDs by the likes of Junior Tucker, Prodigal Son, and Antigua's Judah Development.[14] This was one of other Caribbean gospel sites that devoted themselves to spiritual and commercial activity.

On World Communications Day 2002, in an article titled: "Internet: A New Forum for Proclaiming the Gospel," the late Pope John Paul II admonished the Catholic Church to see the new frontier of cyberspace as being like other developments in human history.[15] He pointed to the Renaissance in Europe and to the Industrial Revolution and urged believers to invest some energies in the Internet by way of "helping those who first make contact through the Internet to move from the virtual world of cyberspace to the real world of Christian community." This view has been shared and disseminated by ministers of other faiths. Inherent in this viewpoint is the suggestion that the virtual realm is only temporary and must give in ultimately to the real world. Therefore, the believer should enter into the virtual domain in order to retrieve those in need of salvaging.

What I want to point to here is the notion that the world of cyberspace represents a discreet space that the evangelist can enter into and capture others and retrieve them for salvation. This is indeed a very engaging concept of the Christian message, of evangelizing and winning souls. The assumption here is that in cyberspace only partial conversion and salvation is possible, whereas full salvation can really be achieved in the world outside of cyberspace. This is a reasonable way of looking at cyber reality and its relationship to the real world. It suggests recognition or even a warning that the world of cyberspace is temporal, limited, and limiting and depends on its other, the real world, for full expression and actualization. Perhaps this way of seeing the Internet and the real world is informed by the current knowledge that the Internet is still in its infancy. It is an open system of communication, transaction and confrontation. But it is highly unstable. It is a fabrication. It promises to approximate and stand in for the real, but most people do not believe it can do so. It has not yet matched the real. So, people's confessions and spiritual transformation and salvation must be retrieved back into the real world where virtual intention is translated into real effective meaning.

Worldwide, there are other agencies that have taken the gospel even further than John Paul II. There are those who are less concerned about the pending evils of interconnectivity but seek to exploit its facilities in order to create new structures within their organizations. In March of 2004, the Church of England announced the creation of its first "virtual parish" and advertised for a "Web pastor."[16] The Internet church, or "i-church," was created "for those who wish to explore Christian discipleship but who are not able, or do not wish, to join a local congregation." They advertised for a vibrant, robust individual who could build and nurture a virtual community of believers and nonbelievers. The creation of such institutions and associations pointed to recognition that new methods of ministry were demanded by the changing times and by the exciting facilities built into new cultural mediums and machines.

The gospel movie industry was making important strides beyond the late 1990s. With movies such as *The Omega Code* (1999) and *Megiddo* (2001) making their way to multiplexes, there was a sense of excitement among gospel teens especially. Other releases included *Woman Thou Art Loosed* (2004) and *The Gospel* (2005). There were debates among Christian critics concerning the quality and content of gospel movies. They debated the state of the gospel movie industry. The 2004 screening of Mel Gibson's *The Passion of the Christ* brought to the fore the distance between specific kinds of religious projects and the mainstream of Hollywood's film industry. The refusal of large distribution companies to take on the production of *Passion* reflected the reality that Hollywood's major interests were not willing to touch potentially explosive creations with strong religious images and messages. Caribbean audiences, like audiences elsewhere, went to see the movie in droves. This movie was perceived by some evangelicals as part of a new drive to infiltrate the space inhabited and controlled by secular popular culture. It is reported to have grossed $110,000 U.S. from twelve screens in Trinidad March 19–21, 2004, and $121,000 U.S. from eleven screens in Jamaica.[17] Movies of this kind are not as high budgeted as are more mainstream productions. Whereas some mainstream productions that deal with issues surrounding the end time, like *The Chronicles of Riddick*, were produced for some $105 million U.S., *The Omega Code*'s production budget was approximately $8 million U.S., with grosses of around $13 million U.S.[18] The Caribbean Christian community consumed many of the new releases being produced. Given the movement towards the relatively cheap digital video, some religious organizations and churches in the United States started to explore funding of small-budget movie and television projects; for example, the Sherwood Baptist Church in Albany, Georgia, funded the movie *Flywheel* for $20,000 U.S.[19] Caribbean churches have not yet contemplated entering into these kinds of ventures, but many denominations are in possession of video equipment and have already begun to record and informally distribute their church services or special religious programs recorded by them.

The rise in popularity of the Internet and the expansion of its peripherals was accompanied by the rise of a new breed of believers who were being fashioned throughout the decade of the 2000s. Whereas traditional evangelism was conducted through conventional mailing of tracts and lessons, by the first decade of the twenty-first century, the cyber believer had access to a range of church resources on the Internet. These materials were in many cases offered online for free. This included Sunday school lesson materials and resources; resource for sermons, special religious holidays, and celebrations; and critical studies on special Bible topics and debates. Given the phenomenal popularity of Western-style praise and worship culture in the region, many believers locked into and shared common interest and fellowship through sites that provided daily devotionals, as well as the lyrics and music to the popular praise and worship songs composed by leading praise and worship ministers and songsters in the West.

Crosswalk.com, for instance, carried links on their home page to "faith, family, fun, community, news and shopping." Many believers logged on to this for-profit site because of its many features and resources. The site's online resources were used by some religious radio stations in the Caribbean as part of their news and inspirational-word broadcasting. Such was the influence of this online "religious corporation dedicated to building up the Church."[20] Its "About Us" page described its mission as bringing glory to God, equipping people, enhancing fellowship, and fostering the care of human needs. In the mid-2000s, its home page splashed the banner "Bibles for Iraq: sharing the gospel with the people of Iraq." Web sites of this kind were therefore not out of touch with what was taking place within the wider global space. In one sense, the reference to Iraq reflected the religious ambition of Christians who saw an opportunity to answer the great commission of Christ, but in another sense the Web site's banner also reflected some sort of complicity with the American military initiative.

The facility of cyberspace therefore did not exist by itself but often functioned with some reference or connection to the real, hard world. This hard world is more often than not driven by political, national, cultural, racial, and economic imperatives. Although Caribbean believers shared in and consumed much of the material put up on these leading religious and evangelical Web sites, there was relatively little input allowed to Caribbean subjects. Similar sites promoted the books of metropolitan authors and the work of larger, more established Christian book publishers in North America.[21] Caribbean Christian colleagues could not therefore appear on such sites, even though they wore the same religious banner. Religious institutions, as other institutions, are hemmed in by a set of political, national, geo-political, and economic conditions. Cyberculture brought this situation more starkly into focus. Some religious surfers found it offensive that they were denied equal showing on sites whose faith was similar to theirs. Caribbean Christian writers and authors found it difficult to break into the tight knit arena of mainstream gospel publishing. In effect, large publishers of popular religious texts were no different than their secular counterparts in respect to editorial policy. As a result of this, many regional authors turned to self-publishing. New technologies also facilitated this trend. Some other authors turned to regional publishers, some of which were thriving, while most were small entities.

Whereas in the real world, it is possible to easily identify a company's financial or social standing within the global business arena, the Internet posed a challenge to such an easy identification. On the Internet, entities could mask their true intent. You could never discover very basic truths about a product or organization via the Internet. One never really knew what stood behind the web of fiber optics. The canvas of cyber conductivity that stood between every navigator and the thing being displayed or sold on the screen was really a codified reflection of the hidden agenda of the site's creator. Because there was so much concealment, many Caribbean religious institutions seemed to approach the setting up of their virtual presence with caution, candor, and transparency.

Caribbean Christian Publications (CCP) is a publishing house that started in 1976 and continued into the 2000s. Its niche has particularly been in Sunday school and evangelistic Bible study. Their Web site is not the sophisticated cluttered frontpage of Crosswalk; it is much easier to navigate, and its links are indeed gateways to the various missions and departments of CCP.[22] If Web sites like Crosswalk hope to breathe life into their virtual presence, Caribbean Christian Publications (admittedly a sharply focused company) wants to maintain some sense of distance between its real and virtual incarnations. Crosswalk's commitment to a virtual identity is conveyed by the careful announcement of their Web personality, complexion, and spirit. A major aim is to "offer the freshest and most compelling biblically-based content to Christians who take seriously their relationship with Christ." To achieve this, they source materials from "qualified, respected Christian sources, including major ministries."

Crosswalk is but one of several dedicated Web sites that fall under the Salem Web Network umbrella. Others include *CCM Magazine*, TheFish .com and SermonSearch.com. Without doubt, Crosswalk is an extremely well constituted virtual institution. It takes its virtual self seriously and wants its users to take it seriously as well. In the attempt to convince believers and Web users about how committed and forthright this Web "for-profit corporation" is, the site forgets to provide a link that discloses who its real owners are. Some people might suggest that this is a deliberate attempt to conceal authorship, but this kind of oversight is an intrinsic feature of the Internet. The absence of disclosure is a defining quality of virtual presence. When the visitor to the site does not readily get access to information about the site's owners, she or he explains this as reflecting a growing custom in cyberculture. It is also explained as a technical occurrence. It is a failing of technology. It is not so much a case of concealment on the part of the site's owners and authors as it reflects the trend towards Web autonomy, where the Internet is its own defining space. Given its autonomy and agency, it therefore does not depend on the real world for validation. It can stand on its own set of conventions, codes and practices. Crosswalk.com is therefore an evocation and celebration of the virtual. It vests less interest in the real than in the possibility of fiber-optically transforming those people who enter the matrix of the World Wide Web. As John Paul II did, it implies that the wired Word can have "practical application," but unlike the late Pontiff, Crosswalk does not so differentiate between the real world and its surrogate or simulation.

Caribbean Christian Publications is not a site identical to Crosswalk. For one thing, Crosswalk is a multifunctional, multipurpose site. It offers a range of products and services, such as religious articles, books, music CDs, DVDs, cards, humor, news, chat, weblogs, and online shopping. Caribbean Christian Publications' primary service is to provide "biblically-grounded, culturally-relevant and evangelically-sound" material to the people of the region.[23] It also provides teacher training videotapes and cassette song tapes for children and older children. Whereas Crosswalk claims to be a universal site that wants to touch all Christians, CCP has a Caribbean target market. Crosswalk has ambitions of being a high-tech Christian experience. CCP is a text-based site that is reserved in its apparent employment of technology. But if these two sites hold anything in common, it is their underlying mission to, as the CCP splash page boldly declares, "facilitate the evangelizing, nurturing and equipping of persons . . . through the production of . . . materials."

CCP appears less sophisticated in its employment of technological facilities. But it is an effective site in some respects. It is transparent in its declaration of who it is, what it does, who its owners are, and who are the authors of the site. There is a brief history of the organization, and much information is shared about its religious and denominational affiliation. Where sites like Crosswalk conceal, CCP lays bare its motives. This apparent honesty allows you to enter the site's matrix without the distraction of technological excess. It does not pretend to have far-reaching international coverage, and hence it limits its sphere of influence to the Caribbean region. Crosswalk wants to speak to the world but falters in its obvious inability to connect with the experience of people outside of industrialized Christendom. CCP has clearly defined links for "Prayer Requests" and "How to find God." Its intimacy and apparent concern for real souls sets this Web site apart from some other, more commercially driven, religious docking stations.

It is evident that CCP has a long tradition of marketing its hard copy literature via the conventional mail. This is reflected in their quite healthy catalog. It is surprising that this company has at all taken to the Internet. Its web presence appears tentative. Whereas it embraces this medium as another means of promoting publications and literature, it stops short of providing facilities for electronic distribution. They do not distribute some of their lesson books electronically, although these could effectively be "shared" through that medium. Here, then, is a publishing company that appears to be in continuous dialog with itself about its role, the past, and the future. While it stands at the threshold of embracing virtual outreach and marketing, it hesitates. The company appears to have determined that its primary domain remains that of the real world of commerce and distribution. They seem to have taken to the Internet only to inform a wider audience about the company's presence in the real world. The sparse use of new cutting-edge features and facilities on the site makes it appear to be a construction of the mid-1990s, when in fact it has only recently come into cyberspace. Although the site appears out of step with what is happening at the cusp of cyberspace, its total disregard for the delights of Web architecture and functionality smacks of a virtual snub of what the Net stands for. A closer examination of the site might find it to be a revolt of sorts against the Net's sleek and smug pretensions of going one step better than "true-true" experience.[24]

Denominational/Religious Bodies in Cyberspace

Caribbean religious organizations saw the Internet as a duplicitous construction. But individual members were more willing to experiment with the Net than were the institutions to which they belonged. Like nonreligious users of leading-edge technology, Caribbean religious tech junkies immersed themselves in the pastimes, innovations, and community activity afforded by the World Wide Web. Many took full advantage of newsgroups, operating within and outside of them, sending religious messages in bulk e-mail to various addresses. Some sites with Caribbean inflection were actually the creation of an individual or individuals. For example, Prayline.com was started by Pastor Nigel Best with the intention of uniting Caribbean and other believers around the common bond of prayer. It did not evolve as a denominational initiative but bore the stamp of the individual who had a vision of entering cyberspace and connecting with people in need of prayer and helping to transform lives. The site's affiliation to a denomination is secondary.[25]

While casual observers of cyber activity in Caribbean religious circles were aware of the intervention into cyberspace by individuals, fewer people might be aware of the presence of religious denominations on the Internet. Religious organizations have tended to be conservative in their use of the World Wide Web. Churches have tended to make muted noise about their exploration of cyberspace. Some people might therefore overlook the very fact of that cyber presence. Closer examination reveals that churches and denominations have contributed quite significantly to the enhanced Caribbean Christian presence on the Internet in the first decade of the twenty-first century.

The Web site of the East Caribbean Conference of Seventh Day Adventists relayed many of their dedicated programs.[26] Whereas less well-structured organizations vacillated about the Net's usefulness, this body in the Eastern Caribbean seemed committed to employing the Internet to at least buttress their on-the-ground programs. They therefore offered their Sabbath School Lessons online as well as, of course, resource materials based on the writings of Ellen G. White. A shortcoming of the site, however, is that its listing of individual churches within the circuit does not provide active, open links to these individual churches. Realistically, supporting and sustaining a Web site is a significant undertaking. Not all institutions therefore can do so. In the absence of dedicated local sites, the master site has the power to harness and promulgate the hard-line, undiluted message of the denomination minus the subtle cultural murmur that local church outlook would bring to a representation of the Adventist faith. Given Adventists' reputation for adherence to the letter of the Law of Moses, the absence of several local mini sites allowed navigators to focus on a single well-defined set of virtual laws.

Like the Adventists, the Church of the Nazarene is also represented by and through its larger parent association.[27] Nazarene Missions International provides some information on the various islands and their congregations' composition. It hardly has a well-constructed Caribbean signature. The parent Web site of the Wesleyan Church International does not provide a link to its churches outside North America. But some sites could be found for individual churches in the islands anyway. Haggatt Hall Wesleyan, for example, put up a spare site that gave general information about church meeting times. Carrington Wesleyan went one step better in 2006 with a more engaging Web presence. The New Testament Church of God's international Web site provides dedicated links to many of its churches across North America but does not offer seamless connection to churches abroad. Many of its churches on the outskirts of the central branches in the United States have a presence through New Testament's world missions Web site.[28] But beyond this, they hardly exist, on the Web.

I do not want to suggest that headquarters of organizations have a duty to put up information on all their affiliations abroad, but the fact of the existence of branches throughout the world for these organizations would necessitate basic recognition of these links. It is significant that by the mid-2000s most local churches in the region had not been sufficiently convinced about the rewards of investing in dedicated sites of presence on the Internet. While many of their denominational headquarter centers outside the region were constructing a visage of the denomination's virtual features, local churches stood outside of their construction. Caribbean churches were on their own with respect to constructing a cyber presence. In the world of real relations, these churches were also asked to manage their own day-to-day affairs, while the central headquarters paid keen interest in their structural, administrative, and financial affairs. The distance that developed between local assemblies and formal Web evangelism was partly a reflection of the belief in the region that radio, television, word-of-mouth, and face-to-face witnessing were still the most effective and efficient mediums of spreading the Word. The Internet was still an unpredictable creation in the minds of most congregations. It was still unstable. Caribbean religious bodies could not yet trust this agent of the "end times." Many organizations were therefore contented to use more conventional mediums and facilities until people were better placed to trust the Janus-faced fiber optic machine that promised to possess us all.

Well Able: Wired for Song and Ministry

Undoubtedly, it is religious performing artists who led the way in pioneering the use of emerging technologies for spreading the Word and engaging bigger audiences. If their controlling organizations held back for fear of loss of control to the machines, individual artists and groups were more confident in their exploration of them. Religious bodies could not afford to immerse their entire presence into the arena of virtual possibilities. Such a baptism could not be attempted in the early stages of the rise of the machines. Individual artists and groups were different. These could enter the matrix of cultural and spiritual representation to spy out the land. They could also beat a speedy retreat. And like Joshua and Caleb of old, they would be able to return to report to others about the prospect of entering, infiltrating, and taking the land of virtual delights and pleasures, the Internet (and its accompanying manifestations). They would be "well able."[29]

Like their counterparts in the literary arts, Caribbean gospel artists and performers were very dependent on their industry affiliations to help them establish a presence on the Internet. Many singers have therefore been represented online by way of affiliation with a record company, being featured on Net (radio) stations' rosters, and being featured within online newspapers. A random search for St. Croix's female vocalist Harella Goodwin, for example, throws up her connection through the Bahamas-based Caribbean Gospel Network Web site, where she is mentioned for her performance at a past Barbados Gospel Fest and listed on *its* Web site. But she is also dependent for her cyber presence on the native St. Croix Source, a Web publication devoted to news, information, and advertising. She also appears by way of a reference to her performance at the Church of the Open Bible, as mentioned on *its* Web site. Someone like the fast-rising gospel calypso singer Sean Daniel owes his fiber-optic presence to his country's National Library and Information System Authority's Web site and to articles on gospelypso, as well as a special 2004 *Trinidad Guardian* feature on his many achievements.[30]

Relatively few Caribbean gospel acts vigorously sought to establish their very own virtual identity on the World Wide Web. Older artists tended to be less concerned with cyber construction. It is mainly the younger artists who have been more determined in their efforts to "represent" (slang for "identify one's self") on the Internet. This has to do with the much more progressive outlook of younger artists generally and with the impact of global and secular popular culture on this age group and on their lives and sensibilities.

Part of the fear and caution exhibited towards the Web had to do with its negative symbolism. Although there were relatively few national debates among the Christian community that focused on the Internet as human creation, there were many smaller discussions that abounded. Many local churches brought their particular doctrinal worldview to an understanding of the Internet. The Net was seen by many believers as an extension of extant facilities like radio and television. But further, it was regarded as the near-final development of these secular monoliths, constructed to propagate the tenets of secular liberation. Many churches therefore unconsciously treated the Internet with much skepticism. The rise in Internet pornography and Net crimes were all proof that the Internet was pouring more harm than blessing on to the nations. In line with their reading of Bible prophecy, some Christians saw the Internet as facilitating the movement ultimately towards a one-world government and as heralding the emergence of a global network that would be infected by the virus that in the New Testament is called the Antichrist. Speculations about this connection were rife, and not only among Christians. Some sites on the Internet named Bill Gates as the Antichrist; some others explored the pervasive power of the World Wide Web. Some religious denominations were therefore intrigued by this suspicion, and as a result, the wholesale embracing of the Internet was not a reality within Caribbean religious space.

Cutting-edge gospel acts have become some of the most vibrant participants within the Internet. For example Lionofzion.com showcases Christafari, Sherwin Gardner, and other leading reggae, dancehall, hip hop gospel artists.[31] The Bahamian Monty G, who appears there, is part of the vibrant Bahamas crew calling themselves Lion of Judah. This crew also features other acts like Mr. Lynx and Mighty 1. The Intellect and

Monty G appear on *Trinity Mix 2001*, singing on the "nightrider" rhythm, and Monty G's acclaimed CD *Voice of the Youth* provides significant audio samples, but no sample of the actual lyrics. Whereas many secular dance-hall acts like Capleton center the word and text as critical to their doctrine and image, relatively few Christian dancehall acts tend to provide the lyrics that reside somewhere beneath their progressive high energy post-dancehall, post-soca, and post–hip hop rhythm tracks. What is clear, though, is that leading reggae Christian musicians are locked into the possibilities of technology and its ability to popularize them and their music. Their Web sites and pages are no less flamboyant or formulaic than those of their secular counterparts.

Differentiating some religious and secular acts on the Internet is not an easy undertaking. An examination of a number of sites and pages that feature regional gospel acts reveals their closeness to their secular counterparts at a number of levels. But perhaps this has less to do with the intention of gospel acts to mimic their secular counterparts than it does with the pressures exerted by technologies like the Internet. Leading-edge technologies often promise flexibility, open-endedness, and difference in theory, but in practice they usually evoke a series of formulaic traits that are as much a reflection of the controlling politics that guide human expression as the inherent codes that drive the machines.

Many gospel reggae artists, like Jah Pickney, make excessive use of Rastafarian iconographic motifs. His Jahpickney.com submerges itself in colors of red, yellow, and green, in contrast to the more festive and cheerful Web page of the Grenada-New York country-gospel group Joe Country and the Islanders.[32] This is not to privilege the latter Web site, for in fact, the layout and architecture at Jah Pickney's site is in keeping with his iconography. His use of a black background is arguably more effective than its use by the United States Virgin Islands artist Aquannette Chinnery on her Web site Aquannette.com. The Jah Pickney site uses this color backdrop as a core motif. It creates the visual impact that sells the site. Aquannette's site is not as dependent on this color and visuals for its viability. The interest in her site rests in its other features. Aquannette's site is replete with hyperlinks that connect her to a range of record companies, radio stations, purchasing outlets and even to other artists.

The impact of commercial imperatives is very evident on the Internet. But there are also other kinds of associations that are in evidence. The Web site of the Silvertones of Barbados, as viewed in mid-2004, reflected some of the other relations at work within religious and gospel culture. Their home page, Silvertones.net, acts as a buffer to the more substantive pages that actually feature the group. The home page is more or less a cluttered splash page dedicated to well-wishers and corporate sponsors of the group and its Web site. Appearing at the top of their page are logos to FedEX, UPS, DHL, and a range of credit card companies. Two images of the group and their CD *Victory* are placed below. They then provide links to Barbadian radio and newspapers. Two of the boldest visible links are embedded within the words: "Our House of Parliament" and "Tourism is also our Business." The links to these latter sites is a reflection of the submersion of gospel and gospel culture within the nationalist project. In Barbados in particular, the ruling administration throughout the 1990s professed to embrace culture as an integral part of their project of developing the nation. Though this was a nice-sounding initiative, the reality was that many groups and artists seemed to lose their sense of independence and lacked the critical edge in terms of their expression of opinions on the range of problems facing the country, especially when these problems were connected with the ruling administration. The hosting and promotion of a number of governmental agencies on their Web site therefore reflected the extent to which gospel had given over part of itself to such drives as tourism. Indeed, the Barbados Gospelfest was started as a Tourism Authority initiative and has remained embedded within a nationalist project. Its longstanding organizer has done an excellent job over the years, but the festival's relationship with successive governments has arguably stifled the festival's ability to impact and transform its society through a much more overt critique of social, moral, and spiritual decay within contemporary society.

George Banton's home page, Georgebanton.com, represents one of the better artist-dedicated gospel Web sites of Caribbean performers.[33] It is well laid out. It is easy to navigate. It provides clearly thought-out headings for ease of access to "biography, albums, videos, photos, press and contact." Its aesthetic qualities are complementary to the message that the artist provides. Photos and sound and video clips are well produced and deliverable on their chosen platform. Indeed his musical style, forthright, unpretentious, and structured, resonates well with the kind of Web architecture employed on the site. It is also devoid of cluttered messages and distracting advertisements. An alternative Web critique might, however, describe the site as boring. It might suggest that the construction of Banton's Web site is too squeaky clean and perhaps would best suit a high-profile Western corporate entity. George Banton might retort that he sees himself in that way.

In spite of the high status achieved by some gospel acts who converted to Christianity, relatively few of them moved to host their own official, dedicated Web site. YouTube began to attract gospel artists by the late 2000s. The construction, hosting, and upkeep of a Web site can be a time-consuming and laborious task. Many artists have rather therefore opted for allowing unofficial Web pages. These pages are embedded within larger Web sites, and because pages are not stand-alone and do not require a server, owners of Web pages can leave the work up to owners of the Web site in which their page is embedded. Papa San, for instance, relied partly on his label Gospo Centric to project his work and image.[34] At his artist page at Gospo Centric, the small number of links to products, tours, news, and events and video reveals the impersonal bulk handling often associated with major record companies. Gospo Centric's most liberating act on the Papa San artist page comes through their sharing of the music Web video to his "Step Pon De Enemy." The Web video (offered through either Windows Media or Quicktime) celebrates the lyrical emphasis on overcoming the enemy. It features the singer driving through his native country, hailing a taxi driver, driving along, and then bursting into song and dance with a group of energetic disciples. The dance moves are assigned some choreography but are not overworked, as in some secular videos. This video is much closer to the Kirk Franklin video mentioned earlier, but its greater influence is post-dancehall culture. The video seeks to capture the energy of young people and to transmit the message of Christ's victory over Satan into the youthful community within society. In terms of filmic narrative development, there is little attempted. Much more important is the director's intention to connect to viewers through the rhythmic and visual energy of Papa San and his cast of celebrants.

King Obstinate's posting on Bigupradio.com is his prime location. He is bundled along with other secular artists as well as with "posters," "girls," and a file-sharing facility called "weed." Other artists like Nicole Ballosingh-Holder, Joseph Niles and Shine the Light are scattered across a range of locations with no single identifiable center. Their virtual image, message, and focus is therefore left to be composited by the outside observer or curious navigator. They remain as de-centered fragments in the matrix of cyberspace. Their parts are yet to be retrieved in the world of the machines.

End Time

While much of the discussion has focused on the failure by Caribbean religious institutions and artists to establish their own dedicated sites, the obverse viewpoint to all this is that the diffusion of pages and presences by artists also has the potential to create greater interest and marketing buzz. This diffusion is mooted to be the real triumph of technology, of the Internet. Some artists who are aware of this have taken full advantage of manipulating multiple virtual presences. Many more have stood helplessly by, watching in amazement as day by day their image and traits are replicated and contorted within the matrix of cyberculture. As virtual technology advances, more and more Caribbean people are forced to stand outside of *their* own construction.

Caribbean artists who host their own pages have come to realize the challenges of this exercise. It is costly and time consuming. There are therefore many dead or dormant pages scattered across cyberspace. In light of this problem, many groups have sought in the first instance to make visible their products. Recordings are therefore often lodged with online vendors. Amazon, for instance, distributes a growing number of Caribbean artists. But many others also place their wares with more regionally based vendors, whether these are located in the region or have some regional interest. In this regard, it is quite common to witness gospel artists on the sales roster with their secular counterparts at a range of diverse Web sites. Artists are not always in control of where their names or products appear on the Internet. For instance, some regional gospel from the early 1980s and prior can be located at the sites of second-hand vendors, some of these as far away as in Europe.

Part of the challenge faced by Caribbean gospel artists who practice their craft in the era of the rise of the World Wide Web is that this facility is regarded still to be in its infancy. It is still relatively unstable and holds out hope of facilitating even greater feats in the near future. Given its potential and promise, artists have at one time or another embraced and retreated from it. Many are currently engaged with trying to manage and manipulate it for their own purposes. But then, some others have not sought to tweak it as much as they have tried to ride on the wave of its uncertainty and instability, allowing its quirky and amazing qualities to carry their individual wares and ideology to wherever the Net would take them. But up to the late 2000s, no single clearly defined pattern of usage or exploitation had evolved within Caribbean religious and gospel culture. There were various streams of engagement.

It is clear that Caribbean religious culture acknowledges the presence of these emerging technological phenomena, but various individuals, groupings, and personnel within the arena have responded quite differently. One does not sense that Caribbean gospel culture in its core areas has developed a strategic response to the current and future intentions and ambitions of the Internet. An underlying principle that does seem to exist is that the region's response will be driven by moments of engagement and moments of retreat. The Internet continues to be an object of admiration and fear among the Caribbean religious community. It is also regarded in this way by other sectors and groupings. Because of this dilemma, it continues to dog our sensibility up towards the end time.

CHAPTER 4

Caribbean Entertainment and Music Culture Pre- and Post-Internet

Part 1:
Media, Communications, Programming, and End of the Real

The State of the Media and Communications

Trinidad and Tobago was one of the first territories in the region to acquire television. In the early 1960s, Trinidad and Tobago Television (TTT) came on air as a state-owned corporation. Many other media houses in the region were constituted in a similar fashion. Some of these are Helen Television in St. Lucia and Caribbean Broadcasting Corporation (CBC) in Barbados. Most of these stations were started with a mandate to provide information, education, and entertainment. Over the years, the cultural, economic and political climate has changed. Stations have therefore had to reconsider their mandate in light of contemporary developments.

By the early 1990s, some annual reports of Government-run television stations began to espouse the imperative of economic sustainability above all other objectives. CBC, in Barbados' annual report of 1993, for example, spoke of "improving programming" for the express aim of "obtaining more revenue."[1]

One very potent factor that has brought about transformation has been the increase in television service providers. Cable channels and other private entities have gotten into the fray. Because the advertising markets within the region are comparatively small, it has meant that traditional state-owned corporations have had to rethink their formulae. Most corporations have been forced due to worsening economic times to operate like private entities. Governments have found it increasingly difficult to subsidize these corporations to the tune of more than three-quarters of their operating costs. Many of these stations have therefore had to cut back on local productions and have resorted to purchasing syndicated films and programs for an attractive price. Many regional governments have held on to these stations primarily because of the mileage that their political parties can gain from controlling their programming and the propagandistic messages they send out.

Next to salaries and wages, the other major area of operating expense by television corporations has been through the importation of programs. In the case of CBC in Barbados, close to 1.6 million out of a 12-million Barbados dollar budget was being spent on imported programs, especially from the United States, during the mid-1990s.

As with TTT, little attention has been paid to legislating a quota for the ratio of locally produced to foreign programs. Governments have tended to maintain a monopoly of television broadcast for most of the time until the late 1980 and 1990s, when a proliferation of other stations came about. In Trinidad, for example, by 1991 two other stations were born: CCN TV 6, and AVM TV 4. Two years later, there were some thirty-three cable channels available, including the more popular American channels like Cable News Network (CNN), Showtime, Cinemax, and ESPN. Lashley reveals that by 1995 more than 95 percent of all television programming was American.[2]

Throughout the region, the response has tended to be the same to suggestions that the region needs to develop and produce its programs. Whereas it might cost less than $400 U.S. dollars to produce a program in the United States, locally (it is said) a similar program costs in the region of $15,000 U.S. An American soap opera in the vein of *The Young and the Restless* or *The Bold and the Beautiful* might be obtained for less than $300 U.S. per episode, whereas a similar local production like Trinidad's *No Boundaries* might cost more than twenty times the American soap.

This argument, though it has some bearing, does not factor in the value of projecting and protecting a sense of one's identity. Although marketing buffs have been selling the terms *globalization* and *global village*, the world is no less politicized than it always has been. Indeed, globalization is marked by a new insidious politics of covert enslavement. Even in the domain of academic discourse, there are discursive statutes to this new way of thinking. The tendency by many new thinkers to scoff at the suggestion of protecting identity reveals the extent to which postcolonial, postmodernist, and poststructuralist dogmas have taken over bodies of knowledge.

Current advances in video and production technology and in cultural product consumption should be seen to shatter the old argument about the cost of local productions. Because popular culture is willing to consume raw images and sound, it seems to me that local producers can indeed tap into that craze. Even some directors, producers of major Western blockbusters, show a proclivity for different textures and styles of production. Many music videos in the late 1990s mimicked the method of the handheld home video camera. A movie like *Crash*, for example, shows how the industry has taken on the "amateur" feel in filming and has created an art out if it. The movie the *Blair Witch Project* depended on the amateur feel for its success. The initial filmed movie cost no more than $40,000 U.S. It was acquired by Artisan for approximately $1.5 million, and after hefty promotion that followed its underground Internet buzz, it shocked the box office with eventual returns of over $200 million U.S. worldwide.[3]

It is now possible to produce amateur-type programs for wide consumption. Popular culture permits this. Programs like *Foul Ups Bleeps and Blunders* were negotiated programs that built their legitimacy on creating lighthearted moments edited from real life situations. But the 1990s gave birth to another kind of rough-edit program agenda, programs that utilized the feel of the amateur camera to alter the audience's perception of the works and the subject matter that they treated. Many movies increasingly utilized this method as integral to their production agendas. Two early 2000 movie releases dealing with race issues employed the integration of film and video shots for dramatic effect. They were *White Lies* and *Divided We Stand*. It is the music video that helped to inspire this new trend, valorizing the raw feel. The straight-to-video film *Starship Troopers 2* appeared to be situated somewhere between the amateur feel and the texture of traditional film. The expansion of reality television worldwide also gave scope to people who were producing their work using digital video. Many producers and directors showed a liking for the less costly yet clean texture of digital video.

Death of Caribbean Culture

In the first decade of the twenty-first century, on Friday, January 4, 2002, the Caribbean Media Corporation (CMC) announced its closure. St. Lucia's Director of Information Services, Embert Charles, in a press release on Tuesday, January 8, 2002, suggested that the closure had not only to do with finding financing for the institution but that the closure reflected a low level of support for regional initiatives.[4] The CMC's closure and subsequent rebirth reflected the uncertainty of regional projects, even in the face of global infiltration into the region's information and entertainment space. The breakdown of such an important institution could be equated to the closure of a major network (say like the BBC or CNN or Fox) within Western information space. The closure was tantamount to the dislocation of the hub of the regional information system. Its closure, though temporary, signified the death of regional information and culture. This was the symbolic reality.

But perhaps its demise was neither striking nor catastrophic for many people, because by the early 2000s, a large number of information systems and networks had proliferated in the region. The death of the CMC was therefore seen as a minor occurrence. For after all, there were other avenues of getting information, though not necessarily in the same compressed and packaged form as provided by the CMC.

Whereas CMC died, newsgathering and dissemination were still being carried on by individual national news corporations. The BBC's Caribbean broadcasts still remained. Other international networks were still alive, so there was no need for the region to worry at all. People still had their televisions, cable channels, radios, newspapers, and, of course, the Internet. The death of the CMC and muted reactions to its passing therefore reflected the low regard in the Caribbean for many regional initiatives and signaled the eventual displacement of the regional project in the age of the machines.

The retreat to local information and communication entities reflected the last stand against the influx of nonregional communications and information corporations. But if international corporations were targeting the region, the region also began to enter into the domain where in turn its islands could be accessed and heard in the international world. Internet radio became increasingly popular by the mid-2000s.

Throughout the late 1990s AM radio was being replaced by FM, primarily because FM allowed for better quality. The opting for FM meant that AM's wider coverage across significant parts of the region was sacrificed. Shortwave radio was long dead as a mass broadcast option. Internet radio, however, surfaced as an alternative. By the mid-2000s, radio stations in places as diverse as Antigua, the Bahamas, Barbados, Bermuda, Grenada, Guadeloupe, Guyana, Haiti, Jamaica, Martinique, St. Kitts, St. Lucia, St. Vincent, Trinidad, the United States, and the British Virgin Islands, set up links for broadcast on the Internet. Newspapers were also a part of this process of expansion onto the Internet. This was recognition by local and regional information corporations that their constituency had changed. No longer were they only catering to a market defined by neat geographical and national space, but also to a wider audience, to an expanded community of virtual participants. David Gauntlett, in the introduction to the second edition of his book *Web.Studies*, agrees with Michael Goldhaber's suggestion that on the Internet there is an "attention economy": what is most sought after on the Net is not money, but attention.[5] While this is a compelling reality about the Internet and society prior to the death of the real, the Caribbean experience reinforces the centrality of economic, political, personal, and spiritual end-time prophecy to the playing out of relations with technology.

End of the Real: Print, Radio, Television

As with traditional news corporations worldwide, Caribbean media houses invested in cyber publishing and dissemination. Most leading and other electronic and print establishments made sure they gained wider constituency by way of hosting a Web site on the Internet. Some establishments offered online subscription, while most others offered surfers free access to selected stories and pages online. Guyana's *Stabroek News*, for example provided Net readers with some access to their daily editorials, as well as to a range of other stories. While the *Stabroek* prides itself with the volume of information it provides online, like that of the *Nassau Guardian* and *Grenada Today*, its use of photos and images is measured. Other online editions like the *Trinidad Express* have invested effort in providing video clips to counterbalance the otherwise text-laden experience. As expected, most of the online editions of newspapers and magazines are heavily dependent on advertising. As is true in the real world of the popular press, so too in the virtual realm, Caribbean publications are laden with advertisements and links to major international, regional and local businesses. These ads are in addition to the virtual classified pages and can be found on the main page of online newspapers and magazines.

One of the more commendable features of Caribbean Web newspapers is that they tend generally to provide links to their other regional newspapers. Apart from this, Web sites like Caribbeannewspapers.com and Cananews.com provide a one-stop link to a set of regional publications like the *Antigua Sun*, *Belize First*, *St. Lucia Mirror*, *Bermuda Gazette*, and *Haiti Online*, among others.

By the mid-2000s, Caribbean radio and television corporations also moved in earnest to have a presence on the Net. Because some news conglomerates dabble in more than one medium, it is not uncommon to have Web sites that reveal this structure. But many other online radio and TV outfits have bracketed and streamlined their real offerings by way of establishing an identifiable product on the Net. Some radio outfits, like Antigua's Observer and Dominica's Dominica Broadcasting Corporation

(DBC), existed primarily in the way of a standalone media player that produced an audio feed of the live broadcast. Other networks had their own dedicated Web sites, on which they sought to consolidate their real and virtual corporate image, giving a face to the company's symbols, personnel, and location in the real domain. Bahamas' 100 JamZ Radio 100.3 FM and St. Kitts' Winn FM 98.9 both held solid presence in cyberspace. Radio and media companies of this kind were frequently those that appealed to younger audiences. Inherent within this nexus is the supposition that it is the younger segments anyway that make greater use of the Internet, so that in fact, most Caribbean youth-oriented networks have noticeable presence on the Internet. Other, more traditional, networks also have a presence, but they often seem to lack the vigor and robust energy that is commanded by FM radio and demanded by youth FM and the emerging XM culture.

It might therefore be useful to briefly compare the Web pages of radio NBC St. Vincent and Barbados' CBC radio 900 AM with those of St. Kitts' Winn FM and Jamaica's Irie FM. The more traditional radio stations seem to cover the basics on the Web. They give a bio and short description of format and target market. They do not all provide a live feed to their on-air diffusion. The FM stations on the Net seek to connect online navigators with what is taking place on the ground. They seek to create a seamless experience. This is done by providing live webfeed, e-chat, entertainment ware, and merchandise, as well as inviting surfers to visit the establishment through other experiences and media where possible. The youth-oriented Web pages are hyped. They often splash the faces of contemporary stars across the screen; they use outstanding color motifs and favor cluttered screens of flickering images and links. All this casts the impression of movement, fast paced lifestyles, and hype, which are said to be defining features of youth popular culture in the Caribbean and abroad. A random search for the Web site of any other leading local FM station would reveal the investment being made in online popular culture.

In the same way that Caribbean popular gospel culture revolves around a set of real and imagined institutions and communities, likewise secular youth culture continues to be driven by the wider world and primarily Western popular culture. The Web site of the organization Research and Markets reports that by the year 2015 a new era of leisure will dawn, wherein half of the United States's GNP will be generated from entertainment and leisure products.[6] The regional entertainment industry continues to be driven by global trends. It is very conscious of what is taking place abroad. It is in some instances following blindly without a clear sense of future direction. But regional entertainment entities that host, manage, and shape tastes within Caribbean popular culture are also independent units in some respects; they are not all directly controlled by larger parent companies or associations. They can therefore determine their own direction, in some respects. This having said, though, regional pop culture institutions like radio and entertainment networks, retailers, and promoters continue to be under immense pressure to adhere to the doctrine of commerce, sexual exploitation, misogyny, violence, abusive language, immorality, and slackness that have increasingly come to be driving principles of the region's popular entertainment culture.

Many of the Web sites that have harnessed, consolidated, and stand at the cusp of Caribbean popular culture are those that have a strong association with the entertainment industry. The "informal" sectors are most responsible for shaping tastes within youth culture. The early 2001 hosting of the first Caribbean Fashion Week in Jamaica reflected a step in the right direction towards showcasing regional fashion trends.[7] One would hope that the establishment of such events could influence the shape of Caribbean fashion. Although the Internet exhibits the designer ware of Caribbean fashion, the reality is that day-to-day fashion trends are driven by what is being projected by larger Western companies through film, television, music television, and endorsements by leading international and regional artists. By the mid-2000s, Caribbean society had firmly connected to this Western mainstream by way of the computer and other technological peripherals. This connection was a lifeline to information, pleasure, competitive advantage, and survival; it was the end of the real and the rebirth of culture through virtual experience and simulation. This connection marked the expansion of machine culture.

Part 2: Entertainment Culture

The Music Video (and Entertainment Television): MTV and Beyond

As early as the 1930s, some "international" musicians were attempting to provide visual accompaniment to music. By the 1960s, groups were making movies as promotional tools for their songs. But it was really in the 1980s that music videos and music television came into vogue. Music Television (MTV) was born in the United States in 1981. In its first year, it lost millions of dollars. British bands like Duran Duran and Culture Club were heavy contributors to this new medium. American groups caught on. Huey Lewis and the News was one of few acts of the time to see the benefits of music television and promotion. In the early days,

MTV was only available in 15 percent of American homes. But it represented a radical change in the presentation of pop music. MTV would redefine the way in which hit songs were made, how they were marketed, and how they were brought to the public.[8]

Prior to MTV, music videos were produced and shown after the official release and popularizing of a hit song. While a new record might be broken on major FM radio, its video release was often staggered. MTV gave the prospect of a simultaneous national and international release. It was felt within white mainstream radio that adult rock dominated play lists. A new system was required that would give greater possibility of airplay to a wider range of artists. MTV was conceptualized to break the monotony and monopoly of adult-oriented FM rock stations. MTV approximated national radio status because it sought to be broadcast across the U.S and everywhere simultaneously. It therefore would assume a status that could see it shaping a national taste and consciousness as no other popular entity had done. MTV soon became known for some of the things that it despised in white adult rock radio. It became a scandal when MTV refused to give airtime to black artists. Inasmuch as this book explores the handling of "minor" players by large industry entities, it is revelatory to consider the politics that has played out between the MTV "mainstream" and black performers. This can shed some light on the kinds of prejudices that also characterize the relationship between larger conglomerates and smaller so-called marginal cultures, like those of the Caribbean.

About two years after the introduction of MTV, artists began to complain that it did not show black artists. The *New York Times* and influential publications like *Rolling Stone* picked up on this criticism. It was revealed that of the more than 740 videos aired on MTV over its first year and a half, no more than 24 featured black performers. Artists and agitators like Rick James and MC Lyte were extremely vocal. MTV's executives countered that the white rock audience was more excited about its music than black viewers about theirs. MTV was not the only avenue for music videos. In 1981, BET also began to air music videos in its ninety-minute show Video Soul. But MTV represented muscle. It aired videos for 24 hours. It appealed to a wide national market, including the important twelve-to-thirty-four-year-old group that it initially targeted.

Michael Jackson was the first black artist to break into MTV. Around the time that his mega album *Thriller* was released, there could be no silencing of his rock-tinged music and progressive funk. Songs like "Billy Jean," "Beat It," and "Thriller" spawned this album. But there was still some resistance to his videos by MTV. It is widely held that CBS executives threatened to withdraw all their artists from MTV if Jackson's "Billie Jean" video was not shown. His "Thriller" videos broke into the music video mainstream of MTV and charted the course for many more black acts. Lionel Ritchie, the Trinidad-born Billy Ocean, and Prince were given easier access and thereafter exploited the facility. But this was only temporary, because with the popularizing of hardcore street rap by groups like Run-D.M.C., MTV executives were uncertain. They felt that such groups would scare their advertisers. Black acts were then forced to meet MTV halfway. Run-D.M.C teamed up with the rockers Aerosmith, and the Fat Boys also teamed up with the Beach Boys and gained significant airtime. Many subsequent videos by black rappers sought to diffuse some of the direct confrontation of black artists by employing a range of cultural motifs. The Fresh Prince and Jazzy Jeff, Salt N' Pepa, and others made use of colorful and also cartoonish videos as part of their strategy to gain access to music television. By 1988, MTV started an all-rap slot called *YO! MTV Raps*. But with the advent of gansta rap, MTV turned away and played less offensive work by the likes of MC Hammer. In the late 1990s, MTV continued to alter its programming. By the mid-2000s, it had transformed itself into a reality television channel. Although it played some videos, it had divested much of the emphasis on music videos to sister channels like the country music channel CMT and, in the Caribbean, TEMPO.

This race politics has been treated by a number of scholars writing on American music. But there has not been much acknowledgement in the Caribbean context of filtering down impact of that kind of politics on Caribbean artists. In Trinidad and Tobago around 1989, when MTV was discontinued there, there was a significant debate that surfaced in the twin island republic. Some observers and writers to the newspapers suggested that the continuation of "Video Soul" and the discontinuation of MTV amounted to a racial practice by Trinidad and Tobago Television (TTT). Viewing practice in Trinidad revealed a preference by Afro-Trinidadians for the dance and R&B format of "Video Soul," whereas other racial groups tended to prefer the rock-oriented format of MTV. The debate continued in spite of the fact that MTV ceased to be available outside of the United States, except by cable.

Trinidad, arguably more than any other territory in the region, continues to exhibit a taste for the kind of programming that defines mainstream and alternative rock. There have been a number of international rock acts that have appeared in Trinidad. Indeed, in the mid-1990s, there was an attempt by regional promoters and industry bosses to popularize that music throughout the Caribbean, a region that the industry acknowledges as having a strong devotion to rap, hip hop, rhythm and blues, dancehall, reggae, and soca. A number of strange occurrences took place therefore on national radios, even on the AM band. Prime time listeners to AM confronted, for example, Tears For Fears' "Break it Down Again" interspersed with their usual diet of song. One of the most hyped tours by pop rock bands featured the 1995 Starship and Survivor concerts within the region. This was well attended in Trinidad. In other territories, the crowds were moderate. In Barbados, where blacks make up more than 92 percent of the population, these blacks represented less than 2 percent of those who turned out to see the two classic rock bands. It can be suggested that throughout the region, viewing patterns and preferences are to some degree determined by race, though one should caution that there are significant numbers of young viewers who have come to accept the goods of popular culture as their own and so are prepared to accommodate different genres of music. Race is therefore a fixed as well as a floating signifier within Caribbean cultural expression and practice.

By the 1990s and 2000s, music television was relayed by a range of different providers via television and cable and on the Internet. Traditional music television enterprises like MTV 2, VH1, Nickelodeon, and Country Music Television (CMT) have altered their programming in recent years, offering a mix of reality shows, entertainment news, and music. But they all used the Internet as a support and real medium for audience contact. Entertainment media, like radio, took to using satellite technology to produce an ubiquitous connectivity to radio through XM. XM carried MTV radio, in addition to sixty-eight other commercial-free radio stations; thirty-two news, sports, talk, and entertainment channels; and twenty-one instant traffic and weather channels, all for just $12.95 U.S. per month (in 2007). Networks like E!, which has been on cable for much longer, launched on to the Internet on August 5, 1996, with its Web presence trying to capture the irreverent through its signature offbeat approach to treating entertainment culture. Other entertainment entities like A&E, BET, and a slew of other corporations enhanced their range of locations through traditional media, but also did so on the Web and newer emerging platforms.

In 2001, CD sales were said to have declined in the United States. As had happened back in 1978, when record sales started to fall and the recording industry blamed the new technology of cassette tapes and early video games, the industry in the 2000s blamed the Internet, among other factors. By the mid-2000s, no facet within Caribbean entertainment and related expression could ignore any of these critical developments within

Western popular culture. The Web and matrix of technology had already been spun.

The State of Music and Entertainment Culture: 1980 to Post-Dancehall and Post-Soca

Prior to the 1980s, Caribbean music, as other musics worldwide, depended largely on traditional means of dissemination. Radio was a major medium. Magazines also worked, as did word of mouth, gossip, and other avenues of popular culture dispersal, such as live concerts and popular film. But around the early 1980s, Caribbean musics like reggae and calypso were undergoing radical changes in terms of their attitude and tone. Reggae proper, for instance, was becoming increasingly a digitized music. Calypso was also moving further from its roots, as perceived by purists, who by then had reacted strongly to the developments surrounding calypso's offshoot dance music called soca.

It can be suggested that Caribbean music was facing the crisis not only of art form consolidation and definition but also of expansion. How far can these forms expand beyond the parameters or boundaries of their traditional construction? Marley had blazed the trail for reggae throughout the 1970s. Island Records through Chris Blackwell had popularized reggae worldwide. Bob Marley became its iconographic image. The locks, the guitar, and the I-Trees in ritualistic garb and chant became inscribed as semiotic referents for reggae. More than twenty years after the death of Marley the iconic image still lingers. Yes, the companies have milked his catalog, issuing boxed sets and re-mastering rough edits and previously unheard band house performances, and so on. But this perpetuation of reggae by the industry is cleverly built around well-enshrined reggae imagery. There are recurring visual symbols. There is Marley smoking his cigarrette or spliff—in portrait. There is also Marley with guitar strapped over the shoulder—in full body. Disney makes use of him to market its world of fantasy, as on its billboards: "Can You Imagine Stars This Big?" Few other Caribbean genres have achieved this type of modern popularity. Yes, a few calypso exponents have captured the international limelight, but their achievements have never transcended boundaries in the way that Marley's have. Belafonte's "calypso" singing has made the widest impact for calypso. Sparrow cannot make claims of sustained international status. Arrow has a stronger case. His 1983 "Hot Hot Hot," a soca song, is still his major and only claim to international status. This appears as a fleeting moment when viewed more than twenty years later. Individual post-calypso acts have made noteworthy impressions over the years. Nigel and Marvin Lewis' "Follow the Leader" is heard off-scene in the Hugh Grant-starred movie, *Notting Hill*; RPB's "Ragga Ragga" appeared on one of Sony's Dance Pool volumes; Gabby's "Boots" appeared in *TIME* magazine, "Jack" in the movie *Water*, and "Gimme Soca" in *Mosquito Coast*; and Beckett's "Disco Calypso" was on the sound-track to *The Deep*. Machel Montano signed "Come Dig it" to Sony, David Rudder was involved with London Records, Super Blue appeared on *Sesame Street*, Krosfyah achieved gold album sales in Canada with the CD "Ultimate Party—Pump Me Up." Eddy Grant reaped phenomenal successes with songs like "Johanna" and the ringbang version of "Electric Avenue." By the 1990s, most calypso acts were consumed with the desire to go where no other calypso act had gone. One of the perceived conduits for mass popularization was the recorded product, touring, and, of course, exploiting the music video genre.

In the early 2000s Eddy Grant brought his music style called ringbang to world attention with the Peter Black remix of his 1980s hit "Electric Avenue," now marketed as the ringbang remix. By the mid-2000s, VP Records had entered a deal with Atlantic Records, which meant that many more reggae artists on VP's roster were given breaks. Elephant Man and Wayne Wonder came to the fore. But this alliance with Atlantic also opened up the way for a few post-soca acts like Kevin Lyttle of St. Vincent and the Bajan Rupee, who both secured deals with Atlantic. These were not the first. Some years previous, the undisputed leading post-soca exponent Machel Montano had also copped a deal with Atlantic but walked away from it after he felt he was not being allowed to create soca music. There are a number of similar advances and retreats within the calypso arena, but up to the present, calypso has not had a sustained presence in the international industry. This is so even despite the projected hosting of a category for calypso in future Grammy Awards.

By the mid-2000s, the artist Bunji Garlin (Machel's compatriot), though not gaining a major contract, was nonetheless still leading the pack. He established and maintained his persona through live stage per-formances and through participation in Trinidad's festival competitions. But he also shrewdly fanned the buzz surrounding his name by investing in cyber marketing. On his impressive platform Bunjigarlin.com (back in 2006), he was proclaimed as "the king of ragga soca." By 2007 he had transferred himself to the more popular MySpace location.[9] Other outfits like Xtatik, Square One (before the 2004 disbanding), and solo acts like Destra, Faye Ann Lyons, and TC all engaged in negotiated promotion via the Net, as on Queenofsoca.com.[10] By the mid 2000s, there were a few signs that soca culture was gaining some ground and increased popularity beyond the region. Many of these strides were brought about by soca's high energy performers and the support of carnival culture at several centers across the world. By the mid-2000s, it seemed even more pressing for soca acts to redefine the seasonality of their music, which was still attached to specific festivals. Many more artists were doing compilation recordings and collaborations. These collaborations were also being done with artists in dancehall. Soca was becoming increasingly dancehallified. But soca, like dancehall, was also borrowing from hip hop and Western black popular culture. This was very evident in the music being produced. In the same way that hip hop in the post-2000 period was founded on the sampling of existing beats, likewise Caribbean dance music was sampling popular beats within hip hop. Hip hop was also discernable in the accompanying codes, fads, habits, style, and language that surrounded post-soca culture. In the absence of lyrical creativity, soca music often descended into the quagmire of banality and lewdness. In cyberspace, soca culture celebrated a newly found freedom. On the Internet, you did not know who was watching. Featured artists on the Net could possibly be catapulted to international stardom if the right person viewed them, but it was also felt that those people who would censure soca culture for its vulgarity and experimentation were less likely to be surfing the Net. Given the Internet's mystique and surreal qualities, most new wave artists with ambitions of stardom saw it as a virtual corridor and arena to international success. By the mid-2000s, emerging soca acts still found it difficult to capture the attention of international and well-placed record executives. But at this time there was more buzz among soca culture than any time before. Rupee's rise to greater recognition was partly attributable to his serious employment of the Internet, where he launched his site, Thisisrupee.com,[11] also the name of his 2003 pre-Atlantic CD. Despite the gains reaped in the post-2000 period, many artists have still declared that the international entertainment industry retains many of the established structures that have defined it for decades. Artists have also quarreled that in spite of the Internet's wizardry, much of the moving and shaking within the corridors of power is still dependent on what takes place on the ground. What emerging artists of soca have found, however, is that the new information and communications technology has created many more opportunities for lateral movement within their arena, and within entertainment culture. It is these lateral shifts and interactions that still hold out most hope of success for Caribbean artists. Soca culture seemed to recognize and catch on to this nexus of relations a little later than dancehall.

Reggae performers have made more significant strides with respect to internationalization of their image and products. Throughout the 1990s, a set of performers rose to prominence. In the early 1990s, Shabba Ranks and Patra were signed to Epic. They are often seen as the pioneering dancehall acts that first crossed over into the arena of international music culture. After these, a number of other performers gained major or large independent deals. Many of these newer artists contributed to the evolution of dancehall into an even more technologically driven music. Dancehall interfaced with such styles as soca, hip hop and R and B to produce a series of post-dancehall creations. Some of its artists deliberately immersed their creations in proudly offensive lyrics that degraded their women and the very society they claimed to represent. Just as had happened with hip hop, likewise soca and dancehall music forms were being highjacked by commercially-driven, unimaginative filth.

Some of the leading artists in the post-2000 period benefited from the inroads made during the previous decade. But post-2000 artists like Sean Paul, Wayne Wonder, Beenie Man, Bounty Killer, Lady Saw, and Elephant Man worked with greater individual freedom than had been allowed of earlier acts. To some extent, their more sustained standing in music culture was based partly upon a wider range of technological platforms on which they could stage their presence. For example, the growing importance of the Internet and its democratic principle meant that artists did not have to rely on established institutions to have their individual wares available to the public. Yes, artists could gain major publicity by being posted at the Web site of large entertainment groups, but there were also other avenues available at underground sites. It is through these sites that some artists continued to ply their trade and promote themselves. Many of these underground sites were responsible for maintaining the buzz on the streets. If by the mid-1990s, Shabba Ranks had lost much of his appeal on the ground at home in the Caribbean, in the 2000s, acts like Elephant Man not only targeted leading entertainment franchises like VH1,[12] but could also be found on less well known sites like Rudegal .com.[13] Jah Cure and Gyptian brought a freshness to the arena and established sound Web presences. Within the digital matrix of cyberculture, you could be located virtually anywhere and at any time.

By the mid-2000s, Caribbean entertainment culture had circumvented a number of more traditional avenues and media in the quest to satisfy the demands and ambitions of those involved as consumers and creators. New technologies like the computer, satellite, wireless technology, and electronic peripherals created a wider range of opportunities that artists and consumers could exploit and consume. Caribbean cultural expression, and its promotion and production, was still preoccupied with more traditional notions of breaking into the big league. However, the lessons of contending with and exploring culture in the real and virtual realms more clearly suggested that regional culture needed to exploit lateral as well as vertical associations.

How Music Television Came to TV in the Caribbean

Although music and music television is but one segment of entertainment culture, its function and functioning do reflect the state of play in other areas of Caribbean cultural expression. By the first decade of the twenty-first century, Caribbean music on CD and video represented a substantial body of work. The expansion of music and video—of sound, images and digital fashioning—now threatens to become the major area of culture dissemination in the future.

Relatively few "recent" books conduct sustained analysis of Caribbean culture as it interfaces with and is mediated through television, film and sound. *Ex-iles* comes to mind as an early 1990's production from Africa World Press, as does, more recently, Keith Warner's *On Location* from Macmillan. There are, of course, selected essays on Caribbean Communications scattered throughout journals like *Small Axe, Caribbean Quarterly, Journal of Eastern Caribbean Studies*, and *Wadabagei*. These works begin to create a discourse surrounding Caribbean film and cinema. But there is still a noticeable absence of uninterrupted and sustained discussion of Caribbean culture as staged on these and new emerging media.

The calypso music video, like other genres of music video, has undergone significant developments since the 1980s. Popular calypso performances have, of course, been experienced, mostly in the "early" days, on radio, as well as in the "live" context, in tents and other forums. Live calypso performances have also been transmitted on television seasonally, during regional festivals. Of course, most calypso performances that were aired throughout the year on Caribbean television around the early 1980s were taped telecasts of "live" performances from popular venues.

It is important to begin to consider one route by which filmed calypso and other performances developed into carefully directed and tightly packaged marketing tools. In the early 1980s, many music performances appeared year 'round on television as program fillers. After their initial showing in some longer program format, television stations were in the practice of playing segments of the longer film, in short clips, to make up time between regular scheduled programs. They were usually short excerpts, between one to five minutes or the duration of a song's performance. An antecedent to the music video form in the Caribbean might therefore be located in this practice by Caribbean television stations. It is reasonable to suggest that even before Caribbean society was shocked by the music video format, as institutionalized and legitimized by MTV, they were already being confronted by disconnected and unexpected sound and image chaining on locally run Caribbean television stations. Caribbean music video discourse must trace the development of the genre to this set of programming practices that were in effect long before the category called the music video was formally birthed in the United States. Any detailed analysis and theorizing of Caribbean music videos or video clips must consider this situation. Some might shrewdly argue that the excerpted video clip filler represents an earlier textual fashioning of the genre. And this is a valid point. For throughout the late 1970s and in the early 1980s, many acts had little control over what segments of a recorded live performance would be aired. This depended solely on the directive of programming personnel at national television stations.

Many writers writing on the birth of music videos point to the ways in which the music video form proved a break from the accustomed flowing narrative of televised programming. Although cable television shows like *Nightclubbing* predate MTV, in the pubic consciousness MTV is the music video's originator. For many commentators and some academics, MTV and the music video genre are synonymous, one not existing without the other.[14] Many observers therefore consider MTV to be the mother of this form and go on to consider the music video as challenging the logic of conventional screening and programming: it is a form of textual intervention. It established itself as different from what went before it.

There is something similar to this breakage in the Caribbean context, a process that was happening before MTV's 1981 birth. The insertion of unscheduled musical clips between regular viewing predated MTV. These clips were transmitted across national space and were viewed by many, because at the time there was one major television station operating within each of the nations of the region. Television program directors resorted to short video or audio clips to compensate for breaks in the regular programming. (They were unaware that the audio and video clips would lead to the institutionalization of both the clips and the breaks). But because programming in the region has always been dogged by many technical difficulties, it meant that the compensatory insertion of singing and musical performances (between programs) was bound to evolve into something more. Because of recurring difficulties faced in sticking to program schedules, many regional stations resorted to stopgap measures. But their stopgap practices have turned upon them. What began as the spontaneous exploitation of "unwanted" fillers has over time developed into a recurring programming necessity. These fillers became encoded into the program sequence.

Because viewers were experiencing the fillers with some patterned frequency, the fillers eventually became an integral part of the viewing process for them. So in effect, the early excerpted music performance began to claim some pride of place. The negotiation of programming space should be considered, then, in light of this system of technical slip-ups, leading to unplanned intrusion and inclusion and eventually the recurring video segment. The eventual result of this process might very well be the contestation for space within the sequential layout of television programs. Inasmuch as there is such a thing as a television guide, then, that document poses as some sort of controlling text. It seeks to impose a format and tight structure to the viewing process. Because television guides are published by media houses and act as supporting texts for the viewing process, they therefore claim a measure of power and authority.

Some viewers have always complained about the inefficiency and nonprofessionalism of regional television stations. These shortcomings manifest themselves through the numerous breaks (or even breakdowns) within program schedules. Conversely, others respond to unscheduled programs in a positive way. Because they have resigned themselves to the reality of television's operational inconsistency, they have come to accept the inevitability of untimed video inserts. There are also other viewers, of course, who are, who have become, fonder of the unscheduled rough insert than of the major narrative that the edit is supposed to be supporting. Because there are many people in the last category of viewers, it raises the question of the relationship between the scheduled or legitimate program and the nonscheduled or nonlegitimate program. If this relationship is perceived in structural functionalist terms, then they can be considered as coconstituents. And indeed they are. They both contribute to flowing passages of film and sound. They both contribute to giving viewers the number of broadcast hours promised (as in TV guides, etc.). So that at the end of a broadcast day, program managers might go home, after a shift, with the knowledge that they have provided eight or more hours of broadcast time. From their perspective, despite the distortion of the broadcast schedule (as textualized in TV guides), the hour quota has been reached. There has been a near-unbroken broadcast, a form of running commentary, if you will, an ongoing narrative of sorts, with as little disruptive pausation as possible.

Indeed there is the possibility also that the scheduled program and its "other" do not necessarily share a functional relationship. They are in tense association on a number of counts: one type of program is legitimate while the other is nonlegitimate; one is lengthened or carved out, the other short or rough; one is anticipated, the other unexpected; one is inscribed within television guides, the other not textualized in this way. Television guides are indispensable in this new era of multiple channels and multi-timbral dissemination.[15] But many Caribbean viewers of the 1970s and 1980s brought up on regional television know of television meta-guides. These were being written daily within the region. The meta-guide is indeed much more accurate than the printed guide that forms the text of programming schedules. It is on account of the meta-guide's greater accuracy (in defining programming) that the video insert puts its case for greater showing and consideration overall within the history of Caribbean television programming. The scheduled program and the video insert have therefore contested on these terms. The written television guide and the meta-guide have also shared a relation of some tension.

Invariably, viewers are aware of which program is a scheduled one and which one is filling the gap. There is always a break (of some kind) that marks the cut and paste connecting discrete entities. I suppose as negative and positive connections are marked by their difference, by male and female ends, likewise the connecting of regular programming to unscheduled tracks of video calls attention to the polar opposites. Because of this, viewers always react to the technological splicing between regular programming. Sometimes they walk away from the television. Sometimes they turn it off in disgust. Sometimes they are pleased by the unexpected airing of a clip. Sometimes they thank God for the breaking of programmed monotony. There is always invariably some sort of reaction that acknowledges the transition. It is the very presence of this marked reaction that establishes the unease between regular programming and fillers. This heightened reaction has also anticipated the level of emotion that the video clip would continue to evoke over the decades.

The divide between and the reaction to the splicing of the two types of material is not defined or driven by badly edited insertions, although this can certainly highlight the point of break and cause some irritation among viewers. But not even cutting-edge technology's pristine editing capabilities are able to mask the point at which the regular feature and its post-text video edit do interface, so that the two types of programs always share a relationship of recognition. They are always distinct. They are always identifiable as being separate in some way. Because Caribbean viewers have lived and experienced this type of splicing, they have always been shaken into some sort of reaction. Caribbean television has therefore always been unsettling in some ways. If MTV and music television derived their dynamic format through planned strategies, it might be said that Caribbean viewers came to cut-and-paste music television much earlier and by another route. So discussions of Caribbean music videos must begin also to consider how Caribbean viewers and audiences were directly or indirectly influenced (not only by MTV but) by experiential viewing realities in the Caribbean. This needs to be investigated further.

Cut—Begin Example

Sunday March 5, 2002, C.B.C Television Barbados: At 4:30 in the afternoon, the video of Kirk Franklin's "You are the Only One" suddenly appears. It is not scheduled. It follows a showing of the travel and leisure show called *Caribscope*, one of the growing number of regional programs produced and disseminated throughout the region. After *Caribscope*'s host Andree Brathwaite says her goodbyes until next week, and after the credits are shown, you confront Kirk Franklin. He is unscheduled, but not unexpected. Here viewers recognize the distance between the *Caribscope* program and the hyped, upbeat, fast-paced video clips of Franklin. His gospel message is appropriately inserted within programming on this holy day. Viewers can hardly be thrown off. Still and always, there is a reaction of recognition on their part. The song does not begin from the beginning of the music video, so this further compounds the breakage. But this is permitted, because this insertion is spontaneous anyway. No one can complain therefore of poor presentation. You should be thankful that the screen's dialog with you is not broken. When this video ends, you are thrown into another Kirk Franklin performance, "Revolution," which, unlike the previous video airing, is not allowed to come to its natural ending, as when the title of the artist, of the video, the album, and the video's director come up near the conclusion. After this five minutes of diversion and intrigue, you must again negotiate, this time with the reconnection to the regular track of programming. Depending on your preference, likes, dislikes, mood, and state of mind at that time, the station's appeal would be established, temporarily (and possibly for a much longer period of time).

End Example—Paste

Up to the present, the nondedicated video clip filler is still a recurring parenthetical inclusion within the sequenced playing out of daily-nightly television programming. Indeed, when the music video program "Caribbean Rhythm Express" aired on regional television in the mid-to-late 1990s, it was their accepted practice to treat excerpted live performance as constituting a "music video." Fireman Hooper's live performance from the 1999 St. Vincent soca monarch finals of the song "Fireman (Push Up De Wood)" became inscribed as a music video. In the double entendre composition, its female speaking voice urges her male counterpart to "push up the wood under the pan." The video recording from St. Vincent's finals night performance became a hot number that aired regularly. The video's appeal stemmed largely from the interaction between the energetic performer and his lively audience, which in the live videoed performance are just an arm's length away from him. What this video lacks in choreographed directorial cinematography is made up for by its pure energy and the spontaneous combustion between Fireman Hooper and the crowd of young revelers. The St. Lucian calypsonian Bachelor also benefited from this program production practice with his popular though less-frenetic composition "Hypocrites."

Caribbean calypso and reggae acts have sought to enhance their standing by engaging more and more the power of the music video. Especially in the early 1980s, acts did taped television studio performances to advertise themselves. Many leading performers saw this type of video recording as a major avenue for gaining access to television and garnering wider national support. As discussed in the previous chapter, many of these taped studio performances pretended to be live studio performances. But because acts wanted to project the highest sound quality possible and because they wanted to remain as true as possible to the recorded text, they kept the recorded audio track and performed with their bodies "live" while they lip-synched. When these artists undertook this venture, they came up against the intimate yet highly contentious relations that play out between audio and video, sound and image, the recorded and the live, the master text and its "others," the original and its copy.

When Caribbean performers began to contemplate the serious production of music videos in the mid-to-late 1980s, they had substantial ground to cover to catch up with international standards, but within their midst, luckily, there were some regional acts that had achieved international standing. The airing of a number of Eddy Grant videos therefore served some reassurance to Caribbean acts that the Caribbean music video was indeed possible. It did not always require the most elaborate of productions or major capital outlay. Early videos like Crazy's "Parang Soca" gave way to even more sophisticated productions like Arrow's "Groove Master." Arrow's video experimented with the interface of real-life players and musicians and the wizardry of on-screen animation. It is like Eddy Grant's chart-topping "Johanna" of the same period. Grant's prior release "Electric Avenue" was even more of a foundational video in Caribbean entertainment culture. It aired on many of the major entertainment networks worldwide. The video to "Electric Avenue," like much of his music, was built around well-stated and repeated motifs. The revving motorcycle and its journey through the heart of darkness of Caribbean street life helped to define the narrative structure of the production. It was sufficiently appealing to the international market, but retained some traits of its origin. Caribbean entertainers have continued to wrestle with the challenges of electronic and digital display of their work. Unlike most Grant videos, not all Caribbean projections by rising international acts are able to exert the leverage that Grant has, by way of control over aspects of the production.

Part 3: Entertainment and Music Culture on the Internet

Television to Computer

In early April 2007, Caribbean Def Jam artist Rihanna launched the first single ("Umbrella") from her third album on her Web site. The launch predated the June 5 release of the album. This was by no means the first such occurrence. The prerelease online reinforced the centrality of the computer and the Web to entertainment culture.

The Caribbean video sector evolved within the context of world entertainment culture. Videos have been made available for sale around the region, sometimes as dedicated packaged videocassettes; other times they have been available through rental at video outlets. The television set has supported entertainment culture in a way that no other medium has done. The role of this technological wonder cannot be understated. Throughout the latter decades of the twentieth century, Caribbean society invested heavily in this hardware. Consumers moved from black and white sets, to color, to interactive brands and high-definition flat panels.

In the post-2000 period, other mediums entered the market and began to alter the balance of power in entertainment platforms.

By the mid-to-late 1990s, it was indeed possible to see video clips of selected Caribbean acts on the Internet. This is not to suggest that there were countless videos available on demand in the mid-1990s, for indeed, this was not the case. Television still remained the preferred medium for video display and promotion at the time. Some agencies within the communication and entertainment sector predicted negative growth for broadcast television, radio, and newspapers between 1996 and 2003. Conversely, the Web medium was expected to achieve a 159 percent positive growth. Given the multifunctional potential of the computer as a broadcast platform, total entertainment via the computer is a stated ambition of the entertainment and technology industry.

An August 22, 2005, article by Paul Eng, "Wi-Fi Companies Help—and Hurt—Efforts to Build Metro Networks," heralds the building of wireless networks around some major United States cities.[16] This initiative would open up the space for endless connectivity. The construction of such networks allows for freer seamless interactivity between users but also heralds the expansion of corporate and industry interests, particularly in the area of sale of goods and services to the general public. This future vision is endorsed by many legislators, industry players, and inventors. Many believers in the supremacy of digital living anticipate the replacement of more traditional technologies, like the dedicated television, by the computer and World Wide Web technologies. But on the other hand, there are those who caution that even with new advances in leading-edge technology, there are still many imperfections within critical processes such as audio and video streaming on the Internet. Streaming Video Primer, for example, draws attention to the many technical, practical and conceptual challenges of Web streaming and its effects on broadcasts such as entertainment productions.[17] Some additional challenges noted by people in the industry have to do with the fears of creators and producers about their copyright in the digital arena, and about "fair use."

Internet (P[l]ay as You Enter)

Over its history, the Internet has developed from being a text-based medium, offering ASCII-based hypertext, into being a multimedia platform. Of course, streaming media is at the center of current and future developments. Streaming media has to do with the transfer of images and sound to desktops across the World Wide Web.

Simply put, streaming involves a process of compressing data sent from a source (like a video camera) onto one of the Internet's streaming servers. These servers are able to store and distribute the data sent to them. This data content can then be accessed by other users through a process through which it is decompressed. These streams can be viewed through media players made available on the Internet. Three of the more popular media players include RealPlayer, the Windows Media Player, and QuickTime. Streaming developed partly to make sure that users of the computer did not have to wait for long periods while downloading an entire data file and then playing it back after recording it on their computer system. Through streaming, you can have easier, immediate, real-time access to audio and video files. While the media player is requesting data from media servers and relaying it, the media player is also caching the data internally through its memory buffer. Through this process of buffering, the media player has some blocks of data in store that it will sequentially relay, even in cases where there is interference of some kind. In an ideal situation, where users have broadband connections (T1, ISDN, DSL, ADSL), streaming can be fascinating. But caching does not guarantee seamless relay of sound and video. There are still some teething problems with this technology.

Some of the failings of streaming video have to do with jerky motion, nonsynchrony of sound and image, and a less-than-pristine image quality. The video-audio industry has therefore had to negotiate different ways of surmounting these challenges. Some video streams have had to sacrifice tight compression in order to achieve a smoother stream of sound and video, but in the process, they have had to maintain their size as big files. Although some video has been placed on the Internet as good quality, this has not guaranteed that all viewers will see them in the same way. Apple Trailers, for instance, which showcases the latest movies, provides good quality at its site. A new PC with a 3GHZ processor and matching multimedia capabilities will play any of these quite well in a favorable climate. But a slower machine in a less favorable climate will take longer to load and buffer and play the same video. The issue of the environment of interconnection (with the technology) is a critical one. It foregrounds the question of the Net's democratic and nondemocratic manifestation.

A vital concern for Caribbean users of the Internet and new technologies has had to do with the cost of staging one's presence in cyberculture. Hosting and managing a site can be time consuming and also a recurring financial cost. Although the World Wide Web claims to be democratic, there is still a monetary price to be paid for its access and exploitation. Discussions of Caribbean usage of the Internet should therefore be cognizant of the economic and other encumbrances that confront artists and creators who perceive the Net as the go-to medium of the very near future. See It First, a Californian interactive streaming media solutions company, provides quotes for the task of producing streaming video on demand under a number of permutations of usage and accessibility for a six-month period. Their creation and production and delivery on-demand cost hovers in the region of $20,000 U.S.[18] Though Caribbean users of the Internet were not faced with this upfront cost when staging their presence in cyberculture, this costing reflects the seriousness and depth of financial resources expended in the arena of cyberspace. The magic and democracy of the Internet is therefore firmly upheld by solidly entrenched financial and economic realities. Given these costs, Caribbean artists cannot hope to stage their presence alone; they must also find creative ways of circumventing the demands of some media solutions companies.

Other challenges posed to potential Caribbean creators have to do with the distance of Caribbean players from the major corporations that control the wider global and Western communications network. Given the peripheral placing of the region in digital culture construction, its peoples have had to compete from a position of greater weakness than, say, another set of people who are much closer to the owners of the means of technological construction. The present state of Caribbean culture in the current communications and technology revolution is a reflection of the varying degrees to which regional individuals and institutions have been able to navigate their presence and space in a highly competitive and preferentially skewed global system and its digitized cultural matrix.

Net video critique has therefore to take all these processes in mind. It should therefore, in cases where it analyzes Net data, give some insight into the particular experience of the critic and something about his or her machine and their relationship to the tools and processes of cyberculture. My discussion does so to some extent. It does not set out to fix the sites and experiences presented as universal (cast in stone), because, as users know, each experience on the Net is different from every other one. But what I want to do in this book is to create a point of some relative reference for people who have an interest in Caribbean and world culture in the context of changing technologies. The insecurity and uncertainty that the region has felt in the presence of digital culture has also translated into the arena of critical discourse. It is possible that the Caribbean cultural interface with digital media such as the Internet could go unnoticed at the critical point of early contact with the machines, within the matrix. The failure to consider the dynamics of this contact could create an empty space of knowledge about the evolution of leading-edge Caribbean cultural expression and about worldwide frontier culture.

When Caribbean entertainment culture started to consider the Internet to be a viable and real medium for its use and exploitation, it was not the first to do so. It is perhaps misleading to speak of people as coming to the Internet first and second and so on, in a way that creates the impression of a linear march towards the technology. It is possible to suggest that some nations have been quicker to use computers and Web technology in wider numbers than others. Again, some societies tend to reflect greater technological proximity than others. Indeed, the notion of the digital divide examines the imbalance of access to resources and technologies due to economic and geopolitical considerations. But at the level of individual usage, there are really relative positionings of individual users. So although entertainment culture was attracting much more attention in industrialized Western corporate locations much earlier, there were nonetheless some regional people who were ahead of their fellows in those very locations with respect to new technological applications and use.

This being said, the point cannot be avoided that Caribbean entertainment culture has always looked beyond the region for guidance. The trend in Caribbean cultural expression is often marked out by larger international and nonregional agendas. When Caribbean cultural practitioners began to consider the Internet as a place of expression and exposure, they were taking the cue from developments at the heart of Western popular culture. The focus here on entertainment culture provides sharper focus for understanding how other social, political, and spiritual transactions are controlled by global interests and association.

Videos: From Sexual to Digital Bodies

A central focus of many Caribbean music videos has been their establishing of a storyline or some other kind of meaningful filmic narrative. The authors of the book *You Stand There: Making Music Video* suggest that, relatively speaking, music genres like hip hop, which share a link with the storytelling tradition, still maintain a strong sense of narrative video in some productions.[19] Calypso, of course, is founded on the notion of storytelling and clear narration by the singer to the audience. Reggae is similarly rooted in narrative and experience. As these two forms have evolved, things have changed. Soca, dancehall, and what I call post-soca and post-dancehall music are further removed from their root tradition in Caribbean experience. So it is reasonable to assume that their music videos have felt less pressure to express a clear narrative, whether lyrical, filmic, or otherwise. As with post-hip hop, leading-edge Caribbean music and culture forms have tended to be about festivities, dancing, violence, and sexual play. The Caribbean music video can be said to have evolved through three stages over the past three decades.

(1) Music videos like Arrow's "Groove Master" and "Oh La Soca" reflect some of the intricate traits of music videos of the 1980s. The former video captures the live band performance on a sound stage. Although it makes use of postproduction effects and graphics, and although it is one of the more self-consciously created videos of the time, it still maintains a certain positioning of humans and their electronic instruments that defines many a Caribbean video of the 1970s and 1980s period (as with the Promise video discussed in the previous chapter). These Arrow videos do not permit a total abandonment of the musical track, and musical instruments in the visual display of soca's leading outfit of the mid-1980s. Arrow knows that his music has ridden on the strength of strong musical motifs. It has also ridden on the strength of key musical instruments. Bass lines are well stated. They groove. Horns are bright and sharp. They are some of the best in the soca genre in the Caribbean at the time. They sometimes take on the impact of horns in the "Latin" music category. The lead guitar has played at the center of many Arrow songs. Arrow and Eddy Grant ascribed a new position for this instrument within Caribbean dance soca. A review of earlier television videos in reggae and calypso would also reveal recurring features and patterns. There is a fascination between human subjects and their sound instruments.

　　In discussions about popular music instrument semiotics, the guitar has often stood for the phallus.[20] Arrow's liking for the guitar in his productions does provide an avenue for some discussion of its symbolism in the progressive soca of the 1980s. In Arrow videos, as in some popular video interpretations of Marley—for example, "Get Up Stand Up"—attention is called to the guitar. In later post-soca and post-dancehall videos of the late 1990s and beyond, such instruments are not as ritualistically positioned. The camera's fixation with the lead solos of Arrow's white guitarist in the 1980s is not extended into later filmic productions.

(2) By the 1990s, human manipulation of the machine is replaced by human manipulation of other human objects. Chiefly there is the male manipulation of femaleness. In many Grant, Arrow, and Marley videos, the guitar is a thing to behold. In later videos of the 1990s, especially by other artists, the instruments themselves are subordinated

to and are often replaced by other objects of fantasy and mastery. The female object or instrument therefore replaced the musical instrument of the previous decade. In the 1990s, the male ambitions of the entertainment industry transformed the female subject into an instrument of production, gratification, and sexploitation.

(3) If entertainment culture throughout the 1990s was driven by fascination with human subjects, particularly males and females and relative presences and absences within selected media, in the post-2000 period these objects are still important within entertainment and communications media, but they now experience some subordination in the presence of other grand objects of mastery and control. The third stage of evolution within entertainment culture again returns to a concern with technology. In this third stage, the technology is not only contained within the actual video production, but it operates outside the production as well, engulfing the entire production (and all *its* viewers) in a real and virtual expansive matrix. Technology and promise of "the better" have created a new set of principles that not only controls the viewing process but also impacts the kinds of creations on display by artists and corporations. Over the years, producers of entertainment have ensured the continuity of their work by launching them on new platforms. The promise of better media in the future has given new representational emphasis to more traditional works and idioms. It would be fair to say that a large percentage of Web video is traditional music videos that are recast on newer media. But Web videos are mediated by the newer emerging medium of the Internet and therefore are surrounded by a set of considerations, some of which I mentioned earlier, but others that are yet to be discovered and discussed.

Machel Montano and Xtatik Video—"Big Truck"

Machel Montano and Xtatik's video "Big Truck" exhibits traits of early soca, of 1990s soca, as well as post-soca aesthetics, especially when the video is experienced as a Web video. The song's lyrics are about the music sound truck, whose cargo of Xtatik's band members act as pied pipers for the crowd of revelers on J'ouvert Morning (Carnival Monday in Trinidad). The televised and Web video reflects the idea of the big truck that attracts more and more party people as it makes its way through the streets of Trinidad. There is therefore an identifiable narrative that both sound and video project, no matter the presence of postproduction cut and paste. The video also features the band of musicians on top of the moving engine, with their electronic gear strapped to their bodies or in close proximity. The presence of instruments and the central place of these in the video hark back to a pre-1990s trope, that of musicians in control of their gear. If the introduction of digital technology in the 1980s threatened a radical shift in the way Caribbean musicians related to their instruments, then mid-to-late1980's videos sought to feature musicians still in control of the instrument. The Xtatik video reminds one of the 1980s fascination with mastering emerging digital technology, which had supplanted analog electronics.

But the "Big Truck" video was also a product of the 1990s. Its treatment of the big truck as a metaphor for the woman's anatomy places the video in sync with the filmic and aesthetic creed espoused by Caribbean dance videos of the 1990s. This preoccupation was not the only defining feature of many 1990s music videos, for like some others, the Machel video reflects some attention to postproduction. Given Machel's obvious fascination with fusion and an unmistakable influence from alternative music, his videos often reflect tinges of technological experimentation and wizardry. The "Big Truck" video therefore reflects a fair degree of editing and postproduction reconfiguration. A detailed listing of the early frames of the production might illustrate how the video gestures to enhanced technological self-consciousness but falls back into a familiar Caribbean dance video formula, where the female body is exploited and violated. The early frames do not necessarily fit logically: they are fast frames, they stir up some intrigue, but they eventually give way to the 1990s fascination with exploitable human objects.

The video begins with a close up shot of a glass of water that shakes on a table. It vibrates due to the horn of a rig truck (heard off-screen). There are indecipherable images of parts of the truck very close up. We think we see the truck's horn, close-up. The glass drops. It breaks. Water spills. There is traffic in the street. It is a busy street. We see a big music truck in the midst—this from a front shot. Then a tighter shot. The angle cuts to side-on. There is an assortment of other shots as the song builds up to vocals. There is an aerial shot looking down on the truck as revelers gather. Then there is a close up shot of men dancing on the truck. The soundtrack sings the refrain: "Ride de truck." Then Machel sings a call as he is located in a close-up. The audience's response to him sees the camera focusing on them. There are shifting shots. Band musicians and the crowd share the focus along with Machel. No one other person is given focus early on, save a woman on the vehicle who dances behind Machel's body. She again captures the video's focus in the crucial "breakdown" section of song, when the music slows, and thereafter. Throughout the video bodies dance, gyrate. This is the video's point of intrigue.

This video appeared on the Web much later than the televised version. By making mention of two versions, I do not want to suggest that there are separate and distinct versions of the video, one for television and the other for the Web. But I want to suggest that the Web environment throws up its own context of viewing and that the Web experience is defined by the expansive intrusion of the technological. So although some videos on the Net are quite the same as those televised, they are rendered as altered versions because of the set of concerns that are attendant to the highly technologized matrix of current leading-edge media. There is a certain familiarity among most audiences with the televised viewing experience, a familiarity that does not exist on the same scale and degree with newer technologies. Because the computer, computer technology, PDAs, and mobile interface are still rapidly evolving, users of these technologies constantly have to renegotiate their relationship with these extensions of their experience and of their bodies. The relay of information and data such as video over these media is therefore always at risk of data loss, either due to the imperfections of the new technologies or due to the fact that many users of these technologies have to look beneath the veneer of the machine to grasp the data. In some cases, the presence of the machine overpowers its function, which might be to relay and receive tracks of data. Online videos by Machel and others are therefore well placed within a new category of post–twentieth century cultural productions. This category now no longer only presents human subjects and objects in positions of control, exploitation, and confrontation based purely on social, economic, and political conditions (as defined by pre–twenty-first century expression and media), but they are also virtually situated. The technology is therefore a central agent and determinant of experience in the new arena of Caribbean and world expression. To experience a Web video of Machel's "Big Truck" is therefore to experience the technology that stands before, beneath, and around the machine that promises to reconfigure said video and much, much more in the not-too-distant future.

Web Video within the Machine (Calypso/Soca/Post-Soca)

In the Web environment you do not just watch a video. You do not simply plug and play. The entertainment industry and technology retail franchises often disseminate the myth of seamless transaction in the dispensation of the machine, but leading-edge culture does not come without a price. There are always layers of technology to be circumnavigated.

It is this web of possibility that both conceals and reveals the wonders that lie within the machine.

In the Web environment Xtatik's locating of videos under the heading of "e-mag" acts as a gateway to video streams on demand.[21] When a list of videos is given, the user is cautioned that they should have Macromedia Flash Player 6 in order to see the Xtatik video. Machelmontano.com, a previous Web site hosted by the band, used Quicktime.[22] The video provided on that old site was of some of the best quality seen on the Internet by a soca act in the late 1990s. The main difference between the older site and the one that replaced it is that the older site concealed its functions and prevented you from gaining full and free access to the band from the word go, on the front page. Whereas the older site took you through the loading process, the new site opens up almost immediately to offer you a range of facilities for meeting Xtatik. The earlier Web site was much more ostentatious. It sought to display the trendy possibilities of the Net and of the band. This was a feature of Web designs around the time. The more recent site is much more sophisticated. It attempts to be more functional, but it still maintains some of the trendy posturing of its earlier representation or life.

The new Xtatik "Big Truck" Web video is contained within a small viewing screen. You are not given different connection speeds for playback of the video. Based on its display, the video gives the feeling of being streamed at 56K playback. The video's Web size and its quality are the two most noticeable features that invite critique. The small display screen makes it more difficult to detect detail within the production. But perhaps this smaller screen protects the video's quality, because a larger screen might also tend to display lower quality video. The challenges of following the production are helped by the fact that the camera work on the production is not as unstable and disorienting as has come to represent music video delivery. The action in the video is fast paced, but there is a narrative logic within the lyrics as well as within the filmic production. The presence of a story line (however tenuous) allows you to compensate for the Web video's less-than-pristine output quality. The lyrics speak about carnival day and the pleasures of following the music truck on the highway. The video begins with the gradual gathering of a crowd of people behind the truck as it snakes its way onto the major highway of activity. This is a video therefore that, in spite of the limitations surrounding its promotion here on the Net, still works because its production features compensate for the imperfections of the technology in the new environment of music entertainment culture. Once you are able to get the technology to work, and you are able to negotiate the glitches in the matrix and to compensate for technology's failings, then the viewing experience can be a thing to behold.

A more recent video, "It's Carnival" with Destra, featuring Machel, is not as effective in terms of grounding you in clearly stated motifs. Its images on screen are much faster and disjointed and flickering. But this method can also act as a camouflage for the failings of Web streaming, because the flickering image, while pretending to conform to music video convention, also masks some of the underlying failings of Web technology. Because new technologies tend to call attention to themselves (and indirectly to their creators and owners, and the society/culture that brought them to life), it is impossible to experience their data without all this baggage being strapped to the experience.

Other Web videos provide more options for viewing through a range of connections, from 56K to broadband. Some dancehall videos featured on MTV's Web site have this facility. But larger sites do not guarantee a more pleasurable and seamless experience with the performances. In early July 2004, for instance, it was not possible to see a Web stream of Elephant Man's "Pon De River" and interviews on MTV's site, although they were advertised there. Still, videos of good quality were available at other big sites like iFilm, and also at the popular Realvibez. Realvibez, a Florida based company, displays its objective of increasing the penetration of Caribbean music into the world market.[23] It provides video connection at 56,100 and 300 kilobites per second. But it is also an informative and demonstrative site in that it provides you with onsite links to a range of songs online, as well as videos and riddims like the Baghdad, Tunda Clap, and Star Wars. Although the video streams provided here are buffered and play more cleanly than the one by Xtatik mentioned earlier, one is still aware of the conditionalities of viewing videos on the Net. For instance, Morgan Heritage's "Don't Haffi Dread" runs without glitches in the stream. But because you are aware of the potential for interference and so experience anxiety, you expect something to happen, and in the absence of something going wrong, you fix onto other minute details, such as the fact that the video and audio, though in relatively good sync, do not match perfectly. Whether this is so or not in the televised video, the point is, that in the Web domain, you are acutely aware of sound, image, and video, and their individual presences in production and dissemination. This is also the case with Web videos after 2005 and with videos from outside the region. For example, the Web video "Summertime," by Japanese dancehall act Minmi. Even The medium calls attention to itself. Indeed, in the environment of cyberculture, there are some kinds of activities and productions that call greater attention to the medium. Although new technologies have attempted to forge a more seamless relationship between the real and virtual places, improvements in technology have also served to remind users of the inherent distance and difference between worlds and realities.

There are many other Web sites that devote themselves to videos and music. But there are also others that do not simply present video as centerpiece. Some sites simply have an objective of promoting and indeed keeping up with various aspects of popular culture. On the Internet, it is easier to keep up with "the popular" than it tends to be on more traditional mediums. But keeping up often demands much effort, energy, time, commitment, and know-how. The beauty of the Internet as a document and agent of popular expression is that it can be updated at its present location. It does not have to be totally retracted and reprinted and physically replaced. It can be tweaked, amended, and enhanced, and a condition of virtual redeployment is created. But this process can also be challenging, given the demands of putting up new material and given the particular challenges that are associated with updating pages. This notwithstanding, entertainment sites devoted to Caribbean cultural expression have played a pivotal role in upholding and celebrating the immediacy of Caribbean cultural expression. Their role is unsurpassed by any other single medium at present.

Web sites like CarnivalPower.com and Timeplusbeats.tv are engines at the heart of Caribbean popular cultural expression within the Net. Timeplusbeats has Grenadian origins. It gives text-based information on a range of artists from the Grenadians Ajamu, Inspector, and Super P, to Kevin Lyttle, Sean Paul, Sherwayne Winchester, and the New York-based Request Band. It also provides a photo gallery and an advertising space, and its centerpiece is its TV-like facility that shows on rotation, videos, interviews, and commercials geared towards youth and entertainment culture. Very significant also is the fact that the Web site provides links to other associated Web sites engaged in promoting entertainment culture. Some of the links provided connect to Toronto-lime, Islandmix, and Bashmentradio.

The really exciting projection of a shared Caribbean entertainment culture can be found on Web sites dedicated to activities around the region. There are few Web sites more regionally embracing and active than sites like Carnivalpower.com and Calypsoarchives.co.uk.[24] These sites are different in their appeal and motives, but they serve a similar function of drawing their audience to a central space in order to locate the raw material of their distinctive cultural identities. Although Caribbean cultural expression at the cusp of experience was predominantly driven by real and virtual deification of sex, female exploitation, violence, and materialism, there were also other frontier sites of knowledge and experience that stood at the other end of the virtual domain. Such sites were more informative, educational, and archival in intent, offering themselves to Caribbean and other peoples as alternative agents of the region. Carnivalpower and Calypsoarchives are therefore in many respects sites representative of Caribbean cultural expression.

The Vincentian-inspired site Carnivalpower is even more eclectic than Timeplusbeats. Carnivalpower revolves predominantly around carnival culture. It also promotes and updates patrons about regional and local fetes. You can e-mail your address to the Web hosts and receive information about upcoming events of all types. Carnivalpower's strength is its immersion in the regional and extra-regional activities of carnival. It therefore promotes the happenings across the region and world. Carnivalpower is not an outstanding site in terms of construction aesthetics. But it is pleasurable in other ways. When you open on to the home page, it strikes you that the page is very busy. It is difficult to keep focus on a specific object or image or text. But this is an attraction. It casts the impression that there is much to do here. What sells this site to surfers of cultural activity is partly its appeal to a number of nationalities. It provides information, music, video and still shots of carnivals in Trinidad, St. Vincent, Antigua, Barbados, Miami, New York, and Toronto.

Web sites of this kind exude a certain energy and hype. This site is therefore not dissimilar to dedicated publications like the once popular "Dub Missive" in terms of its sacrificing of organization and aesthetic appeal for raw passion and cultural involvement. This is an important point, because this book recognizes that the Internet and new technologies are not born of themselves. They are a reflection and continuation of existing systems and phenomena. The "hard" publication of entertainment magazines is a forerunner of sites like Carnivalpower. Web sites have not totally replaced these more conventional means. In some cases, carnival magazines still exist side by side with newer sites of celebration and information. Indeed, the hosting of culture and carnival on the Internet is not done in a vacuum. Many people who surf these sites on the Web are also actual participants in the real activity on the streets and other actual venues, though there are many more virtual participants. Carnivalpower is a virtual arena that reflects the goings-on throughout carnival culture. It not only celebrates the events of the past and anticipates the future, but it also celebrates its ability to capture and reinvent the mystique and role-play of carnival. There are many other sites that, though not achieving the popularity and buzz of Carnivalpower, nonetheless are achieving underground status, like Kingdomofsoca, for instance.[25]

Calypsoarchives.co.uk is arguably the most comprehensive site dedicated to archiving calypso and soca music culture on the Internet. Its impressive presence has to do with its catalog of old recordings by a range of artists and with its provision of JPEG images of countless album jacket covers. It is a virtual and real source of cultural data. It is not a commercial site, so you are not bombarded by distracting pop-ups. Unfortunately, it does not have interactivity built-in. Researchers cannot easily correct or contribute material. But this is also possibly a sign of tight management over the site.

While these sites work hard to keep up-to-date with activities, they also challenge entertainment culture within the region. As these sites become even more popular, performers, patrons and people with other interests are forced to reassess the ways in which they experience the activities that they have depended on traditional media to convey to them. The increasing investment in multimedia, in sound, in video, and in virtual live Internet, means that increasingly the new technologies promise to take you on location at the actual event. Ultimately, there arises the situation of the virtual experience substituting for (the absence of) the real thing. Once Caribbean cultural experience reaches this point, it will conjure up the stuff of science fiction. People will talk of being at an event that they experience live via Web streaming. That is still a little way off, but not beyond the horizon.

In the present, there is much more available to entertainment culture than there used to be. The Internet challenges performers, patrons and researchers to reconsider the means by which it is possible to experience and produce culture. In the first decade of the twenty-first century, Caribbean culture has come to depend more heavily on emerging technology than on any other single phenomenon. It is significant therefore that as technology reproduces the culture that is in demand, the very fact and act of popular culture gives even greater energy and presence to the technology. It would seem that these two phenomena are mutual beneficiaries one of the other. But it is also possible that in the future, as people compete for prominence and presence, that technology and the culture it reproduces will increasingly come into contention for pride of place. As we view expressions of ourselves through the technology, it is becoming increasingly more difficult to ignore the enhanced facilities and trendy, sleek functions that are onboard. Technology therefore not only produces and reproduces culture, but by route of this very replication of culture, technology holds up itself as an indispensable agent.

Web Video within the Machine (Reggae/Dancehall/Post-Dancehall)

In the cyber realm, dancehall and post-dancehall cultural expression also undergoes technological contortion. You do not get to this culture without first navigating the matrix of reconstruction. As happens with other expressive Caribbean cultural phenomena on display, you come away from the virtual dancehall experience with bouts of stress, adrenalin, and anxiety from the process of wrestling with the medium, the machine. A simple illustration reflects the niggling challenges that either wear down or sharpen the determination of the Web entrant. A simple search for the main official page of a leading act like Morgan Heritage could see you being directed to other sites, due to the system of site ranking that under girds the virtual matrix. The uninitiated might very well find him- or herself washed up at one or more of the locations that package Caribbean bands.[26] But a more prolonged and a better-focused search might eventually lead to a more credible dedicated homepage.[27] This much enhanced, interactive, and relatively self contained site features "history, text, sound clips and streaming video" using the Quicktime platform. When the site is finally located, you might or might not feel that it is actually worth the energies expended in cyberspace, wrestling with the kinks and protocols lurking within the technology.

Some of the more popular sites on the Net feature multiple artists. These tend to have commercial appeal. They are therefore low on aesthetic appeal and creative content. At Artistsonly.com, the New York record company of the same name features reggae acts along with blues and new age, as well as dance artists. Here you find such acts as Sizzla, Beenie Man, and Baby Cham. Because the site seems to bundle a lot of artists onto its roster, individual artists do not get their own individual touch on their featured page. Each artist's feature page comes with the Web site's standard iconographic banner colors of red, yellow, and green horizontally painted across the top. Beneath this, on the right-hand side of the page, is the body of text, which gives the artist's background. On the left, there is either a photo of the artist or a bold representation of a recent CD release, beneath which is a listing of the tracks. There are no other links, except links to Amazon, Tower Records, and the Reggae Source. Through these links, navigators have the option of purchasing the work of the artist. The link to Tower provides sound clips to many of the songs through Media Player.

Other links offer soca artists to the public in a quite similar, though stark and limited way.[28] Realbuy is an established Web site devoted to selling items, including recordings in a range of genres. Its thrust in soca music is with compilations like "Soca Anthem" on the UK based Hot Vinyl label and the "Soca Gold" series by VP Records, the reggae dancehall powerhouse. It is hyperlinked to the larger warehouse of Amazon .com. Its prime focus is to promote and sell records online.

Afiwi.com is a much more credible site. Its emphasis is squarely with the Caribbean. It posts articles and links relating to various aspects of Caribbean life.[29] In the area of music, it also serves as an advertising site for recordings. It is a well-constructed site, which though a little congested on some pages, still does manage to provide substantial resources for investigating the different facets of Caribbean culture. It too has links to Amazon.com and offers gateways of connection to other sites, establishments, and personalities. This lateral relationship that is based on the interconnectivity of sites epitomizes the multi-layered structure of the Internet. But this also serves to highlight the set of relationships that exist both in the hard world and in the virtual domain of art, entertainment and commerce. It is clear that the virtual world is dependent on the kinds of networks and affiliation that characterize business culture in the real world of marketing and promotion. These hypertextual links are therefore similar to interlocking networks and affiliations in the real world of commerce. Caribbean reggae evolved in the 1980s and 1990s by route of music exportation and market exploration. But while reggae was gaining new markets and popularity, there was also an accompanying process of genre exploitation by external interests. Reggae has therefore always survived in a context of creative expression, niche marketing, and transnational exploitation. It is therefore not surprising that on the Internet, its commercial potential is foregrounded on many leading sites. Soca's presence on the world stage is not as big as that of reggae. But soca has also evolved in response to calypso's inward-looking orientation. Soca is therefore calypso's commercial arm. It too has therefore been embraced by marketing entities, and its artists have often stood alongside dancehall's superstars. Those Web sites dedicated to exploiting and selling recordings in these genres have therefore tended to offer their wares, hard sell. Those addresses like Artistsonly.com cannot therefore be primarily assessed for aesthetic and creative input, for in fact they are clearly set up for a dedicated purpose of hosting and routing artists and curious navigators to other sites and other kinds of activity.

In *Travels in Hyperreality*, Umberto Eco discusses the ways in which Western society re-creates fabrications that are more appealing than the real.[30] He also uncovers the lurking presence of the sales pitch. The Internet is a creation of that very society and culture. The Internet in many ways engages in a process of simulating and outdoing the real. It has evolved to a position of importance largely because of the economic potential that it both nurtures and conceals. Those sites that bundle Caribbean cultural expression are in many instances reflections of contemporary ambition. They are in competition with other similar sites. The competition is driven by a quest for economic and cultural power. This quest has resulted in crude, creative, and formulaic methods of capturing attention and markets, so that the highly commercial Web sites that project Caribbean entertainment are at times either crude or creative, but many are formulaic. In the final analysis, they both mask and reveal their deeper objectives by way of the features and strategies they employ in the virtual realm.

Admittedly, not all Web sites are like those mentioned above. There are other types of representational arrangements of reggae artists on the Internet. While it might be true to say that Internet Web aesthetics are pretty much set in relation to reggae, in that many Web sites that feature reggae acts tend to be formulaic in terms of their treatment, presentation, and representation of said culture, there are indeed some interesting, creative, and imaginative Web interfaces. Capleton, like many other reggae acts, appears through the facility of the record label. Capleton can be found "big up" or "live and in color" through his site hosted at VP Records.[31] In terms of color imagery, the Web site does not overindulge in its splashing of the traditional reggae colors. The dominant color motif is a black background; other colors are not allowed to share frame space. The dark reflection that overshadows the two-framed layout is only lit really by contrasting flickers of red fire. All in all, the Web site wants to capture and express what the front page to his "Morefire" CD calls his mission to "draw light to the plight and upliftment of Black people."

This site is adequate in terms of its providing a range of links and gateways. It offers four major links to "The prophet," "His evidence," "His words," "His friends." Some critical perspectives suggest that in the age of enhanced technology, Caribbean culture will forever be disconnected from the roots of its development. For instance, people tend to look outward into a world where and when the fast-flickering images of MTV and music television overpower and disconnect Caribbean traditional forms from their social and political functions. The Internet, however, has not yet done this. Technology is not the only determinant of cultural presentation and fashioning. Human beings are also a part of the process. Caribbean culture is not without its own agents who wrestle for power in the digital arena. Some post-dancehall and post-soca Caribbean artists on the Internet have tended to maintain quite consistent use of text and "message" as important to their politics of representation. This is a point also made earlier with respect to selected performance poets. Capleton's presentation therefore devotes an entire link to "His words," giving access to the lyrics of selected songs. This is balanced against the facility of access to words in motion, where through RealNetwork's RealAudio and video, you can listen to and view Capleton's discourse on his career, or on "fire" or "bunning (burning) cable television." This sober discourse is not replicated on all sites of leading pop culture icons. The majority of sites have little interest in this studied verbal discourse. The majority place greater emphasis on the spectacle, on motion, interactivity and on hype. The Internet is an effective medium of hype.

Barbados' leading reggae act of the early 2000s, David Kirton, has appeared at his official Web site, Davidkirton.com, which has not been updated since May 31, 2001, in spite of the fact that it has attracted 14,121 hits.[32] His debut album, *Stranger*, was released by the popular RAS Records in 1999—not a small achievement for a new reggae act from the Eastern Caribbean. In contrast to the iconography of Capleton, the tone of the official David Kirton Web site is much happier, bright, and perhaps upbeat as well. This has not only to do with the colors selected for the Kirton site, but also with the overtly showy, near-playful movement of text and image across the screen once Apple's Quicktime takes its leave upon announcing its platform control of video and sound on Kirton's splash page. Like the Capleton site, this site also provides audio and video clips, but it does not foreground Kirton as philosopher, or man of words as is done with Capleton at his site. Kirton's site does provide access to lyrics, reemphasizing the importance of the word to some categories of pop culture artists. The retention of the lyrics sets these artists apart from some gospel acts, but it reconnects them with those performance poets and their poetry discussed in an earlier chapter.

Guyana's leading dancehall act, Arawak Indian (not to be confused with the British-based Apache Indian), appeared at Arawakindian.com back in 2006.[33] This site was not too fussy about projecting dancehall and reggae motifs. In fact, there was a noticeable de-emphasizing of the formulaic traits present on other dancehall Web sites. If this Web site foregrounded any iconic motif, it played on the racial makeup of the artist. His East Indian and South American Indian ancestry came across very strongly through his symbolic name. But there was still a connection to dancehall mainstream established by the Web site's posting of photos of the smooth looking Dj, with sunglasses, gold chain, bling, and other outstanding motifs of post-dancehall, post-hip hop, and post-soca acts. Although the site provided links to his biography and discography, strangely, it did not give access to sound clips, preferring to privilege photos. It was here that the Web site seemed to establish its central space of interest. Here Arawak Indian posed with the hard core of dancehall performers, like his idol Apache Indian and others like Sean Paul and Super Cat. These are also racial hybrids that have infiltrated dancehall's center. This Web site therefore represented the forefront of Guyanese dancehall culture and turned upon playful gestures to mainstream dancehall, while vigorously maintaining a sense of place, space, and uniqueness.

Grenada's King Ajamu, like many other artists in the region, is a hybrid performer. He is not a racial hybrid but is predisposed to singing good calypso and soca, as well as reggae. At the site Belgrafix.com, there are some twenty-two audio samples that reflect the extent of his dexterity.[34] Many islands of the region, especially in the Eastern Caribbean, continue to produce entertainers who straddle genres and thereby redefine boundaries. Given their propensity to explore new frontiers, Caribbean entertainers have taken to the virtual arena in hope of self and genre redefinition, but also with full knowledge that they cannot always control or determine where their exploration will lead.

Apache.waria.com was the site of Arawak Indian's compatriot Apache Waria. Like Arawak's site, Apache's site also gives a sketched introduction to the artist, with much emphasis on still photos. Waria's splash page promises sound clip and active graphics, but its sound clips are not all easily accessed.[35] Another compatriot, Daddy Fire, proclaims his brand of music as a new style, ragga hip hop. His front page makes no pretensions. It offers few links but is most concerned with giving access to samples of Daddy Fire's music. His "Mek A Who Feel Good" fuses a straight up but driving hip hop drum rhythm with sub woofer bass tones that gesture to reggae. The song's lyrics center recurring imagery of dancehall and hip hop culture. It deals with male and female relations, the ghetto, uptown, downtown, "nigga," and Benz and agony, among other central tropes. The extent of his experimental work now released with VP Records, is two or three mixes of a single "joint." All in all, the presence of these Guyanese performers is well stated in cyberspace. Their audacious confidence is a reflection of their talent. But it also seems to stem from a belief that they are starting something different. They give props to dancehall mainstream, but one feels that they are more intent on negotiating their path by route of the new technological medium. If mainstream dancehall creates the tradition, dancehall cyberculture has the potential to set new standards that are not encumbered by traditional national projects and agendas. These acts are therefore post-dancehall to the extent that they look beyond the traditional locations of dancehall and traditional discourses about dancehall but instead vest more interest and energies in the machinery that reconfigures the genre. Technologies like the Internet therefore provide the impetus for these artists. While some people look into the tradition for inspiration and leadership, iconic figures and many contemporary entertainers peer into the matrix for the secret, for the codes to success. This is the nature of Caribbean reality in the first decade of the twenty-first century.

The Internet Underground Music Archive (IUMA) seeks to provide a platform for new acts to get heard by others and to bypass the distributor and record company. Listeners can sample all the new songs being offered by using Real network's RealAudio, and then they can download entire songs as they wish. The Montserratian Mykee Mystic, who once sang with Dub Culture back in 1983, also appears on IUMA's Internet roster of artists.[36] Through such mediums, Caribbean artists have sought new relationships, alliances and strategies of not only getting up on the Internet but also of confronting the more traditional structures and procedures that have controlled the entertainment Industry. Many artists have become disgruntled with the repressive bureaucracy that controls the international industry. Caribbean artists are quite visible as part of the new emerging category of performers who are prepared to gain wider audiences by way of new, nontraditional methods of performance. In the first decade of the twenty-first century, they are not satisfied to be tied down by traditional practices and discourses; instead, they have turned increasingly to technological advances to go where no other Caribbean artists have gone before.

Alternative

Caribbean alternative bands have continued to challenge the representational and cultural stereotypes that we all hold concerning the constituents of Caribbean culture generally. It is possible that an assessment only of Reggae and Calypso performers leads to a set of limited and limiting conclusions about the aesthetic, artistic, and technological imperatives that Caribbean musical acts bring to the desktops of virtual reality. I am not suggesting that Caribbean artists are one track in their approach to the Internet and to their employment of the virtual stage, but my analysis does suggest that there are indeed recurring motifs, themes, procedures that have as much to do with the shared experience of Caribbean place, space, and history as with the ways in which the Internet forces artists to package their images by way of lateral and vertical links, main pages, access to clips, and connectivity to peripheral facilitators like audio and video and streaming networks.

Caribbean alternative music is already situated outside the core arena of interest among Caribbean mass audiences and Caribbean cultural critics. It is precisely because of this that it is worthwhile to examine the way in which Caribbean alternative music culture interprets its difference from other Caribbean-derived music forms. Perhaps the distance from the center of Caribbean cultural expression warrants a different approach to and response within the technological domain.

There is the widely held perception that such genres as alternative are extrinsic to the Caribbean experience. Many commentators consider alternative rock music to be "white people's music." This is not an informed reading of music history at all, because it does not recognize the disputed evolution of rock and its racialized construction. The entertainment industry has also perpetuated racial myths about certain styles of music.

Caribbean alternative cannot be understood only by the route of comparing the ways in which Caribbean artists sound or look like or have the attitude of say, REM, or Green Day, or Linkin Park; rather, one must also come to understand the extent to which Caribbean alternative gestures to other, more centrally rooted styles like calypso and reggae. It is clear though, that Caribbean alternative troupes have representation throughout the region. They are quite diverse in their styles of music and also in the attitude that they bring to the Internet.

Geocities.com provides a listing of Caribbean alternative groups. The Caribbean Web ring was formed in July 2001. The Trinidad group Awakening's Web site captures the red, yellow, and green of many other Caribbean acts but blurs the color scheme to project an outfit that performs somewhere beyond the moon's dim light, where the molten redness of the sun casts a glowing shadow. Gregory's Dream is less elemental and grand on its home page but gives greater emphasis to MP3 and Real Audio downloads of cuts and studio demos alike.[37] Guyana's Tech 21 holds no pretensions; in fact, as many other bands do, it emphasizes its style as Caribbean Rock. Barbados' Desire presents one of the most provocative sites and rich assemblage of pix, links, and songs. Other striking sites that challenge the repeated tropes found throughout calypso and reggae are owned by groups like Overdose and Big Eyed Grieve.

Most Caribbean rock bands though, do not offer real moving video, and so in this regard they have not caught up with reggae and soca acts. It would seem that alternative bands have invested much energy in providing lyrics, bios, photos, and audio clips. Additionally, they have devoted much energy to text, colors, and other graphic detail. They do not seem yet trusting of the limitations of moving video via the Net. But perhaps they do not require the deeper resources and functionalities within the matrix, when basic Web technology already allows them to dismantle and to reconfigure the real.

Mobile Culture

Du Gay, referring to the pace of culture and experience in contemporary society talks about the Walkman as an extension of the body.[38] John Urry, writing in his article "Mobile Cultures," discusses travel and tourism and their relationship to notions of mobility.[39] Although he is more concerned with tourism, his study nonetheless reinforces the extent to which modern societies are societies in constant motion. Although I use the term "mobile culture" here in a broad sense as well, I want to briefly make a few observations about the growth of cellular and mobile culture in the Caribbean and its relationship to entertainment and social and cultural fashioning.

Advances in cellular and mobile technology correspond with the information industry's attempts to keep pace with quickening lifestyles and to make technology perform at the speed of life. Cellular and mobile culture worldwide has also found an outlet in Caribbean society and especially in *its* popular culture. The international communications industry made significant shifts in their market tools over the past three decades. The dedicated desktop was a vision from the 1970s and 1980s. The laptop and broadband were 1990s preoccupations of computer users and seekers of information. In the early 2000s, cellular and mobile culture reflected the ambitions of research and investment by leading communications and technology companies. In addition to the dedicated cellular and mobile phone, other hybrids also began to surface, offering a range of functions and services to people on the move. In the region, the telecommunications market had been dominated by the transnational company Cable and Wireless for many decades.[40] By the early 2000s, regional markets were being freed up. By the mid-2000s, there were effectively competing telecommunications companies across much of the region. Much of the fight took place for the mobile and peripherals market. Digicel, AT&T/Cingular, and Cable and Wireless were some of the major competitors.

Caribbean society changed in some significant ways. It was now cheaper and easier to make local and oversees calls and connections. People therefore talked and interacted on the move. They sent short text messages (SMS) on their phone display screens. By the mid-2000s, many more users aspired to wireless connection to the Internet on their mobile phones. Taking photos, recording sound, MP3 capability, Bluetooth, and expanded memory were all features that came standard on the devices that most young people carried around. They were connected to their peers, with whom they could communicate across unencumbered space.

It was only logical that music culture embraced and was embraced by this emerging technology. Not only were artists referring to the cellular and mobile craze in their songs, but the said technology was also sampling the very artists. The mid-2000s ring tone craze was but one aspect of the new way in which culture was sampling and being sampled by technology for the purpose of shared gratification. Because the mobile phone was an extension of other electronic ware, it was compatible with a whole set of other technologies. It could therefore send and receive data by route of the computer, for after all, the phone was a mobile computer. Ring tones came into vogue by the decade of the 2000s. In the mid-2000s, the Internet offered free and for-sale ringtones of all sorts of sounds. Many of these tones alluded to sounds within global popular culture, from television shows, to voices of people, to edits of popular songs. The acquiring of ringtones moved from being an active crave into an ordinary practice by the late 2000s.

With the passing out of monophony, polyphony meant that ringtones were richer in texture and were able to more accurately reproduce the harmonic character of songs; hence the popularity of polyphony over conventional monophonic ring tones. Sound polyphony technology that emerged through music technology in the 1980s opened up possibility for even more intricate interlacing of sound and video. The marketing buzz over ringtones of familiar songs also signaled the anticipated interplay between communications, wireless technology, and the music and film industry.

Ringtones were available online for artists in a range of Caribbean music styles. Web sites like Bashmentringtones.com have offered ringtones of current post-R&B, post–hip hop, post-reggae/dancehall, and post-soca tracks, for example Elephant Man's "Pon de River," Sean Paul's "Like Glue," and Soca's Kevin Lyttle's "Turn Me On," Machel Montano's "No War," Rupee's "Tempted to Touch," and Rihanna's "Pon De Replay." As was true for other artists elsewhere, Caribbean artists did not always benefit from this craze directly. Indirectly, they were able to increase their popularity, and symbolically, the sampling of their songs served to entrench them within the heart of popular culture and popular commodification.

But mobile culture was not interfacing only with the music industry. It also appealed to the gaming industry, as the chapter on video games will attest. Even the most primitive of mobile phones came with built-in factory games. But increasingly, cell phone companies negotiated with the gaming industry to provide users with a wider range of leading-edge games. These games would be built in at the factory, but they would also be downloadable via the Internet and through other network facilities. The mobile phone was but one handheld gadget that aspired to workstation status. There were other handhelds, like Apple's iPod, which were primarily music oriented. But the cellular phone's primary emphasis on providing contact between distant callers for a range of reasons (from business to pleasure) and its universal appeal made it a leading technology in the race for workstation status among handhelds.

If the use of the computer and interaction within cyberspace forced Caribbean users to reassess their relationship to traditional activity and to technology itself, then mobile technology sought to bring these questions much closer to an even wider group of individuals. Given the rapid expansion of mobile phone ownership by individuals within the region, Caribbean culture is now even better predisposed to being wired than at any other time before in its history.

Not Quite There: Virtual Porn

Many Caribbean citizens have tended to be critical of the most daring and risqué movements within entertainment culture. As are all societies, Caribbean society is preoccupied with the perverse, the transgressive, and with violence, and with illicit and explicit sex. The Caribbean has continued to flirt with sexual stereotypes through tourism marketing, aspects of which I explore in the final chapter. If Caribbean entertainment culture embraced the facilities on offer within the Internet, it must be said that the Internet's preoccupation with porn and sex also infected the region.

Caribbean entertainment culture has spawned a number of sites that base their salability, presence, and popularity on a range of enticing attractions. Most leading commercial sites devoted to Caribbean popular entertainment generally invest in the suggestive language, imagery, and symbols that define their virtual presence in cyberspace. Increasingly, women, the body, sex, and sensuality are indispensable cyber marketing tools. Many sites have therefore skirted the borderlines of promiscuity and pornography. Some of the sites mentioned before in this work, though not specifically dedicated to the display and selling of the body, have used the body to give their sites added attraction.

But there are other sites originating within or relating to Caribbean society that do not mask their use of the body. The relationship between overtly and covertly pornographic sites is not always as well marked on the Internet as one might feel. Indeed, the Internet has become a medium from which it is virtually impossible to escape some intrusion of the suggestive, if not the blatantly pornographic. Given the level of hyper-connectivity at work on the Net, even clean entertainment sites are in virtual proximity to a connection to restricted sites, or sites that display subject matter of an excessively sensuous type. A site like Mvpvideos.com offers videos of "bashment" parties and events for sale. Its marketing on the Net also therefore attempts to attract buyers through its posting of, among other things, bashment girls and "badbwoy." Whereas the badbwoy photos present the men in a range of attire from street gear to cool dapper threads, the women are almost always scantily clad or provocatively attired, while others pose with their derrieres pointed at screen. This method has also been used within other music culture networks as part of the process of gaining attention or enhancing Web presence, but it is also done for self- and other-gratification, ultimately with a view to gaining financial wealth and power.

The experiences of women on the Internet are considered to reflect their experiences with science and technology. Writers like Helen Fallon have shown the contribution of women to the development of the Internet. She also makes note of how some of their work has been reconstructed as "men's work."[41] Given the excessive emphasis placed on (and the virtual exploitation of) the female within many sites that prey on the body, it would be reasonable to suggest that Caribbean Net hermeneutics cannot at all avoid discourses about gender and Caribbean cyberspace. It does seem to be the case that Caribbean marketing aesthetics in cyberspace is even more gender biased than it is in the real world. That is possible because there is less policing of this emerging domain by Caribbean and other interests. Leading Caribbean cultural critics are also still preoccupied with gender and exploitation outside of the virtual arena. Although it might be argued that women are also responsible for their very exploitation and the exploitation of others by selling their services directly or indirectly, perhaps the more significant point is that Caribbean Internet practices reveal the regressive tendencies of past decades. But maybe this is not so. Perhaps some rebutters of my reading of gendered Web politics will argue that women who appear in the nude and in compromising positions on the Internet are only virtually exploited. They are only performing acts of liberation.

It is realistic to suggest that the Internet's interest in sex and virtual pornography reflects a wider social interest and fixation with the topic. Note should be made of the fact that most new technological inventions that facilitate and promote entertainment have throughout their evolution been similarly critiqued as promoting sex and the body with increasing intensity. Television and the film industry, for example, have evolved to a state today where it is now being made the norm that the "A" word is used on primetime television within many territories of the region without significant debate. The time was when television would not dare utter the word at any time. But the region has reached a stage where it has come to resign itself to the power of machines like the television and to the cultural regimes that technology has instituted due to the region's wholesale embracing of fixed Western codes.

There is still a lobby throughout the region that critiques the perverse intentions at work within the technologies. But increasingly the voice of this lobby fades. There is awareness that new creations like the Internet are responsible for conveying substantial trafficking of sexual content. Caribbean commentators are yet, however, to enter into the wider debate on this evolving phenomenon. In many respects, Caribbean interest groups have seen this phenomenon as an emerging global debate that is yet to bear results, and hence they have hesitated to enter the fray. Likewise Caribbean cultural critics have delayed engaging with emerging technologies. It is therefore instructive that the field of interest for cultural critique within the region remains in the arenas that have long preoccupied critical debates. In the interim, however, Caribbean society experiences the onslaught of international and regional corporations in search of profits and gratification. It is, however, reasonable to predict that by the late years of this decade there will be a significant shift in the field of Caribbean cultural discourse. This is inevitable. The role of technology in our lives is too pervasive. It is virtually impossible to avoid some confrontation with the machines as we experience the end-of-the-real within daily transactions.

CHAPTER 5

Cricket (Sports) and the Digital Dispensation

Part 1: Cricket, Radio, Television: Sound, Images, and Ideology

From Five-day to One-day to 20/20

On July 2, 2003, it was revealed that the West Indies Cricket Board (WICB) had sold the rights for televised series with the West Indies cricket team to Dubai-based Ten Sports. Previous rights holders were ESPN Star Sports and Sky Broadcasting.[1] During the 1990s, the sport of cricket began to take its place as a satellite phenomenon. In the past, it was experienced primarily live at the cricketing ovals around the world, and then radio relay became a primary source for its dissemination. Although there is significant archival video footage that dates back to the 1960s and 1970s, it is only really in the 1980s that cricket and television found a harmonious union. The diehard purists of the sport will say that the five-day version is real cricket. This version drove the sport up until the 1980s, when the more entertaining one-day version began to emerge. Kerry Packer's revolutionary World Series one-day innovation (where each team bowled and batted for fifty six-ball overs) was partly responsible for the refocusing of this game as a spectator's phenomenon. There were those people who found the five-day version of the game too protracted and at times lacking in entertainment. These people, who were not locked into the technical and traditional discourse of the purists, would often take leave of the five-day game until critical moments of play. By 2007, twenty-twenty (20/20) cricket (where each team bowled and batted for twenty overs), was beginning to threaten all other forms of the sport in terms of spectacle, use of technology, and income generation. The first 20/20 World Cup competition was staged in South Africa in September of 2007.

On December 16, 1999 (during the launch of the 2000 Busta Cup season in the Caribbean), the West Indies Cricket chief marketing executive Chris Dehring made the point that West Indies cricket in the 1970s and 1980s suffered because the "technology for televising and radio was not around."[2] His statement hints at the ability of television and technologies to act as a catalyst for popularizing the sport at home. He was not the first to present this argument. Others have made this point long before. But fewer enthusiasts mention the equally potentially dangerous outcomes augured by the popularizing of cricket through television and newer mediums.

Of course, the introduction of the one-day variety of the game back in the 1970s brought new life to the sport. But more so, it brought new audiences to experience a sport that was considered by some to be struggling and in need of a higher profile in relation to other world sports. In Europe, as elsewhere, soccer and other mass appeal popular sports have always captured the imagination, interest, and financial input of a wide audience. In the book *Sports Culture*, Ellis Cashmore considers how from the 1960s, fans were "accustomed to television and expected the kinds of visuals that only television could provide."[3] Cricket did not evolve with the same televised visual flair. In many respects, the advances made in other television sports prefigured and inspired the revolution that took place a little later in cricket production and dissemination. I would also contend that the United States's NBA and NFL, and their baseball league were catalysts that precipitated the interface between television and cricket. After all, the filming within these leagues set production standards for other sports enterprises throughout the world. This gives the impression that the revolution in one-day cricket came about purely as a result of technology. This is not absolutely the case, though I would contend it begins to explain the revolution that has taken and is taking place in cricket. I am not given to an unmitigated belief in technological determinism, because I feel that social and spiritual determinism also play a role in the evolution of human society.

Packer brought the restrictive circle, white ball, night cricket, and colored clothing to the sport. These were integral in repositioning the sport in the consciousness of its audiences. The introduction of these new features also meant that cricket could be transformed by external interests and for the sake of the spectacle. Cricket has always been a centrally controlled game. Rules are made by a governing body that comprises the playing members of the International Cricket Council (ICC). Despite the claim of offering full democracy for all member territories, it is widely felt in some quarters that some test-playing nations have more influence than others. Some test-playing national boards have used their influence to bring subtle but telling changes to the sport. Nations like England, Australia, New Zealand, and, in recent history, South Africa have lobbied the central governing body to bring about changes. The ICC's embracing of the even shorter game of 20-20 cricket represented yet another marketing success for countries like England and New Zealand. Shorter versions of this kind have been played in other regions like the Caribbean, but regional boards have never had the confidence or foresight to formally influence the direction of the sport worldwide. West Indies cricket is therefore caught in a crisis of inertia, where it stands outside the construction of a sport in which it is a willing participant.

Cricket, the WWE, NFL, XFL . . .

When cricket therefore came into contact with television in a big way (through one-day cricket) it was doing so pretty much as a rebel, an off-shoot of the main tradition. Even today, some people have not forgiven that maverick faction of players who conspired with the Australian millionaire Kerry Packer to change the game forever. Many readers of cricket history who are intrigued by the Kerry Packer years point to the pivotal introduction of changes on the field of play. But equally intriguing must be the advances brought to the game by means of technological advances. This signaled that new things were finally possible within the sport. Significantly, the changes in the sport were affected not by the players or creators of the sport, but by another entity with an insatiable passion for repositioning the sport and achieving economic gains. A significant part of this repositioning revolved around new marketing tactics.

Media moguls have always tended to pose challenges to traditional sports. In the American context, Ted Turner, through his media empire, has inspired new ways of perceiving sports. His conceptualizing of the Goodwill Games represented the harnessing of many ambitions. Rupert Murdoch, his counterpart in the European context, has also helped to transform viewing practices within Europe and in turn has redefined the relationship between sports, live spectators, and displaced listeners and viewers. The point will be made that these cultural interventionists are primarily driven by financial imperatives, and so their innovations must be interrogated with that in mind. This is a valid point. But it does not negate the fact of the impact of capital-driven initiatives on *the sport* itself.

Cricket has been repositioned in terms of the medium of dissemination and also because of the medium of dissemination. Television (and by extension the computer) represents the frontier of cricket deployment and popularization worldwide. International sports have been heavily impacted by the media, and by television and new technologies. In the cricketing world, most serious boards host Web sites for their teams. In early 2001, the West Indies Cricket Board launched a new and enhanced Web site, Windiescricket.com.[4] It contained features on the team, team itineraries, online competitions, and free audio and video and picture downloads. The major cricket Web site that claimed to represent international cricket, Wisden's CrickInfo, through its semiotic positioning of icons, logos, and images, reflected either its own bias or the state of global cricket. Any surfer attempting to find out about the West Indies performance against South Africa in the 2001 series could only do so by locating the South African logo on the site. The West Indian logo was not readily on display.

The impact of television and other technologies on sports generally cannot be understated. Inasmuch as cricket and television have only really begun to establish their relationship in the relatively recent history of this sport, it is perhaps instructive to consider (in a general way) another sport of some similarity, but one which has a longer relationship with television. How does baseball (and also other sports) compare with cricket at the level of production, broadcast, and overall representation? It is important to begin to map some of the similarities and differences, inasmuch as one wants to begin to understand the production aesthetics. Cricket on television is therefore ultimately better understood when it is seen not in isolation but in relation to other sports. This kind of juxtaposition can open up other realities, and tracks of knowledge.

When juxtaposed to American baseball, one-day cricket television broadcast compares favorably at the level of production, interest, hype, and relay. In baseball, the camera shots are usually more intimate than in cricket. The zoom is enhanced. There are more close-up shots of players. There are also close shots of coaches and other players in the dugout. Cricket does, however, reflect a greater degree of ongoing production manipulation. By this I mean that there is much more ongoing interspersing of the game at hand with post-ball slow motion replay and filmic over-layering of stats and graphs. Because cricket spans a longer time than baseball, it is felt that multimedia and digital intertextuality are needed to enhance the viewing process. The camera does appear to be consistently busier throughout the course of a cricket (one-day) match than it is in a baseball game. Six to seven seconds represents the average elapsed time between new camera or screen shots in baseball. In cricket, the elapsed time between a new screen or camera tends to be around four to five seconds. In terms of the live audience, both sports pay equal reference to the crowd at the level of visualization, though in terms of sound, baseball sound-mixing practices result in a louder output of crowd sound. Cricket commentary on television is often sporadic, detached, disjointed, uninspiring, and dull. The sound commentary by baseball commentators tends to be much more fluid, engaging, and hyped. Inasmuch as sports production companies are operating in a competitive, yet collaborative, industry, it is inevitable that production practices are learned, copied, sampled by international broadcast companies. The point I am making is that it is reasonable to assume that cricket production and cricket dissemination will be driven by technological developments. One can therefore predict the future of cricket production by observing leading-edge innovation in world sports broadcasts.

In the U.S. context, for instance, the XFL was born through an alliance of commercial, cultural, and technological innovation that promised to redefine the face of world sports production. The alliance between the WWE and NBC prefigures the future of sports and sports production. Before the league started in 2001, many fans wondered about the authenticity of the game on the field of play. This is not unlike the interrogation that cricket fans conduct in light of match fixing, although some misgivings about the XFL sprung from its association with Vince McMahon and his association with the WWE. But the XFL excursion was an instructive exercise in the future of sports television in the digital dispensation. Although it was announced that it would not return for a second season largely because of low ratings and economic reasons, NBC in the early stages was reminding critics that for a considerable time the XFL ratings were way higher than that reached by National Hockey League telecasts. In comparison with the NFL, the XFL promised cheap seats. Players were paid lower sums.[5] In effect, the production was designed for the fans.

But one has to pay attention to a number of comments made about the XFL because this enterprise prefigures the commercial ambition in world sports. In the XFL, the cheerleaders were treated as quarterbacks; they were given a lot of focus. The cameras went to the locker rooms at halftime in order to give the game more dramatic appeal. To one viewer, "Having a camera suspended above the field that follows the ball down the field . . . gives the viewers motion sickness . . . This is a distraction from the sport." For another commentator, the "behind the Quarterback camera . . . looked like they were using a Sony Handicam for footage."[6] These are all commentaries on the digital technology employed for broadcast. They are incisive commentaries on the impact of technology on viewing practices and on the viewing process. But perhaps the most derisive and dismissive comments made, ironically, foreshadow the direction of sports broadcast in the digital domain. Many lay observers commented on the unstable camera work. For one anonymous viewer, the camera work was straight out of *The Blair Witch Project*.[7] On this score, the instability of popular culture discourse surfaces. Is the comparison of the XFL's moving digital camera to that of *Blair Witch* a reference to the original production of *Blair Witch*, or to the subsequent work done by Artisan before official release? You are never really sure in these matters to do with digitization. It is evident that advances in film and music video production will impact in a big way on sports television. The privileging of the amateur or virtual amateur camera is not out of place in cinematographic production. The popularity of high definition video over traditional film derived partly out of fascination with consumer video creation.

SKY Sports has been a leader in cricket broadcast around the world. In 2000-2001, they publicized a number of innovations that they were bringing to the game. These revolved around a desire to create "a brand new innovation to analyse live cricket coverage." Parts of the release read:

> Sky Scope uses the latest missile-tracking technology to measure the exact flight path of a cricket ball . . . As well as analysing LBW decisions, the system of six specialist cameras positioned around the ground will also give viewers a whole host of other useful statistics. . . . Sky Scope is a state of the art computer system. The main computer triggers the cameras when the ball leaves the bowler's hand and three video image streams are recorded. The computers then identify the cricket ball by filtering out any other "clutter" in the picture. Finally, the three images are combined to form a three-dimensional picture to accurately depict the true flight of the ball and make a prediction of where the ball would have gone had the bat or pad not intercepted it.8

Sky Sports Executive Producer, Barney Francis made the assertion that viewers would be better informed than the players, the coaches, and even the umpires. Over the past fifteen years, a number of innovations have been brought to the viewer to make the experience more pleasurable. This has given cricket new life. Where many of the innovations have been spurred on by the shorter version of the game, the longer 5-day version has also benefited. The longer version had been in need of new energy, anyway. Some of the innovations that have been brought to viewers include the super slow-motion camera, stump cameras and microphones, the rail camera, x-camera (a backward-of-point camera to capture action in exciting areas of the arena), the snick cam, and hawkeye. Additionally, viewers and special subscribers have been offered a choice of camera angles at selected game broadcasts.

How's That! How's That . . . Not!

At the end of the twentieth century, television continued to raise some tensions between traditional codes of conduct and new ways of seeing the sport. In December 1999, encounters between Australia and Pakistan, and Australia and India, and South Africa and England, there was much controversy generated on account of what was referred to on sports broadcasts as umpiring errors. One umpire even gave in to the authority of television and technology. The power of images therefore became apparent. This was an indication that umpiring would eventually concede its traditional sole control over the game to images, to television. The television replay, magnified and slowed down, became the unofficial adjudicator of decisions at the end of the twentieth century. Umpires were being judged in relation to what the cameras really said. The Australian Cricket Board reacted to the many criticisms of umpires by restricting the replay of dismissals, especially close ones on the large screen within cricket arenas. The West Indies Cricket Board, as it is wont, followed suit. They took the decision to restrict the replay of some footage of decisions for fear of disturbance by cricket fans. The Pakistani captain Wasim Akram, after their encounter with Australia, called for the International Cricket Council (ICC) to institute a system of all neutral umpires in test series. It is Akram who had in the past also called vigorously for at least one neutral umpire during test series.

Although international cricket began to ascribe some power to the camera at the beginning of the twenty-first century, this did not signal an end of controversy. Indeed, the belief that technology can bring about total fairness is a flawed expectation. When cricket moved to make greater use of technology, it forgot that technology is not itself neutral. Cameras are operated by individuals. The images received are manipulated onto the screen by producers and directors. In pretending to give power to the camera, international cricket was really vesting much of that power in the third umpire. It was not the camera that itself made the decisions. It was the third umpire who on consultation with the images came to a determination. But at the end of the twentieth century, it was becoming apparent that even third umpires were biased and making flawed decisions in spite of the aid of high technology. In some international matches, decisions of third umpires also came under scrutiny. During the West Indies' 1999–2000 tour of Australia, the Caribbean News Agency (CANA) radio commentary team reacted to the failure to give the red light to New Zealand's Chris Cairns, who was visibly out of his ground in trying to make a first ball single (during the triangular one-day series). Tony Cozier was to make the point that "it was the latest of umpteen instances of such umpires getting it wrong."[9] Due to the presence of millions of television viewers, the decisions of adjudicators are increasingly going to be called into question. The limits of technology are being tested in order to bring about "fairness." Television and related mediums are central to this drive.

As with other sports, from basketball to soccer to athletics, television is the principle medium for cricket's consumption by a wide audience. It is inconceivable that West Indies cricket in its many facets does not take full stock of this. A major source of future development is indeed the imperative of understanding the new role that capturing images and attendant sounds will play in controlling and better positioning West Indies cricket. But it is scandalous that over the years, as television's importance has grown, regional interests have not been able to come up with a system whereby the region or its interests can claim greater control of its team and of its icons on the field. Within the Caribbean region, where satellite television looms large, cricket on television is still not a common programming priority. The cable channels that beam into the region ensure that NBA and NFL games out of the United States and European soccer games are the staple diet of most Caribbean households.

It became increasingly difficult to see even test matches featuring the West Indies team abroad by the first decade of the twenty-first century. With each successive tour, Caribbean audiences are never sure if there will or will not be a televised broadcast, sometimes up until the very beginning of the game. The recurring problem is one of finance, which is necessary to be paid to the rights owners of the broadcast. The Caribbean Broadcasting Union/Caribbean News Agency (CBU), which is comprised of the major radio and television stations throughout the region, is largely responsible for administering the broadcasts through the region, but it depends on the willingness of member stations to take the feed. To do so, they must secure sponsorship so as to offset the cost of the fee negotiated by the CBU.

During the 1999–2000 tour of New Zealand, for example, it was released that the CBU would cancel its region-wide radio broadcasts due to developments that were "financially difficult."[10] Although it facilitated television broadcasts, they were not available Caribbean-wide for free, as individual members had to determine how they would finance the televised game. In order to offset costs, the CBU reported it needed to raise at least $400,000 U.S. from its eighteen territories. What is particularly striking about this complex is the claim of statistical evidence revealed by the WICB, which shows that cricket is indeed a marketable item. A Cable and Wireless survey (1999) revealed that 90 percent of the households surveyed had at least one cricket lover. More than 80 percent of those surveyed identified cricket to be the most popular sport in the Caribbean.[11] The fact that Trinidad opted not for live broadcast but for a highlights package signaled the further contraction of televised cricket. The West Indies would perform in the international domain, but its supporters, its guardians, would have limited access to the team's performance. This absence represents the break between the team and its reason for being. To the extent that the team is now lost to its supporters (on account of financial imperatives, wherein it operates in the international domain without the scrutiny of the Caribbean), its demise is signaled, if only at the level of self-reflection. Any performer who cannot be had by his or her support base in the same way that his or her competitors have access to theirs is in a disadvantaged position. Commentators on the game over television are aware of the composition of their audience. Usually, during broadcasts, the commentators will say a welcome to the countries receiving the broadcast. This act of greeting is also an act of confession. By this act, commentators are defining the breadth of their commentary. When a particular entity or country is missing, this represents a space or track that is left void for the taking. Commentators can invade that area, either to speak for it or to erode it. Commentators can control that space without fear of counterattack. Through the act of greeting, they are also signaling to those listening/viewing who will and who will not be in active contention or contestation for control of the multilayered, multitracked discourse. The struggles that are being fought take place in many places: on the field of play, in the commentary booth, and throughout the respective nations who have a stake in the game and its outcome.

In the absence of a substantial representative West Indian audience (as often happens), commentators are free to propagandize without fear of censure. They are free to play to the desires of their heavily politicized audience without any regard for opposing voices. Indeed, there is a perception in the West Indies among the significant majority of viewers that even in the presence of West Indian commentators, other comments persons enforce their own agenda without rebuttal. West Indian audiences have therefore chided its commentators who work for some of the larger networks like the BBC and Trans World International. Michael Holding, Colin Croft, and Tony Cozier have all been severely criticized and accused at one point or another of selling out.

Camera and Commentary

In the first decade of the twenty-first century, cricket (the one-day variety) is a very marketable sport, generating the major part of its revenue earnings from television and related rights. One-day cricket is, in effect therefore a television-dependent sport. This does not diminish the significance of the live audience. There is a marked difference between the privacy of the living room and the live spectacle and spontaneity of the same game at any oval. But to the extent that the moving camera and its sound have entered the arena as a medium that bridges the communication process between the players, the crowds, and a displaced audience, it becomes of extreme importance to begin to examine with a bit more depth some of the discursive relations that accompany the performance of a game brought to an audience at home. What is the relationship between the camera and that audience? Are there any concealed ideological relations between said camera and the competing teams? What is the relationship between the speaking commentary voices and this same camera? How do both of these (camera and commentary) influence the discursive relationship between the audience and their sport?

In this genre of cricket presentation, the camera shares a discursive relationship with the commentary voices. In fact, there is a series of ongoing interactions between sound and image; some are obvious, others are hidden and need to be deciphered and discussed. Also missing from the equation, though, is the controlling power of the producer. To some extent, the producer controls and attempts to regulate the range and parameter of images and sound.

In radio commentary, it is the voice that compensates for the video, attempting to supplement the image's absence. The commentary voice therefore situates itself as the only real purveyor and mediator of the cricket performance. The radio commentator has assumed the role and status of a god. As a mediator between the absent audience and a game in motion, the signification process has largely been controlled at the stage of radio commentary. To the extent that the commentary stage is so heavily vested with ideology, radio's compromise with objectivity has been to position more than one voice as commentator. Usually there are two voices that discourse at any one time during the run of play. One usually provides the ball-by-ball commentary, and the other provides expert comments. These are voices that for all intents and purposes are opposing in some respect. Usually, they carry and represent the interests of competing teams. Most radio commentary panels will comprise experts from the two competing nations. Radio commentary has served cricket well. Where its discursive parley has been conducted between Henry Bloefeld, Reds Perreira, and many other radio commentators, sound has been the winner. Sound has faithfully followed and served cricket well all across the world in the past. The video image and its relay are a more recent phenomenon. Images are the spectacle, but they have still depended on sound for full presence and effect.

I go on here to make some reference to selected televised matches, as for example, the final one-day match between the West Indies and England during the English tour of the Caribbean in 1998. The venue for *this* match is Trinidad's Queen's Park Oval.

The Camera

The British team TWI/SKY, a leading broadcaster of cricket via satellite, is responsible for producing the television coverage. Caribbean Broadcasting Union member stations receive their feed from SKY. But significantly it is not the SKY logo that occupies the top left corner of the television screen, but it is the CBU's logo. This, of course, is not an unusual arrangement in the modern world of television, satellite, and regional distribution. One conclusion to be drawn from the pasting of the CBU logo is that other viewers, like those back in England, receive a different coverage from that which stations in the Caribbean receive. Viewers in the Caribbean do not see the British advertisements when breaks are taken from the game. And indeed, neither do British viewers see local ads that promote the regional sponsor companies of the coverage. But the pasting of the CBU logo in the top left of the screen also masks the reality that the coverage has its controlling center outside of the CBU. If you did not know, you might think that the CBU was totally responsible for all aspects of the production.

At those moments when regional viewers in the Caribbean experience long moments of silence from the commentary team, it can often be a sign that the main viewers in England are on a break, and so is the team of commentators, which awaits the return of leading stations to the broadcast before they resume commentary. Sometimes, before the start of the game, it is not uncommon to see and hear a presenter standing overlooking the field rehearsing the areas on which the opening commentary will focus. At times, local Caribbean viewers experience the preproduction foreplay. It is the experiencing of this foreplay that alerts you to the controlled formulaic production structure in effect during televised cricket. You become aware that there is indeed substantial planning and manipulation of the televised coverage.

During Caribbean tours, TWI cameras will seek out, locate, and reinscribe Caribbean iconographic imagery. The 2001 tour of the Caribbean by South Africa reassured the world that although the Caribbean team's style of play had altered, in no way had the region's cultural symbols. Production directives ensured that there was sufficient pre-, inter-, and postlude reinscribing of sea, and excitable party-driven natives.

This was another way of keeping interest in the tour by locating and establishing a visual track of dialog that would be woven throughout the series, as the cameras and production team moved from island to island. During the third one-day international against South Africa in Grenada, the cameras wandered away from the game as the West Indies struggled to compete. The locating on camera of a small boat in the midst of a paradisial blue ocean made for excellent cinematography. It was the stuff of tourist brochures. This could have been a clip from the popular British program *Wish You Were Here*. Relayed on Barbados' CBC Television, the visiting commentator, Mike Haysman, intervened: "A beautiful place, Grenada, and that's a nice view on the sea. And you could say that the West Indies were all out at sea this morning only making two hundred runs."

The Camera on the Field of Play

In recent cricket production, the visual angles provided suggest that there are at least eight cameras at work on the field of play. During the BBC's farewell to free televised home series in the UK, during the 2005 Ashes series, they made mention of more than twice this number of cameras. I want to stress that I have preferred to discuss the presence of cameras as they *appear* to be positioned, rather than as they are *actually* positioned, because I want to talk about the signification process, not as it is constituted in the realm of logistical actuality, but rather as it assumes its presence by way of the screen. This chapter could well be a documentary-type discussion of the production process as set out by a television production company and crew. But that is the emphasis of another work. In this work I want to discover the ways in which the production aesthetics suggests the presence and function of technology. The value of this approach is that it comes to an assessment of the technological event from the perspective of the viewer. It wants to valorize the experience of viewing within the discursive arena of production and dissemination. If the owners of technology, production companies and their powerful associates, do wield control over staged events, then the ability of audiences to track beneath the layers of technology represents an act of some control.

For some time, I have been suggesting how it is possible to come to a number of startling discoveries about culture and technology by approaching them from the perspective of what I have been calling a multi-track reading. Reading multi-tracked foregrounds slows down the production, or performance, taking notice of its constituent parts and analyzing the data from a range of chosen perspectives. For example, it is possible to begin to speak of the relational politics being played out between competing entities in the digital domain of televised sports from the orientation that firstly interrogates with some precision the intricate strands that conspire to constitute a product or performance. As I do at various points in this chapter, I freeze a particular cricket match and locate the varying strands that produce the composite that is called "the game." This critical functionality of freezing the work under consideration is not unlike the capability built into digital machines and digital video games. Any subjective assessment will and should bring to the analysis the orientation, ideological bias, or interest of the viewer or observer. This is unavoidable—and desirable as well. And how does the reading that I perform based on a multi-tracked method sit with other received, accepted, or scientific approaches (sometimes called "fact")? This becomes the point at which confrontation and/or compromise take over.

Main cameras appear to be positioned high up above either huge colored sightscreens, which serve the function of enhancing the visibility of the ball once it leaves the bowler's hand. Each camera gives the viewer a rear view of the bowlers as they run up to deliver the ball from both ends of the pitch. Two other cameras are similarly positioned at either end of the field, but at the ground level. These either provide selected close-up shots of the batsmen as they stand poised to receive or give intimate on-the-field clips of the bowler as he thunders in to deliver. In addition, there also appear to be cameras that remain positioned above the scoreboards to give wide-angle shots of the game. Two more cameras are situated at ground level on opposite sides of the field but looking side-on at mid-pitch. These would be positioned beyond the boundary at mid-wicket and deep cover. The two cameras in the two middle stumps capture the close-up of a dismissal, a batsman's movement, or a bowler's follow through. Critical to the smooth working of these camera angles is the production and directorial team. It is these who, after all, must legislate what is to be shown, for how long, from which angle, how close, and if at all. They are also for the most part responsible for what is heard on the broadcast.

Sound

Sound in cricket on television plays what appears to be a secondary role to images. Sound's secondary status in televised cricket is illustrated by the tendency of many viewers to deny and negate sound's presence on television by turning off the volume while searching for a more engaging source of sound, maybe on radio. Television commentary tends to be flat. The search for sound elsewhere is found in radio commentary. Whereas television presents images as spectacle, it has relegated sound to the position of insignificant other. At least this appears to be so. Yes, there is this kind of hierarchical relationship that can be gauged based on the production energies vested in images and sound. Images are always present during television broadcasts, except for those occasions of malfunction when the picture goes and sound remains. Sound is not always present in the sense of an ongoing commentary, and so in this regard, it does not command equal space. But sound's commentary can be a direct manipulator of images, in that a commentator's observation on a key player can serve as a directive to the camera to locate that individual in a close-up shot. During the 2005 West Indies tour to Sri Lanka, a second-string team represented the region. During the one-day triangular competition (also featuring India), commentators frequently made statements about key emerging players like Dwayne Smith and Denesh Ramdin. These therefore gained much of the on-screen attention throughout the tournament, especially when mentioned by the commentators.

The value of sound is even more crucial for the uninitiated to the game of cricket. Sound can help make sense of some of the complexities that are said to characterize the game. But even for the initiated, sound is still of significance in that a major component of cricket discourse is the verbal discourse of commentary. Cricket's verbal discourse is an area that has grown in tandem with the development of the game, and for connoisseurs, it represents an important site of contention, signification, and meaning. Although sounds and images are in positions of contestation, they also share to a large degree a relationship of interactive complicity within the broader reading of digitized cricket-on-satellite hermeneutics.

Images

Images are the open spectacle. The images of the field of play, of the players, and of the crowd represent the most exciting component of cricket on satellite. It is easy to overlook the role that sound plays in supporting and enhancing this spectacle. Indeed, sound is the hidden spectacle of cricket on satellite. In order to re-create the arena of live play, it is mandatory to have a good decibel level of sound as a coating constituent. During the World Cup coverage of 1996, Caribbean audiences came up against sound's significance. When there was not always sufficient foregrounding of "background" or crowd sound and noise, the broadcast on television lost much of its appeal. Sound's importance is therefore understated. The fuller presence of images masks the degree of sound's importance. Images promise to objectify the sport. Images promise to place the sport in a position of direct, uninhibited contact with viewers. But the scandal of the image's lack of objectivity and its own obscurity (at the source of production) reveals the broken promises that satellite television makes to an audience of unsuspecting viewers. When I talk of the image's own obscurity, I refer to the underdiscoursed nature of the technological, of television, of images, especially in studies of sport in the Caribbean. This is therefore an unexplored area. It is also an unexplained one. The image therefore remains an unclear, obscure phenomenon. In some respects, Caribbean sports discourse is as conservative as the policies and approaches of management and administration within West Indies cricket.

Cricket, Television, Technology

One of the most telling influences of video and television technology on cricket is its use by the third umpire, whose primary function is to adjudicate in close situations, especially run-out appeals. It is widely felt that technology and television can improve the objectivity and fairness of the sport. But as has already been said, the camera is not infallible and still has to be manipulated by human beings. Even when images are played and repeated in slow motion, the camera itself does not trigger a response or outcome; this is still left up to the human eye and perception. In the England versus West Indies series of 1998, (carried on regional television) Ian Botham as commentator questions the third umpire's failure to see in slow motion that Alex Stewart is clearly run out by a Neil McGarrell throw from the covers:

[Commentary person no.1]: It's going to be close! . . . direct hit! . . . Magarrell with the, eh, initial throw. [The umpire makes a signal—there is a body close-up shot of him.] . . . The umpires have allowed it to go, and now they are going to call for the third umpire!

[Botham]: Well this is either going to be no runs or five. Stewart looks to me like he-e-e i-i-s-s-s-s out! . . . I can't believe that the umpire needs to see more than that; it is clear that the stumps are broken, and Alex Stewart is six inches short. . . . Well, that really does make a mockery of having a third umpire!

Botham's discourse is indeed significant in that it reveals the ways in which we palter with human and technological capability, substituting technology in anticipation that humanity will point the accusing finger and win out over the imperfections built into the machines.

By the end of the twentieth century, there was further talk of devising and utilizing video and other technology to help with leg before wicket (LBW) decisions and a call for the expanded role of television in the decision making process of umpires and other match officials. By the mid-2000s, cricket's ruling body was still divided on the matter and so deferred a decision to later.

While the counterargument suggests that technology itself is not necessarily objective and perfect, serious analysis of this point has not gone beyond the truism of the statement. What I mean is that there is relatively little writing in Caribbean cricket discourse that goes beneath the surface of the game and the medium that it has come into contact with to explore the extant impact that a reliance of one on the other already causes. I would suggest that the contact between cricket and television has resulted in a two-way influence. Television and video technology has expanded to accommodate the demands of five-day action. It is more common to hear talk about the impact that television and technology has brought to cricket at the level of adjudication. There is some discussion also of how it alters the consumption of the sport by a larger audience. There is even less discussion on the experiential reworking of the game; that is, how the current popular mediums begin to wrest the potential of the sport away from the sport itself (i.e., its context, locality, and "liveness").

How then is cricket conceptualized by a society that experiences it vicariously through the prism and matrix of technology? It seems to me that this will be a significant factor in the future structuring of the game. There will be the perpetuation of the traditionalist lobby, those who have grown up on the long, great tradition of cricket. That is, its history and statistics and the politics of cultural confrontation on the field. But the new site for a confrontation will shift. The burning passion that ignites the Ashes or the India versus Pakistan clashes on the field will not die. But it does seem to me that an important site for the contestation of cricket's glories is in the context of its technological reconfiguration. I am really suggesting that the packaged, technologized images and sound represent a reconfigured space in which the passion of nations is played out. Television and newer technologies like the computer and Internet are central to the deployment of cricket and sports culture in the region, as they are worldwide. It is my contention that these intermediary constituents harness and deploy the ideologies at work within global sporting culture. The analysis of future sports cannot ignore this fact.

(This book does not set out to test ethnography of audience theory. It is not concerned with the pleasures generated through popular media by a given set of people within a set location. Of course, domestic leisure is a commonly defined field for audience analysis.[12] Although this study examines cricket as projected domestically, it does not locate the domestic setting as the only or primary context for interdiscursive signification).

Interaction of Sound and Image

Sound theorists have for some time now concerned themselves with the relationship between image and sound. Theorists like Rick Altman have spent much time exploring the relationship between sound and image in the context of film. At the center of many debates concerning sound and image is the suggestion that the image came first and that the sound was the weaker addition, following primarily to support the image. That is one type of discourse in relation to film. Conversely, in the specific context of popular music and the international music industry, there were many music purists who distrusted the inception of music television. It was felt, especially around the early 1980s, that music television would lead to the death of the lyric within popular song as traditionally constituted. It was felt by some popular song purists that images would not only usurp the primacy of sound and lyrics but would alter such things as the meaning of songs. It would alter the way audiences related to lyrical compositions. This would detract from the writing process. Sound and image are always in constant contestation for place and power, at least in the minds of critics, artists, audiences, and academics.

The significance of this debate is that it points to the ways in which technology transforms aspects of culture. This represents the fear that we have of the multi-tracked, multi-dimensional spaces of representation. In the future, with the advent of virtual technologies, there will certainly be further discourses in relation to sound, image, and other dimensions that have to do with virtual appeal (touch, taste, smell, and digital architecture). But what of sound and images in cricket? I have touched on some of that above, but perhaps I need to say a bit more concerning the actual (real-time) play that takes place between sound and image. There is a case for suggesting that cricket broadcast (at least for Caribbean people) is, in the first instance, sound based, and that the televised image comes afterwards as a feature of consumption in the 1980s.

I suppose some individuals will claim that the actual arena of play has always been accessible to West Indian audiences, and hence sound cannot unilaterally claim a dominant role in cricket performance. This is a telling point as well, although in actuality, more audiences in the earlier period experienced the game aurally than otherwise.

Now, when we begin to talk of the relationship between sound and image we are, of course, limiting the discussion to television (and television-related technologies like the computer, though I also talk more about the computer later), and television images and sound. It must be made clear that what we identify as sound and image are potentially complex phenomena to talk about. Cricket sound might have to do with the sound of the crowds. It might be the music of the sound system that plays at intervals at games within the Caribbean. So when throughout the 2005 Digicel Home Series musical acts from Trinidad, St. Vincent, Antigua, Barbados, Jamaica, and Grenada invade the production space of television, this constitutes a track of data with which the critic has a right to engage. Because there are live microphones positioned within the batting area, the noise of the ball hitting the turf, or of the bowler groaning in expectant anguish, all constitute cricket sound as well. The slight noise off a deflected ball (later seen on the clickometer) that hits into a keeper's glove just before a vociferous appeal is also cricket sound. The belligerent retort of Allan Donald to Cameron Cuffy (heard and seen) at the end of the West Indies batting innings late in the test series—"F—— off, Mate!"—is also cricket sound. But ultimately, it is the commentators who continuously make the most compelling case for control of cricket sound. Indeed, there is the fear that with the popularizing of entertainment and sound systems at the grounds, the position of dominance over sound that commentators have will wane and some of their space will be taken over by sound systems and their posses.

Images are not constituted solely by the players on the field, not only by the crowds, not only by the green and red lights that can flicker like stop-or-go-lights at the command of the third umpire, not only by the umpires, not only by icons like Gravy and Mayfield and Mac Fingall and Chickee's hi-fi, and not only by the scoreboard, but it is constituted by all these things and more. For television viewers, the game of play is also mediated by production, specifically computer graphics. Indeed, in the same way that the soundscape is constituted by differing tracks of sound, the visual field is also comprised of competing tracks of images. If the commentators can be said to dominate the production soundscape, then it might be said that the middle (or what takes place in the middle of the field of play) dominates the visual. Sound and image are at once harmonious and on other occasions in some conflict throughout the process of contemporary televised cricket production.

At times, a spontaneous discussion between commentators, as about the new West Indies captain Chanderpaul, can lead the camera to go in search of a close shot of the diminutive superstar. At other times, a "wayward" camera shot can lead the sound commentary team into distracted chatter on some item, as in the 2001 tour by South Africa to the West Indies, when they chatted about Caribbean women and their dancing and the way they move their feet unlike their men. But there are also other times when image and sound disagree, when each resists the insistence of the other. Such moments are not protracted, but they foreground the fragmented cohesiveness of cricket production in the current dispensation. Such moments remind the viewer about the technology that mediates the sport. This points further to the constructedness of the exercise and the potential for interpenetration by producers and directors, as well as audiences.

It is erroneous to believe that a cricket broadcast begins and ends once the feed is cut or stops being relayed. In a practical sense, media and technology companies still have the hardware and software to secure, service, and manage. Preparation for a broadcast takes hours and days to set up, and even longer to plan. But even when the cameras and sound are turned off, its internal discussions and all the attendant sport politics continue to preoccupy the focus of spectators, players, managers, and others who have beheld the spectacle of the field of play. Indeed, the end of broadcast feed only represents a hiatus in one arena of the sport. When the cameras and sound are turned off, then political correctness recedes further into the background. If there is such a thing as an end of feed and end of play on the field, there is hardly an end to the inherent and attendant politics that define the reality of sports throughout the world in the twenty-first century.

The fact of technology and its role in relaying, mediating, and, indeed, fashioning sports and entertainment culture cannot be avoided. The presence of technology as a major player also calls to mind the issue of ownership and access. It is clear that regions like the Caribbean and their team the West Indies do not possess the financial resources to sustain their own satellite network. It is not impossible for Caribbean nations to pool their resources and mount their own satellite network, but like other nations, those in the Caribbean have determined that it is much more practical to rely on extant, tried, and functioning networks, which already have the facilities and experience to relay entertainment and sports from across the world to the region. Sports television has been very popular across satellite networks beamed into the region. Soccer, extreme sports, basketball, and other sports not widely played in the region still draw wide audiences. This anomaly reflects the possibility that there is no direct correlation between viewing and active participation. This apparent discrepancy reveals the extent to which Caribbean viewers have become passive consumers over the years. It is not games themselves that often draw viewers, but it is the realization that through viewing they share in an experience lived by millions of others worldwide. The phenomenon of sharing vicariously with other peoples across the world has become an entertainment industry marketing tool. Viewers in the region are sometimes much more fascinated with the location from which sporting action is broadcast than they are with the sport itself. Major America and European sports therefore draw many viewers who share the experience with other local, regional, but also international audiences. One of the paradoxes of entering into the viewing arena of large global events is that there is often little recognition within the broadcast that there are indeed audiences from many other cultural regions. Regional viewers are often made to take what they get. In the region, for instance, some news corporations that relay sports and other channels have had to settle for feeds that are targeted at Spanish-speaking viewers. Far from regional viewers and media corporations being active participants in global entertainment and sports culture through negotiated Caribbean-slanted packages, the region has had to take what it gets. This is a reality of contemporary sports. The owners of satellite feeds and their companies and affiliates are pivotally placed not only to influence the relay and dissemination of information, culture, and sports but also, if only indirectly, to influence the balance of power off and on the field of play. Given the growing significance of sports on new media, the domain of sports is set to witness the playing out of global and regional cultural tensions with the rise of the machines. In the Schwarzenegger movie of the same name, it is the machines that embody the human potential for either creative action or destructive possibilities. In the present arena of sports, technology is dually a medium, and an icon. It has the potential for creative good, but it is also an agent of some people's insidious desires.

New technologies like the Internet, computer, and video game make it possible to have easier access to sports and entertainment. Because some of this new technology is robust, trendy, and sleek, viewers are prone to replace the real with its substitute. Because of the new technologies, viewers, though not on the scene, are always potentially nearly there.

Part 2: Cricket on the Internet

Cricket Culture, Entertainment Culture

As with other sports and activity, cricket also moved to take full advantage of opportunities afforded by expansion of the World Wide Web. In the wider world of sports technology development, leading sports broadcast companies took to the Internet around the mid-1990s. ESPN Sports Zone was launched in April 1995. Rapid developments in Net technology saw them launch a successor site in late 1998 simply addressed ESPN.com. NBA.com, NFL.com, and Nascar.com also launched around 1995–1996, signaling the rise in importance of the Internet within the corporate culture of sports.[13]

This was not the first contact between sports and the Internet: the Internet has from early days provided users with primitive versions of arcade games. But the mid-1990s and thereafter marked the period of wider use of the Internet and the computer for projecting and propelling the imperatives of sports bodies, institutions, franchises, genre associations, fans, and the sporting media. As sports and sporting culture has developed in close relationship with business, gaming, and other kinds of associated activity, likewise its presence on the Internet has reflected some of these associations.

The level of investment in gambling and gaming within physical location in the Caribbean region is currently also matched by the number of Caribbean virtual gaming sites on the Web. The Whertobet franchise therefore devotes a link on their Web site to the Caribbean, "Caribbean Cyber Casino International." This is a dedicated gaming site. But some other sites, not devoted squarely to gambling, also facilitated betting of some kind, while others made their money through effective advertising. From as early as December 17, 1997, an Associated Press article titled "Internet Gambling Booms in Caribbean" drew attention to the anxiety of U.S. legislators and prosecutors concerning the rise of "virtual casinos" offering blackjack, poker, roulette and professional sports wagering.[14] This was a reflection of other tensions between the Organization for Economic Cooperation and Development (OECD) and some underdeveloped nations, whose offshore tax regimes came under fire from leading developed nations. But the unease about the rise of Internet gaming was also a reflection of the recognition that the World Wide Web made it more difficult to control the behaviors of people. Up to the present, it has proven difficult to police the Internet; it has also proven very taxing to set up workable and functioning rules and laws to govern the set of issues that arise surrounding copyright, exploitation, free use, fair use, and fraud in cyberspace.

In the Anglophone Caribbean, soccer has been a very popular sport over the decades. Arguably, it is the most widely played sport, in terms of participants, but cricket is still without doubt the game with the deepest historical, cultural and political roots. It is the only major sport in which the region plays as a unit. Regional soccer teams from Trinidad and Tobago's Soca Warriors (Socawarriors.net), Jamaica's Reggae Boyz (Thereggaeboyz.com), to Cuban and Haitian teams can be accessed and read about through the Internet.[15] But the case of cricket and its culture provides an opportunity to consider how a group of islands that have fought to maintain a sporting unit fare in an increasingly competitive environment. This case also provides an opportunity to consider the role played by leading-edge technology in facilitating, advancing, and reconfiguring the more traditional ways of experiencing a leading pastime and activity.

A comprehensive examination of the impact of new technologies on sports in the Caribbean cannot be undertaken in a short study of this kind, but it might be possible to begin to discuss some emerging features within the matrix of sports presentation, representation, and simulation. Caribbean sports and cricket discourse has been less enthusiastic about such issues at the level of formal scholarship. Formal cricket discourse from the region has been much more passionate about cricket history and its relationship to politics, regionalism, and postcolonial debates. There is relatively little in-depth scrutiny of cricket and cricket culture in the context of emerging technologies and in the sphere of future sports. An assessment of cricket culture does reveal the significant relationship between the sport and other kinds of activity. Cricket and entertainment culture have become synonymous in recent years. There has been some discussion of the relationship between cricket and calypso, for instance, and cricket and popular music, though much of this has focused on the historical legacy of sport and popular song in the region.[16] Cricket ovals across the region are now turned into large party yards and entertainment venues when international one-day matches are staged. Cricket is driven by accessorized spectacles like music sound systems, party mounds and stands, makeshift swimming pools, festive banners, and a set of unique characters who have attached themselves to grounds throughout the region. It is conceivable that 20/20 cricket will push the entertainment interface to never-before-experienced levels. Like basketball, it will represent a spectacle of never-ending multimedia hype.

It is the cricket-entertainment culture interface that drives the transformation of the gentlemanly sport into a festive carnival. No longer are spectators mere onlookers; they have now claimed greater participation and presence in the spectacle of the game off field. The West Indies Cricket Board, through its longstanding sponsor Cable and Wireless, began to sponsor a set of jingles for radio, television, and the Internet at the turn of the twenty-first century. These jingles featured leading regional performers like Bounty Killer, Machel Montano, and Alison Hinds. Television ads also featured cricket team members in humorous situations. The interlocking of cricket and music culture at the beginning of the new century was a continuation of a long association that has always been there between cricket, sports, and music culture. After all, many calypsos and popular songs have been composed about the exploits of the West Indies and other world teams. But arguably, the more recent interface has been driven by the changes brought to the game internationally by the popularity of the one-day game, the necessity of creating heightened atmosphere for television audiences, and the recognition that cricket has drifted behind other world sports in terms of its rules, philosophies, ethos, and practices. Whereas the ICC maintains tight control of cricket overall, the sport has internally revolted against the conventions of decorum, good manners, and stoicism that have characterised its origin and development. The extent of this revolt was experienced during the 2007 World Cup, when some audiences seemed to stay away from stadiums partly due to frustration of not being allowed to participate and conduct themselves as usual. Local organizing committees and the ICC placed many restrictions on what people could bring to the games. They had to get prior permission, for instance, to bring noisemakers and drums and certain foods. The result was that the West Indies spirit was squeezed out of the tournament until the Super Eight stages, when organizers sought to save a potentially embarrassing situation of empty stadiums. Patrons were thereafter encouraged to bring their culture and come to the game!

Although there are still many sober songs that tell a story surrounding West Indies cricket, and which are played at fitting moments of the game, it is without doubt the new styles of Caribbean music that drive the behavior of participants off the field. It is leading post-dancehall and post-soca tunes that constitute the new soundtrack for the playing out of West Indian desires and ambitions in the arena of sports. These postdigital forms of Caribbean music are above all rhythmically frenetic and hyped. To the extent that this is so, it is possible to suggest that cricket and its culture stands at a pivotal point in the development of Caribbean society. The game's soundtrack belongs to the wider society of supporters; but it is also the soundtrack to the lives of regional sportspersons. The lyrical and musical form of the soundtrack is no longer fixed in traditional patterns and practice. Though contemporary songs from the region tell a "story," the majority of these songs do not set about constructing linear, or even logical, narratives. Many compositions are driven by rhythm, and lyrics are secondary. The preferred soundtrack of our time is therefore one of festive engagement, with attachments of Caribbean and crossover lyrical and musical motifs. When regional cricketers perform, they therefore perform to hardcore notions of Caribbean experience. Significantly, it is these very hardcore actions, behaviors, and rituals that are believed to have infiltrated the regional team. Indiscipline and a proclivity for partying among players have been identified as contributing to the team's decline. During the 2007 World Cup, some players were reportedly seen partying into the early hours of the morning. While it is tempting to suggest that the team's falling performance and lack of discipline are inversely proportionate to the incorporation of hyped entertainment into the sport, this critical formula cannot explain the current predicament of the team. The decline in team performance cannot be simply attributed to the hyped culture of entertainment that permeates the sport. It is clear that there are over-determining factors that have contributed to the poor regional performance ever since the early 1990s, when the new hardcore in entertainment culture was emerging. This was also the beginning of the age of the machines.

Beyond the Virtual Boundary

If Caribbean cultural criticism has gestured to the relationship between sports and music, it has hardly at all considered the possibility that cricket is driven by extra-cricket considerations. It should be said that the birth of new arenas of play reflects the extent to which cricket has outgrown the conceptual, technical, technological, structural, and political contexts that have contained its debates over time. Is it possible that the region's attempt at catching up on the field of play is reflected by the extent to which current advancement of the game in new arenas has rendered our input limited?

While much of contemporary cricket discourse is rooted in more traditional praxis, newer representations, re-creations, and simulations of the sport reflect the distance between future sports analysis and dedicated, die-hard traditional critique. C. L. R. James' work *Beyond a Boundary* has been used by some Caribbean cultural critics as a model of how it is possible to understand Caribbean society through awareness of several activities across disciplines, vocations, and barriers. But perhaps people are prone to read James too tightly. Not enough criticism has factored in the virtual domain as a frontier site for cultural exploration. It does seem now that Caribbean cultural discourse requires a setting out of new parameters. Awareness, at least, of how far cricket has advanced through its representation and simulation on the Internet can provide insight into the state of play on and off the field at present. But this assessment can also give clues about coming trends and practices for the future. Given the frantic search in the region for paths towards renewed performance, it is possible that the playing out of ambitions and visions by way of technology affords an opportunity to navigate the links to future strategies and success.

There are several layers of experience that define the makeup of contemporary cricket. The ICC claims control of the sport at the international level. They set policy and regulations, and they enforce a system of fairness and equality among its members. But there are other systems of control and administration within and around international cricket. As said before, some national cricket bodies assume greater influence than others. It is widely considered that nations such as England and Australia are more equal than others. It is widely regarded that voting blocs exist among test-playing nations. England, Australia, New Zealand, and to a lesser extent now South Africa are regarded to be a staunch lobbying group within the international sport. It is therefore not surprising that in recent times, these nations have inspired changes within the sport based on their own national experiments with the sport and based on a sense of their own national imperatives. But there is also a swell of mistrust for cricket's central agencies by the supporters of nations like Pakistan, India, and Sri Lanka. Because these nations have the largest number of supporters worldwide for the sport, they are able to present a counterbalance within the association. Alas, the political tension between Pakistan and India has diffused the potential strength of this bloc within world cricket.

The ongoing tension between British and Zimbabwean leaders in the first decade of the twenty-first century and the breakdown within the Zimbabwean cricket team due to racial and political events marks the extent to which contemporary cricket is indeed an acting out of past, current, and future relations between nations. The open criticism of Brian Lara's decision to bat on and break the world batting record (scoring four hundred in Antigua versus England in 2004) drew criticism from his gentlemanly colleague, the Australian captain Ricky Ponting. The Australian Prime Minister openly criticized the bowling action of the Sri Lankan spinner Muttiah Muralitharan just before the 2004 series between Australia and Sri Lanka. World cricket is an embattled arena of confrontation at several levels. The West Indies has appeared passive, disinterested, and often powerless in this new climate of the culture wars. This sort of disengagement, though not an active strategy, is in fact representative of a position. The approach of the West Indies of not getting involved, of sitting on the boundary rope, does not position the franchise outside of cricket politics. They are also implicated. Significantly, this apathy and lack of confidence has infiltrated the West Indian game. The future rise to power of the regional team could well be dependent on a reassessment of the team's place within the wider field of international sports politics, administration, culture, performance, and fashioning.

You're Out, Mate!

Curiously, the West Indies has appeared lost within the ongoing nexus of international sports relations. When some stadiums turned up relatively empty during the 2007 World Cup, partly due to local dissatisfaction at not being allowed to participate in the stands freely, the ICC absolved itself of blame, intimating that it was the local organizing committees that set the rules concerning the games and it was *their* management that was at fault. The West Indies cricket administration has been acted upon continuously throughout the last two decades. Many citizens of the region have urged their leaders to take a stand. The cricket board is often regarded as playing from the crease, hardly playing positively on the front foot, seldom dancing down the wicket to score big hits. As a result, West Indies cricket has been trapped at the crease, caught on the back foot, and ever throwing itself to the mercy of an external set of adjudicators. In such circumstances, they have often been called out, by default, not playing a shot.

Web Sites

Web sites reflect some of the overt and covert strategies and relations that define digital cricket culture. It is a worthwhile undertaking to begin to map out their real and virtual politics.

The International Cricket Council's Web site, Icc-cricket.com, is a hub of information about what is taking place in international cricket, but more so the site gives information about ICC matters.[17] It provides a history of the organization, provides links to information about five-day and one-day cricket, "rules and regulations," "development," "world cricket

TV show," and an "anti-corruption and media center"—which promotes upcoming events and offers a free read of the ICC's *Quarterly Cricket Newsletter*. The first three issues, as presented online, tend to foreground concerns impacting on the ICC and international cricket.[18] The articles have tended to feature words by leading ICC figures. Reports are carried with an uncanny sense of dispassionateness. Although this appears so due to an effort to avoid taking sides in sensitive issues, their site nonetheless reflects bouts of subjectivity on occasion. Their bold headline in the first issue, "ICC to Assess Safety in Zimbabwe," pointed to the contentious relationship developing between Zimbabwean and English and Australian leaders, magnifying the appearance of threat and harm to some countries due to the continued presence of Zimbabwe in world cricket. The second issue of the online journal places antidoping policy at the front. The article reminds the reader that "4 of the ICC's full members (Australia, England, New Zealand and South Africa) have longstanding doping policies." Although it is possible to read further into the communiqué emanating from the ICC (which might suggest that the other poorer nations do not and hence are more prone to use illegal substances), it must be said that at least the Web site tries hard not to convey traces of bias. This aspiration to equality is not matched at the level of corporate relations between the ICC and companies worldwide. As is expected, ICC alliances for the purposes of marketing, and upkeep of the institution, have drawn on big business, many of these located in the West and with strong ties to leading political nations. Their reliance on regional and peripheral nations appears less significant. This is less directly a political statement in itself than it is a reflection of how the world of business is invariably set up at a number of levels on the international scene. Cricket is no different, really. Caribbean companies cannot be expected to play in the big league of the international business world.

Wisden's Web site Cricinfo.com is one of several popular Web sites. Cricinfo, like some other Web sites devoted to world cricket, is cramped. Its main page does not endear itself to those concerned with aesthetic appeal, Web architecture, and design. It is a straight-up factory for information about cricket around the world, hosting facilities for betting, casino, poker, shopping, mobile, and live video.[19] Its commercial and gaming interests are supreme, as reflected by the Web site's emphasis on these headings and links. Its live video facility is an exciting offering, also provided on other sites. The growing market in this area is evidenced by their offering England's entire summer of cricket in 2004 for $149.95 U.S. Offering live feed through Setanta.tv, the site previews the quality to be expected. The demo reveals relatively good Web picture definition.[20]

The "clean" picture quality is, however, compromised by the never-ending process of buffering that infects the technology. But when the webcast gets going, the subscriber can zoom up to 200 percent and has three video settings to improve picture quality. The British Sporting Life subsidiary site Cricket365.com is similar to Wisden's site in many respects.

Individual dedicated Web sites for individual test teams reflect their particular bias, as expected. But they are not all alike in terms of functionality, facilities, and architecture. Australia's official Web site viewed in mid-2004 and considered to be a new site, is spare, if not basic. It is surprisingly devoid of frills, and the range of media and connectivity on show at other dedicated sites, but it gives the basics primarily through text-based facilities.

As late as mid-2004, not all playing countries hosted official Web sites through their boards. The Board for Control of Cricket in India, for instance, announced its planned launch.[21] This lateness does not reflect the absence of Indian cricket online. There are, of course, independent sites that have managed to promote the Indian vision, brand, and presence in cyberspace. In any case, some of the nations of Asia were represented on the Net by the Asian Cricket Council. Of these nations, some of the leading ones had not posted an official site. Interestingly, some of the lesser known playing nations like Hong Kong and Singapore paraded their official sites. The Cricket Association of Nepal's official site is a source of information and insight into Nepal cricket history and culture. The relative absence of official sites in Asia reflects partly the pace of technological implementation in some regions but also the priority and value placed on the Internet and new technologies by some boards across the world. The absence of Web sites is not directly proportionate to the level of passion and enthusiasm for the sport in the subcontinent.

Because of the potential for cooptation and appropriation on the Internet, commercial and other interests have often been more proactive in making use of its facilities. Cricket and other sports have therefore been driven by "independent" companies and interests. Cricketfundas.com is a Hyderabad-based interest from India. Their Web site, though young, provides information and services about world cricket while also giving an Indian and non-Western viewpoint on some issues. Whereas some other interests in Australia and affiliated territories have demonstrated their disappointment at losing the world record for the highest individual score by a batsman to the West Indies, most Asian Web sites hailed Lara's achievement.[22] One writer reminds the world that (the previous record holder) Hayden's performance was hardly as impressive as Lara's. This site's tributes pages focus mostly on Asian and West Indian players. Here is a company with international ambitions but with a sense of location in their regional culture and its politics. It is therefore no less and no more biased than other similarly constructed sites in cyberspace. Such sites, though overtly attempting to lure surfers and business in order to gain financial success, are, however, invariably biased with respect to cricket and its politics. The façade of objectivity, of fair and free coverage, is often undermined by the kinds of subtle confrontations that play out. The kinds of cyber debates, positions, and counterpositions that define many Net sites are reflective of the ongoing tensions and conflicts that underpin the world of international cricket. There are few other international sports that have tried to ignore and deny their internal, cultural, racial, national, political, and ideological conflicts than has cricket.

The West Indies Cricket Board's official Web site is actually a much more impressive construction than many other official Web sites of its kind. Its layout, facilities, architecture, ease of use, clarity, and functionality make it quite an impressive location. The board can be lauded for this showing. The site was launched at a time when West Indies cricket was on a downward slide. Its launch was in some ways an act of affirmation in the face of uncertainty and doubt about the place of the team in the international arena. If it could, the Board's Web presence would convince all detractors and sceptics that West Indies cricket administration was in fact very forward thinking in their vision. This is one way of reading the Board's impressive Web showing.

But this high energy, interactive Web presence was not equaled and matched in other corporate and functioning spaces. This is a telling observation, and not about this institution alone, but about the practice of institutions that enter the digital world of display, marketing, and propaganda with a sense that new media and new technologies can miraculously impact on all aspects of an organization. The truth is that the virtual and real world are still very much dependent on each other for fulfillment of objectives. Inasmuch as such organizations like the West Indies Cricket Board function primarily in the real world, they are very dependent on the actions taken in that space in order to achieve goals. But the difference between the impressive showing of the Board on the Internet and its real-life handling of matters such as the 2005 Digicel versus Cable and Wireless controversy serves to reinforce the distance that still exists between the real and virtual world. The virtual domain does not as yet have the capacity to supplant and replace the real in all contexts. In time, this might be possible, but in the first decade of the twenty-first century, any hope of affecting this technological feat is rendered futile. For all of its showiness, the WICB Web site still lacked some grounding in the realities of the affairs of the actual game. The Web site's pretense of accepting and facilitating criticism and debate through its chat facility was undermined by its failure to carry some stories that openly questioned the capacity and functioning of the regional governing body. The Board stood strong in the face of criticism. It kept up its Web appearance. Impressive it was. It wasn't widely known that this appearance was maintained by partnership with SKY and an Australian consultant.

The series of misadventures surrounding the first announcement of the appointment of the Australian coach Bennett King even before an official offer was accepted, the sending of overage players to tournaments, and the sequential firing of coaches and support personnel all represent the vagaries of the Board in the real world. Web and real-life presence are therefore codependent. Observers and connoisseurs have been quick to critique the real actions of the Board in the press on a daily basis. Incidentally, the very instrument used by the Board to expand its agenda has been used by regional organizations to support and critiques the agenda of the Board. The discursive arena in cyberspace is often harder to control and manage than that in the real world.

For instance, Caribbeancricket.com, provides avenues through which the public can comment on the issues within West Indies cricket. In mid-July 2004, it carried stories about Sir Viv's resignation/dismissal, the new deal struck between the Board and Digicel, and the chosen World Cup venues. But this Web site has also gotten into trouble with the Board, a fact that the site does not hide. It is seen in some quarters as a response to the official Board's site. This point is played up by the Web site through its publication of discourses that are provocative and that speculate and provide much more inside information about the happenings behind the scene of cricket administration and practice. For example, in mid-July, it made much of the way the West Indies team was greeted and not greeted when it arrived in England for the 2004 series. The provocative headlines on their site read "Doghouse . . . ECB Mistreats the Visiting West Indies Team."[23] Careful search of the West Indies Board's Web site around the middle of July provides stories about the planned trip and about preparations for the first practice game, but nothing about the well-publicized ill treatment. The resignation or dismissal of Sir Viv Richards as Chairman of Selectors was glossed over at the official Web site. It was mentioned in a report titled "Lara Deflects Sir Viv Issue." But interestingly, in that very article, Lara declares, "Of course you can find out about it on the Internet if you want to."[24] This statement, while avoiding the issue head on, recognizes that official positions and points of view within international cricket only represent bouts of political correctness. His statement passed the question on not only to other sources but also to another medium. Here was recognition that the virtual domain, apart from providing rumor and scandal, was also paradoxically a potential source for getting the real story.

The absence and presence of selected information reflects the varying levels of discourse about cricket that exist in the region. The Board's official position is hardly embraced by the average observer. Its position often represents one of political correctness. This is in keeping with the rules and spirit of the game as enshrined long ago, but it often seems idealistic, bland, and otherworldly, especially given the current ideologically and politically charged atmosphere that defines the sport of cricket.

Proximity to Technology

The great dilemma of cricket appears to be its rootedness in a set of rules and practices that are over a century old. Cricket administrations have fought valiantly to maintain strands of that root. Over the decades, the game has come under immense pressure to stay in touch with the changing social, political, and cultural reality. One of the most telling influences on cricket and cricket culture has been new robust technology. The introduction of predictive tools like Hawkeye technology, which tracks the trajectory of balls and predicts their ultimate path, is merely the latest in what will be an endless line of gadgets that will control the game.[25] One could foresee future cricket where individual players each had minute cameras and microphone feed attached. This would give viewers unmatched coverage. But players could then have direct access to off-the-field strategists who, like military planners, could virtually plot the outcome of a game from miles away.

The struggle between those who favor the use of technology and those who resist it is in some ways a reflection of the tensions that exist between aesthetic and scientific communities. Not that the debate is necessarily split down the center in this way, for there are other competing communities. But the promise of technology does seem to challenge the authority and work of subjective human beings, replacing this subjectivity with the supposedly more objective technology.

Most of this technology is being created and tested firstly in the wealthier cricket nations. This therefore calls into question the motives that inform the creation and implementation of this technology. I would not want to overplay the point that the period of the ushering in of new robust technology into world cricket was coterminous with the decline of West Indies cricket. It would take some further fuller discussion to prove that there is a direct correlation, although I tend to believe it is so. But it is easier to suggest that the past decade and a half has seen the solidification of the position of some nations within international cricket. Regions like the West Indies have hardly piloted the introduction of new technologies into the sport. It is possible that in the future, research conducted in several regions will compete more vigorously for pride of place with respect to application within the international sport. As nations continue to invest more heavily in technological research, it is possible that individual members will through their innovations manage to fashion rules and new conventions that will complement their preparation and style of play.

For example, the studied attention paid to bowling and batting styles and technique has led to a growing perception that West Indian players, especially batsmen, are technically deficient. This discovery has placed the traditional flamboyant or unique style of some West Indian cricketers in great doubt. Players like Chris Gayle, Shivneraine Chanderpaul, Ricardo Powell, Philo Wallace, Dwayne Smith, and others have therefore been deemed inherently deficient, and their style of play outmoded. Everyone now believes this. The players seem to have given in to this. The coaches now concur. Past players waver. The wider public is increasingly coming to feel so as well. The discourse enunciated through cricket's medium of inscription threatens to project the wishes of those who control this medium onto the fields of play. These fields of play are varied. They include the actual playing arena, but they also encompass the mental field of players and regional personnel, as well as the belief systems and spirit of the wider society. The ambition of technology is therefore harnessed by those people who see in it a correlate set of innate desires to fashion social, psychological, and cultural systems of being and existence.

The power of television has the tendency to ascribe to commentators additional powers on account of their perceived proximity to the technology. It is this proximity to the technology that has continued to give some countries even greater powers. Commentators and commentary experts are therefore embedded shapers of cricket consciousness within the culture wars. Pronouncements made on the air during the mid-to-late 1990s (by a West Indian commentator) about the action and attitude of players like the then-promising Reon King of Guyana, prior to his loss of form and place in the West Indies, should not be taken as visionary insight but more so as the psychological working out of discursive will in the era of technological proximity.

Arguably then, all commentators can root for their team and thereby enforce a balance of power. No. This is not how it works. Commentators can assume some power when they come to the microphone on radio or television or the Net, but not all commentators are similarly positioned with respect to the origin and make of the technology. The leading economies within the cricket-playing world, because of the frequency with which they challenge the face of the game through their research and specific technologies, are able to demarcate their territorial claim to technologies and hence to ascribe position: proximity to and distance from the technologies that increasingly run the sport.

Future sport would seem to be built around technological proximity and its relationship to more traditional issues of talent, dedication, discipline, skill, et cetera. It would seem therefore that more and more nations like the West Indies should seek to enter into the domain of creativity. It would seem that other nations should seek to have a bigger stake in controlling the game and dictating its makeup, pace, rules, and implementation of technologies. Inasmuch as it might be difficult for regions like the Caribbean to keep up with technological discovery, at least they should come to a state of awareness about the new kinds of culture wars that define world sports and other activities. Maybe this recognition will see other strategies put in place to circumvent the matrix of techno-cultural engineering. Maybe creation of technology is not the fight to wage. Resistance to technology might also prove futile, given the fact that cricket and other international phenomena are themselves driven by broader global trends and practices. Maybe legitimate hacking of the technological process is an option. Maybe a process of technological borrowing and tweaking can also prove strategic. Indeed, at a deeper level, the region might need to reconsider what technology claims to be and what it really is. Its relativity to the past, present, and future often defines it. In some respects, it is a function that streamlines and reconfigures more traditional ways of knowing and ways of doing. Perhaps the region should reconsider its position relative to the sport, and its position relative to other teams. Maybe instead of playing catch-up by way of following suit to the practices and structures as instituted by more successful teams in recent times, the regional team should be engaged in a process of alternate reconfiguration, a process that is aware of how the digital paradigm has reconstituted cricket and one that is prepared to break into that system, reconfigure its network, and regain some control of the sport. In other words, maybe the region needs to create, employ and deploy its own brand of high knowledge, and technology.

The 2007 World Cup Did Not Take Place in the Caribbean[26]

As the 2007 Cricket World Cup approached, Caribbean nations were placed at the center of cricket's greatest spectacle. The hosting of the 2007 World Cup represented the fulfillment of the West Indian desire to establish a place in the firmament of the digital dispensation. But as the preparations were set in motion, it became increasingly evident to the region that the event did not belong to the region in the sense that the region would have autonomy to fashion the spectacle in its own way, with its own imprint. The event belonged to the ICC. It belonged to the world, to special interests. Caribbean companies and personnel were beholden to the directives and control of the ICC. Some questions raised by people in the region had to do with disappointment that the regional input in conceptualizing, fashioning, and branding was subordinated to the dictates of the ICC and their chosen set of international, real experts.

It was revealed in 2005 that the West Indian mascot would be a mongoose. The region was infuriated. The concept designers denied the mongoose rumor. When the brand mascot was launched in Trinidad around mid-2005, it was not a mongoose; maybe a distant cousin wearing pants and an unbuttoned tourist shirt. It could indeed have just sobered out from a night of riotous partying. The new symbol of the region was designed by an Australian company (which, of course, had done intensive research on the region). It was unveiled for regional acceptance. The region was therefore from early on placed outside the construction of the World Cup and of their own identity. The fashioning of the mascot, a chap called Mello, represented an act of shaping world consciousness about what the Caribbean is, what it stands for, and who can stand in for it. The name Mello (with echoes of "mellow") has various connotations. It is therefore a clever marketing product conceptualized by the Australian company Minale Bryce Design Strategy, who on their Web site boast of doing creative, strategic, realistic design.[27] Audiences and consumers of World Cup culture are therefore free to choose whatever interpretation they see fit. Some will see Mello as a laid-back bloke. For others he is a Caribbean beach bum with links to Australian wildlife. Yet to some others, the meaning of "Mello/mellow" is as the dictionary says: "mildly or pleasantly intoxicated or high"; "especially from smoking marijuana."[28] This corporate vision of the Caribbean might have been garnered from texts like *Robinson Crusoe*, or from watching repeated scenes of cult movies like *Ali G in Da House*, or even from selected episodes from *Scary Movie 3* or *Shark Tale*. These are movies that gesture to the Caribbean. Arguably, they cast the impression that the region is a space of perpetual relaxation, lazy natives, and pot-smoking dudes.

West Indians were asked to volunteer their time and skill informally to the World Cup cause, while at the same time, the region had no knowledge of the salaries to be earned from the festival by nonregional and regional officials and by well-placed companies. As obtains with cricket, there was also a silence among officials about the finer workings of the World Cup, the inside stories of profit and benefit. The region was asked to be thankful that they would be centered for a month. They should shut up and smile for the cameras, visitors, and the pleasure of cricket.

Because most Caribbean citizens would experience the actual cricket games not from dedicated seats within the new expensive stadiums across the region but second hand (vicariously) from the distance of their living rooms; the actual event of the World Cup would not take place for them. Instead, they would receive a version of the on-field action. They would depend on the technology to compensate for their absence at these games. The real details of the actual games would exist within the collective consciousness of the society as technological moments. That is because television, the Internet, and other media would be the major conveyors of the Caribbean experience. The extent of regional input into television and electronic relay would therefore serve to determine the power that the region would exhibit in the worldwide spectacle and its simulation.

While planners spoke of the unlimited gains to be had from Cricket World Cup 2007, the reality was that for most people in the region the World Cup would not really happen. They would observe the games as though on television, they would see the many tourists who had come to go to the actual arenas and ovals, but for Caribbean citizens, the actual participation in the ovals would not come to fruition. They would stand outside the real arenas of play. These would not be their games. Like in a video game, they would behold the sound and images and multimedia graphics on a screen. But they would not experience the real game. The 2007 ICC World Cup would not happen for Caribbean citizens. It would not happen in the West Indies.

CHAPTER 6

Video GameZ: Enter the Machines (Version 3.5)

Mr. Baudrillard, But the Second Gulf War Did Take Place (Didn't It?)

Caribbean culture experienced substantial transformation in the early post–first Iraq war (Desert Storm) years. The mounting of the second Iraq war of 2003 (and its relationship to the first war) provides a point of departure for engaging the new ways in which information about ourselves and others are conveyed. The region's location within wider global space is increasingly being marked, represented, and simulated by leading-edge developments in technology, communication, commerce, and culture.

While Caribbean critics have always responded to shifts in global and contextual arenas, cyberculture's immense expansion has only recently drawn out Caribbean cultural critique. Part of the challenge posed by cyberculture is its instability—and above all, the fact that it is still in its infancy. Critics have perhaps rightly not jumped headlong, but have waited to see how structures and patterns develop, before they bother about logging on to and seizing control within the domains of cyber critique. But in the interim, Caribbean cyberculture represents a growing set of practices and procedures. The immediate future of Caribbean cultural criticism requires an engagement with new technologies (a point I have been making at intervals throughout this book). Part of the challenge of global positioning in many spheres of practice (academic, political, commercial, etc.) has to do with the ability of participants and stakeholders to anticipate and comprehend the new and emerging field of real and virtual engagement.

In the book *The Gulf War Did Not Take Place*, Jean Baudrillard proposes that inasmuch as the war was mediated by television and experienced by many in the West through that effacing technological medium, in some respects, therefore, it did not really take place.[1] This interpretation of the increasing power and central placing of technology in shaping and replacing real experience signifies the eventual ambition of those forces that control the matrix of experience and human beliefs.

If the first Gulf War did not take place, then the second Gulf War sought to take its place. In some respects, it came to stand in for the first war. Whereas the first was relayed on television via one-way networks featuring repeated images, the second war had some degree of interactivity built in. The storage of data (audio and video) in digital form in the computer meant that viewers or navigators could interact with controlled images that might have been present during the real war. Because viewers had enhanced facility, they could claim greater presence. They were therefore closer to the real war. They were closer to experiencing it.

The difference in coverage between the first and second Iraq war can give the observer a perspective of how much things changed between the 1990s and the 2000s. The shift in geopolitical reality also serves as a backdrop for our better understanding of changes in cultural expression and within the media that convey these expressions.

Whereas the 1991 Gulf War was conveyed to the region largely through the perspective and facility offered by CNN, the 2003 war in Iraq was brought to the Caribbean and the world through a number of other competing networks. Fox and other institutions played CNN at its own game. The war was fought in the living rooms. The contentious role of reporting in global conflicts of this kind came to the fore when Fox's Geraldo Riviera leaked supposedly vital information to the public concerning the path of advance of the division with which he was embedded. Networks used video simulation and models to map out the path of the war. There was an air of theater, game, and play surrounding some of the media coverage. You almost felt that here was a new, emerging video or screen genre. Live reporters and fast-paced editing gave to the Iraq and Afghanistan war coverage a sense of blurred experience. By 2007, the news seemed a simulation of the latest PlayStation or PC game.

Video Game History

Video games were popularized largely throughout the 1970's.[2] Games such as Computer Space (1971), Football (1978), and Battlezone (1980), all produced by the leading American company Atari, drove the arcade industry throughout that decade. Pac-Man (1980), Pole Position (1982), and I, Robot (1984) were some leading games of the 1980s. I, Robot returned twenty years later as the title of a Will Smith–starred movie of the same name. The appropriation of that title was a reference to the earlier video game and by extension the 1950 book of the same name by Isaac Asimov. The film's subject matter reminded society that new robust technology has the potential to outstrip the expectations and knowledge of humankind about that very technology. Although home video game systems were in existence during the rise of arcade subcultures, the functionality and affordability of home games made them household commodities only in the 1990s. Nintendo's Super Nintendo Entertainment System (1990) anticipated later evolutions of the late 1990s and the twenty-first century.

Handheld portable games also propelled the industry. With the popularity of the computer, the expansion of the Internet, and the interface capabilities of the PC, the video game industry began to interact with other technologies and sectors within the entertainment sphere. Video games lent their title and plot to big-budget movies (*Tomb Raider*), video game heroes were brought to life on television and on the big screen, computer software made it possible to provide updates to main video releases, and the Internet gave freer access to games that could be downloaded or played on line, either with a single or multiple displaced players. Caribbean society has never been distant from the developments within this sector of the entertainment industry. As this book has suggested, Caribbean popular culture also shared and continues increasingly to consume the creations of world entertainment culture. Caribbean youths, like many across the world, were hooked on video games. The society also had to deal with the complaints from the establishment that video games and the entertainment industry's technological wing were making clones out of Caribbean youths. Although this has proven true to a significant degree, there have always been some active users of the technologies.

Whereas most Caribbean video game fiends of the 1970s and 1980s spent hours on end at arcades and game shops, present-day users are hardly displaced from their real-real homes because the video game is within arm's reach. Whereas the video arcade was an actual space, marked off by distance and location within a commercial business house, today the distance and displacement of reality from the sphere of its simulation is hardly noticeable. You do not have to leave the real space of the home or the backyard to experience a video simulation. The television set, the computer, and the home stereo and entertainment system are all integrated to some degree. Caribbean societies continue to aspire to own and enjoy these luxuries, now seen as necessities.

But Why Do We Call Them Video Games?
Sound in Video Games

Sound in video games, like sound in film and other genres and categories of cultural expression, plays a secondary role in the minds of users, as well as critics. Whereas some critics have sought to compare the interaction of sound and vision only in an adversarial relationship, the advent of digital phenomena such as video games, video conferencing, instant messaging, and cell and mobile gadgetry has challenged more traditional ways of thinking about sound and video. Over the past five years, companies at the cutting edge of research have been offering customers enhanced video or visual features to the extent that the multifunctional palmtop represents the apotheosis of communications research. But the desire for a ubiquitous portable, multitasking, multifunctional handheld also represents the working out of a contentious relationship between seeing and hearing in the domain of techno-human fashioning. In the realm of cyber practice, hearing and seeing, sound and video, are also in some relationship with virtual sensing, feeling, longing, touch, and other capacities.

If technological relaying of sports such as cricket developed by way of a dependence on sound (radio) firstly and then video (television) afterwards, then the development of video gaming was the opposite. Video games are primarily initially visual-oriented. Sound was originally in older game systems stock chunks of data, as with many versions of Pac-Man and Asteroids. Many early games used precomposed and public domain sound and copyright-free popular or folk sound or music. Over the decades, video games have moved to accord greater significance to the accompanying soundtrack. Entertainment icons now have their songs featured as part of the soundtrack of games. The release of PlayStation 2 marked the expanded employment of music icons and the tightening of relationships between the music and video game industries.[3]

At the cusp of gaming culture, where simulation and virtual reality anticipate open-ended play, users also demand a much more dynamic system of sound, where canned tracks give way to freer expression of sound scores. In a review of Cricket 2005, Rich Hingston advises potential users or players to "remember to turn Jim Maxwell off and listen to some relaxing music."[4] The 2005 game reveals little improvement over the repetitive and boring commentary of Richie Benaud and Jim Maxwell.

The attempt of gaming technology to respond to pressures in other sectors of entertainment culture represents an industry consolidation of media, but it is also a reflection of an anxiety about creating games that are so expressive that they can surpass the impact of more traditional entertainment systems. The attempts to better gaming culture is also partly a desire to employ sound, video, and interactive technologies to go one step better than the impact of real experiences. When such gaming and entertainment systems convince us that we are at the cusp of possibilities, then we begin to behold how superior or inferior we are to these machines of our age. In the future, this process will continue. When, however, one is able to determine the process by which the research and entertainment industry causes us to think and not to think about the units of data that comprise simulation culture, then one begins to detect the defects within such tech wonders as video games. In Cricket 2004, for example, the encoded sound and its formulaic style makes one think about the video game's construction and the underlying implication that the sport belongs to certain Western nations (as emblematized in the soundtrack).

Newer Technology (Internet) and the War

Whereas the first Gulf war was fought on cable television, the second war was fought (for many audiences) via the new network called the Internet. The taking of news and conflict and war to the Internet reemphasized the way in which technology was gesturing to itself and reflecting the interface of media and genres. MSNBC, ABC, CBS, and other networks showcased daily simulation of the fight on different fronts. Some of the images viewed through videophone conveyed the stuff of videogame play. In late 2003, the BBC boasted about its breakthrough in news technology, which involved sending sound and video by 3G mobile phone onto television. One of their senior correspondents spoke of the picture composition as bringing "drama to the viewers' experience" and as appealing to younger audiences.[5] The invasions of Afghanistan and Iraq were executed as multimedia events. If the gaming industry was pitched at younger viewers, then older and more serious viewers of cultural relations could not ignore the way in which they too were participants in this display of technology during the war.

Caribbean Critique and Technology

At the 21st Annual Conference on West Indian Literature, held in Barbados 2001, I began tentatively to ask questions about the Internet and its staging of Caribbean culture. That presentation represented a version 1 (V. 1.5) critique. In version 2, at the 23rd Annual Conference in Grenada, 2003, I posed deeper questions about the hidden practices that contribute to the construction of Caribbean culture in the digital domain. In this current chapter, I take these earlier debates even further.

In the industry, it is only at Version 3 that system hardware and software are said to be "right." The kind of critique that defines this chapter, as it does this book, is less concerned with rightness per se than it is with suggesting that Caribbean culture and its criticism have had sufficient exposure to new spheres of production and dissemination to be able to engage these new arenas over time. One of the greatest challenges posed to Caribbean cultural critics is the task of engaging the range, diversity, and interconnectivity of technological and cultural activity. Future culture and its criticism will hardly be able to ignore the culture wars.

Simulation

Over the last decade, the news on major networks has transformed into spectacle, being delivered (as one CNN executive said) at the speed of life. Maybe he really meant at the speed of sports video. This partly explains why exercises like the Iraq and Afghan wars on television and on the Net appear as Xbox, PlayStation 2, and Nintendo adventures. So war and play or sports are in some respects, therefore, interchangeable in contemporary manifestations of technological wizardry.

In his work on simulation and ideology, Gonzalo Frasca suggests that there are three levels of representation or encoding. Level one shares similarities with traditional storytelling, having "scripted actions, descriptions and settings." Level two emphasizes the rules that govern the simulation. Level three has to do with a set of goals; it "defines a winning" and therefore desirable state. Level three is much closer to many simulation games. Frasca suggests that "narrative is based on semiotic representation, while videogames also rely on simulation."[6]

He suggests that whereas narratives are more or less fixed, simulation is dynamic and defined by change. This is very well the case. But I would also want to make the point that many popular games traverse the matrix of formulaic patterns and flexible outcomes. This chapter is even more concerned with examining how simulation relates to and reflects the vision and ideology of its creators. It wants to alert the reader to the importance of simulation politics.[7]

Interestingly, the history of simulation media has significant connection to the military (through flight and battlefield practice). Game, practice, and war are therefore symbolically wrapped up within the evolution of simulation systems. I do not use the term simulation in a purely scientific sense in this chapter or in this work. Simulation is usually based on the mimicking of a real action or object. But simulation does not always follow the real. The virtual is also a leader in the discursive world of meaning (and its construction). I want to suggest that simulation offers the viewer and critic a range of opportunities. It allows us to see the vision of the future. It allows us to observe the codes and strategies at work in the minds and boardrooms of mega corporations. Inasmuch as simulation also creates the real, simulation can also become the subject of the real. Simulation can therefore stand as an indicator of the future. The relationship between the virtual and real are being explored and the distance being challenged over time. The realm of gaming and gaming technology defines the forefront of this process. Does major gaming technology (in simulation video) reference the Caribbean at all; and if so, in what ways? This is the chapter's central focus.

Simulation: Technology, Ideology, the Caribbean

In a popular video game, Grand Theft Auto: Vice City, an actor within the program shouts, "Kill the Haitians!"[8] There were complaints made about this. Though this shout was, in context, a part of the violent exchange between rivaling groups in the game's plot, it was felt that the shout resonated too powerfully within the matrix of game and actual experience.

It is vital to understand how powerful agents of cultural fashioning operate and view peripheral regions like the Caribbean and also to contemplate how the region is simulated in the arena of sports and culture. Perhaps through an understanding of leading-edge programming and simulation of Caribbean iconography, there lie secrets of how first-world technology and culture beholds the Caribbean. Perhaps by engaging the simulation process we better understanding the set of relations and practices that define the hidden codes. The secret of this virtual cultural matrix might very well tell us things about the hard and soft (-ware) ideological politics that will confront us in the future.

Cultural Reading: Theory and Simulation

I do not make a great deal out of the narratology versus ludology debate itself here. I do not seek to align this work on Caribbean video game discourse squarely in one camp or the other, for I believe that both orientations provide useful approaches. Simply put, video narratology approaches the video game as a story, as a cyber drama. It can therefore be read like a book or even a film.[9] On the other hand, ludology views and treats video games as games first and foremost. Ludology often debates the relationship between narrative and simulation in video games. Ludologists acknowledge the presence of plot, narrative, and structure in video games, but they privilege the influence and power of game play.[10]

Julian Kucklich assures the literary and cultural critic that video games are within their critical domain inasmuch as some of these games possess narratology, aesthetics, and plot.[11] But he cautions that critique will come up short if it does not acknowledge that some other video games do not have a rigidly fixed set of codes built in.

Like Marie-Lure Ryan, I believe that simulation systems are not strictly conceived narrative systems but contain a narrative matrix.[12] Simulation builds in flexibility and interactivity. She suggests that in simulation technology, narrative (and systematic, identifiable, formulaic process) is low. I want to suggest that the lowness of this narrative can fool the critic into believing that there is no cultural or construction politics inherent in new simulation video games. Some video games are able to suppress the presence of narrative beneath a highly interactive and open-ended simulation. This suppression cloaks the presence of structure and fashioning in simulation programs. There are indeed principles, rules, opinions, and ideologies built into these advanced games and technologies.

While authors in traditional media are accountable for maybe a few instances of possible actions (which they ascribe to characters, for example), simulator authors are not only creators but also legislators, because they decide which rules will apply to their systems. Ideology within a simulation is conveyed not only through representation but also through the set of rules built into the program, the game, the matrix.

Video Gaming and Caribbean Simulation

The 2003 World Cup of cricket proved that international politics and sport were indeed new and renewed sites of confrontation. The refusal of New Zealand to play in Kenya and of England to play in Zimbabwe, and Australia's early decision not to go there as well, set the tone for a competition with undertones of contentious cultural politics. The Caribbean region has hardly made its official position known or clear on many of the conflicts that have surfaced in recent time. The absence of a strong position by the West Indies within the cultural wars reflects diminishing power and regional impotence in the arena of expressive play. It is therefore not surprising that current gaming simulation of Caribbean reality reflects a virtual undermining of the Caribbean. Oh, how the real and virtual have conspired to reflect and perpetuate the new status quo through the various tools at the disposal of the more influential powers!

So then, how does a brief examination of a leading video game that features the Caribbean, and other nations as well, reflect the traces of ideology? And more importantly—because it is possible that simulations are based on observation as well as ambitions, desires, and hopes—what might the examination of a leading video game begin to reveal about the gaming industry and its attendant politics? Further, what does the virtual re-creation of the West Indies say to us about our relationship to creators of software and virtual culture? What might a video game simulation say about the West Indian cricket team's future? Might a simulation of this kind cast a wider vision of our overall future as a region? If simulation can also inspire and anticipate life, then does the video games matrix present a space within which we can access information about the future? What can we take from that and use in the present?

Brian Lara as Cultural Critic

There are a number of video games that might present themselves for scrutiny. In presenting the series of questions and observations that this short chapter offers, one game that was tempting to consider was Brian Lara Cricket '99 (launched around 1998) from Codemaster developers. Lara has commented on the game himself, saying,[13] "It's very realistic. It's getting very close to the real game. You can look at it and it'll be just like watching a cricket game on the television . . . If it creates more interest from . . . kids, most importantly—they might show more interest in the real game . . . But I don't think it's going to have a great effect on where cricket is heading." These comments begin to reflect a personal perspective on the direction of the sport. Beneath his comments are deeper conceptual issues. The acknowledgement of the fact that young people are the targets of these games is telling. These statements also expectedly hail the positive contribution the video game will make to the real sport in terms of individual interest. But the suggestion about its limited impact on the real game in the future reveals a conservative perspective on the role of technology in cultural reconfiguration. The comment also seems to demarcate a fixed line between simulation culture and the real, hard world of sporting experience.

Ironically, while these comments were being made, international cricket was undergoing radical shifts in terms of the use of video simulation technology. Video game technology had already begun to feed into the real world of cricket. Cricket had already started to alter on this account. At this stage of its development, the virtual game was not attempt-ing to replace the real game as much as it was attempting to approximate it. This quest for proximity through simulation is still a preoccupation of the video game industry. Technology has yet to reach the real. The quest for proximity facilitates a situation in which there is greater lateral inter-play and movement between real and virtual worlds. Lara's comments on the game that bears his name and on its technology is perhaps a reflection of his own vision and ambition for simulation culture. But not even mega stars who give inspiration to games can control the direction and ambi-tions of game simulation. Brian Lara International Cricket 2007 repre-sented an ambitious program. It continued the trend towards pristine simulation. Curiously, the Codemasters Web site does not locate the Caribbean as the site for the game. You must click the cursor on the island of England.[14] Video game simulation gets most of its references from the real world, but the real world increasingly also borrows from advances in video game technology. Televised cricket is increasingly attempting to challenge the conservative symbolism of the traditional sport that is cricket. The commercialization and pop culturalization of cricket reflects the trendy influences that would take over the sport. At the unofficial level, the pop culturalization of cricket reflects the extent to which the sport is a sport no longer of gentlemen but of dogged competitors, fierce national and regional rivalries, and geopolitical skirmishes and wars. Of the cricket-playing nations, the West Indies seem the very last territory to recognize and accept that cricket is no longer a sport but an expression of future desire for superior standing.

Reading Cricket World Cup '99

Instead of focusing primarily on the Codemasters–Brian Lara cricket sim-ulation game, I have opted for the game Cricket World Cup '99,[15] one of the most popular cricket video game franchises, created and distributed by Electronic Arts (EA), the leader in gaming technology, which also makes games based on NBA, NFL, soccer, and 007.

EA claims to be "the world's leading independent developer and pub-lisher of interactive entertainment software for personal computers and advanced entertainment systems such as the PlayStation®2 Computer Entertainment System, the PlayStation®, Xbox™ video game console from Microsoft, the Nintendo GameCube™ and the Game Boy® Advance." Over the years EA has garnered more than 700 awards for out-standing software in the United States and Europe. EA markets its prod-ucts across the world under four brand logos, and it has over thirty three product franchises that have reached more than a million unit sales worldwide. Its headquarters is located in Redwood City, California. Here are some telling observations about this simulation game:

1. As it is being installed, the game begins with a history of World Cup competitions in cricket. History is told from the perspective of England, as though to suggest that the game is targeted at England primarily. It is true that the 1999 World Cup was held in England, but even so, England's success in the previous World Cup tournaments has been, at best, reasonable.
2. The commentators are the British Jim Maxwell and the Australian Richie Benaud. There is no room here for a Reds Perreira or Tony Cozier. Other commentators from Asia are also absent from this arena.
3. Product placement has Vodaphone, Natwest, Pepsi, Fly Emirates, and EA Sports on the boundary boards. These would seem to be sponsoring companies that contributed in some way to the development of the video game production. But what is the nature of the involvement of these companies?
4. The music used is hardly eclectic. It does not set out, for instance, to create regional references that might embrace the variety of cultures being represented at this momentous simulation of a culturally diverse spectacle. The soundtrack is defined by rock aesthetics with touches of dance, synth-pop and funk possibilities. The soundtrack in the introductory show of the game is tightly edited and recorded. This is a carefully produced segment of the game. In the end, credits are given to sound teams. Although this much attention is given to the soundtrack, it is significant that no greater effort is placed on representing the cultural diversity of nations through the game's soundtrack.
5. The demo mode is often an essential part of games, because the demo reflects the flexibility, potential, ambitions that are encoded into the simulation process. The demo mode sidelines the player, and the machine takes over. The taking over of the game by the machine signals the automated process that lies beneath the game's promise of flexibility, interactivity, and democracy. The presence of built-in demo and replay reminds the user that coded programming is still in operation in simulation games. Any hopes of entering an arena that allows for free, fair access on account of dormant technological politics is called into question. In demo mode, an English squad plays *first* with another team, which appears to be Bangladesh. But why is England a default team in the game's matrix?

6. EA expects most of its sales to come from England and Australia. Once the game boots up, the default teams for the several competitions on show are, significantly, England and Australia. Although you can select teams that are listed alphabetically, the England-Australia default reading is not justified alphabetically or otherwise, save that these are two teams that share a similar location and space in cricket's global ideological wars.

7. The players used to model simulation are British primarily. There is no use of players from outside the favored ideological arena. Full endorsement of the game is granted by the English Cricket Board, Australian Cricket Board, United Board of South Africa, and New Zealand Cricket Board. These therefore appear in official and full kit. Why has there only been limited endorsement among test-playing nations? Did the other nations refuse to endorse the simulation video game? And if so, why? Were their boards approached? Does the partial endorsement therefore signal an unequal arrangement within the game? Does the endorsement by some teams place them at an advantage within the game? Are programmers and producers aware of this, and are they therefore biased with respect to the codes and facilities that they make available to the players? Can the game's construction even ignore the fact that some nations are on board and others are not?

All in all, World Cup '99 was a quite impressive game. It anticipated a line of other simulation products. Cricket 2002 was followed by the much-anticipated Cricket 2004.

Reading Cricket 2004

At their Web page devoted to a description of Cricket 2004, EA Sports praised the popularity of Cricket 2002 but sounded the importance of Cricket 2004 as moving the franchise up a level with other PlayStation 2 second generation titles. Some of the special features of the new creation Cricket 2004 are the[16] "inclusion of all the international teams and players; detail in the players' faces and bodies, and sizes; full licenses from the ACB, ECB, NZ Cricket and the South African Cricket team; seventy-five accurately modeled stadiums; various pitch types and conditions; manual fielding, or allowing the intelligent AI to position the fielders."

Cricket 2004 was indeed an advancement and improvement on some of the earlier simulations. Its animation and other built-in features were improved, revealing an ongoing quest to bring game simulation even closer to the actions of the real world. Part of the appeal of this product has been the creation of official and unofficial individual sites by gamers to provide additional downloads to users of the game. For instance, Cricket2004.co.uk advertised its England Test Sweaters, as well as Natwest paraphernalia, and a New Zealand players' face pack.

But like other versions of the sport in simulation, the 2004 installment continued to reveal some of the features of older editions. Apart from the purely technical shortcomings in simulation technology, there are even more telling and worrying features that reveal the ongoing ideological and cultural politics that have permeated the real world of cricket culture and have seeped through the impermeable domain of virtual display.

It is possible that such games are indeed only that: games. It is possible that these are to be enjoyed and consumed for the simple sake of leisure. It is possible that most people who play these games do so solely for excitement and recreation. It is possible that readings of the kind I have been urging in this work are only "academic" and have no real bearing on the actual sport. All this is possible, I confess. Depending on how you approach cultural and social reality, one is bound to see or not see threads of connection and underlying relations. Arguably, there is no relationship at all between sports on the real field of play and sports on the field of animated play. It is very possible that West Indies cricket has solely to do with the game on the real field of play. The creators of simulation sports cannot afford to be bogged down with trying to undermine the real performance of some teams when in fact their greater priority is to enhance digital modeling while satisfying patrons of the game and reaping financial returns. It is true that the West Indies does not constitute a large market for sales, but this would be no reason in itself for cricket simulation developers to sideline the West Indies and similar teams. Some believers in the pure innocence and total fun of video simulation would therefore prefer to think that there is a clearly demarcated space that exists between the real and its sketch. Such a space does exist, though increasingly, it will become harder and harder to locate.

When you consider how the video game has changed over the years, then you begin to understand the processes that have brought about the conflation of the real and the virtual world. Many early arcade games of the late 1970s and early 1980s, like Asteroids, drew young people into arcades to play them. Many of the leading games of the period were based on science fiction and on the excesses of confrontation. By the first decade of the twenty-first century, this emphasis was being counterbalanced by other kinds of social reality simulations. Games like Asheron's Call 2 embraced political notions and motives. Some online clans and guilds shared in online games for the sake of bonding, but also to perpetuate their sense of community. According to Kevin Parker, in the article "Free Play: The politics of the video game,"[17] "Political ideas are infiltrating not just the back-stories of games but their 'play mechanics'—the inner workings that shape game behavior. It may be the scripted parts of the games that explicitly state political notions, but what's ultimately more significant is the way games can communicate doctrine by demonstration, the same way sports communicate physics."

Although he suggests that many contemporary video games are moving towards physical modeling and advanced artificial intelligence, and hence privileging greater player freedom and control over the game and its author, he however points to the existence of game rules that are embedded, consciously or unconsciously. It is the very fact of rules and codes and authoring that invites questions to do with the politics of the very industry of simulation, replication, and modeling. In the present climate of culture wars, it is increasingly difficult to think of production without its cultural, economic, and political objectives. Cricket 2004 came into the market at such a time. The culture wars were on the rise.

Here are some telling observations about the simulation game Cricket 2004:

1. The buzz phrase for Cricket 2004 is "It's in the game"; this suggests that if anything is there in real life it is here in the video game. And, of course, if it is in the EA Sports simulation, then it must be in the real game. Such are the subtleties of marketing.
2. The game's promotional introduction on the CD is termed its "movie soundtrack." This movie clip to the game has become even more hard rock in its musical reference than in the earlier Cricket 2002. In the movie, England and other major players within the international arena appear to have greater presence than others.
3. The game credits and acknowledgements lists the EA Team in Europe, Australia, New Zealand, and South Africa. These are evidently the main contributing territories, prime marketing places for the game, and also constitute the strongest lobby within world cricket.
4. Cricket 2004 is advertised widely on the Net in the noncombat category, but this general placing within the industry marketing system ironically obscures the covert inherent combative codes at work within the gaming matrix.
5. Because Cricket 2004 has greater flexibility and functionality built in, the user can also play a range of county teams from the territories of

major cricketing powers. Usually the degree of difficulty in conquering one's opponents in the virtual realm depends on the strength ranking assigned to these opponents by the game authors themselves. Curiously, however, some county teams are actually assigned a higher ranking than the international West Indies team. This is puzzling. It is inconceivable that this ranking can ever reflect the true weight of teams in the real world. It does appear therefore that there is some degree of fanciful projection. This can perhaps be termed as ideo-technological wish fulfillment within the machine. Is it possible that through some reversed process of affectation or influence that the game begins to construct its own vision of how it desires the real world to function? This wish fulfillment calls greater attention to the input process that seeks to define and control the matrix of virtual and real experience. Because the user of this game detects these kinds of anomalies, she or he turns inward upon the game itself and questions its very construction.

6. Cricket 2004 professes to have seventy-five accurately modeled stadiums. You can play simulated matches in the Caribbean: in Antigua, Jamaica, Guyana, Trinidad, and Barbados. The Barbados simulation is set at Bridgetown, at the well-known Kensington Oval. Through virtual display, the game provides its own vision of the Caribbean. Anyone who knows Bridgetown and its cricket arena Kensington Oval would know that it is located near the heart of the island's capitol. Kensington is surrounded by buildings and houses. Some of these are modern, others are just residential houses, but all in all there is a harbor and industrial estates, the landscape is flat, and road networks define that location.

In Cricket 2004, the simulation of Barbados' capital is modeled on a primitive and rural topography. The game even has a few mountains in the immediate and far distance within the program. This simulation is less contemporary Caribbean and more primitive West Indies. Even 2007 cricket simulation games perpetuate a vision of the region as unexplored, exotic space. It might be argued that this depiction is in keeping with old stereotypical perceptions of the region as cultural jungle. This is a vision similar to that projected in older imperialist texts. This complex is explored in such literary works as *The Tempest* and *Robinson Crusoe*. Because these games also have a life of their own online, where they open up a world of images, sounds, and simulations to all and sundry, their influence cannot be understated. Some mainstream films have also perpetuated this process of cultural misprojection. The final chapter of this book examines aspects of that phenomenon.

The Eventual State

The video/palmtop/mobile game is the latest domain to be colonized. Inasmuch as Caribbean people either ignore, don't know about, or actively participate in this cultural arena, the region is implicated. Where in *The Tempest*, Caliban promises to learn and use Prospero's language to curse him, Caribbean video and technology users also have this potential to declare a revolutionary virtual-postcolonial project as their own in contemporary society. However, the language and practice of technology is widely regarded to be beyond the reach of our societies. By technology, I do not refer squarely to actual technology, and gadgetry as much as I mean the kinds of activities that are associated with the rise of the information communication technology digital age. Yes, I mean the computer, movies, communication tools and so on, but I here refer to an awareness of the deeper cultural workings of these tools. Caribbean societies are hardly taught and educated, whether formally or informally, about the wider cultural implications of techno-cultural domination and control. This is not a science or scientific assignment of which I am speaking. Rather, it refers to a process of knowing about and actively manipulating the systems and networks that are at work within modern society so as to assert fuller control in the future. This is part of the greatest challenge facing Caribbean society in the midst of the culture wars. For instance, the opening up of trade and economic and political systems worldwide means that Caribbean societies have a wider field of play in the international world, but this new set of international governing principles signals the handing over of boundaries to the more powerful agents and agencies that would control the world in many sectors. The region's level of preparedness for the handing over of control can affect the kinds of strategic responses and alliances that it makes in anticipation of the eventual State.

All of this prepares the world for the centralized system of domination that will one day rule. This process is inevitable. What is perhaps more significant is the distance there will be between this central ruling government and "peripheral" regions like the Caribbean. It is possible that there might be relative blind spots or resistance networks within the emerging global system, but given the fact that Caribbean society is widely becoming always connected to technology, it is inconceivable that surveillance and control will not also extend to the region. Simulation technologies and video games are therefore reminders and symbols of the way that real and virtual actions can begin to intersect. Such games and their flaws remind us that they are ultimately the creation of human beings; they therefore reflect the ambition, desire, vision of the powerful corporations that are themselves at the center of refashioning society in preparation for the future, a future driven by innovation and total connectivity, one in which real and superreal ambitions will converge in expectation of profits and religious and spiritual rule. Commercial profit is but a surface component of deeper ambitions. Cultural and spiritual control is the unstated, submerged preoccupation of contemporary and future civilization.

CHAPTER 7

The Caribbean in Big-Budget Film: The Caribbean in Tourism

Part 1: Caribbean in Tourism

In the movie *Shall We Dance*, Richard Gere's character, John Clark, expresses the fantasy of going to the islands.[1] On the Web site of the extra-regionally owned tourist liner Royal Caribbean International, the white leadership of the company declares: "No one knows the Caribbean better than we do."[2] Potential tourists are offered the dream of a lifetime in the Caribbean.

Caribbean society exists in the wider world as a set of stereotypes and tropes. Perpetuation of these stereotypes is supported by popular media but also by regional actions and initiatives. Western big-budget films and Caribbean tourism marketing are but two areas in which notions of Caribbeanness are represented, simulated, and refashioned for popular consumption. While Caribbean society has used tourism as an economic tool of development, this has had the effect of streamlining notions of the region. Web marketing reflects the frontier site of tourist-related imaging of the region. The cruise industry and boards of tourism across the region have turned to technology for economic salvation. But what is the nature of this co-option of technology? Is the technology passive in the whole exercise? Does technology come away from the association with anything of its own? The images of the region perpetuated through the international media, and through the entertainment industry, are no less reconfigured and fixed within the technology of film, video, and sound. A closer examination of the international treatment of the region via big-budget film can help to make sense of the relationship between large capital interests and "peripheral" regions that exist beyond their imagination. But an assessment of the relationship that Caribbean audiences share with some big-budget films can also open up an awareness of the potential for regional-international connectivity at the level of cultural fashioning in a digital world.

Caribbean Tourism: Just beyond Your Imagination

Caribbean tourism has always been a phenomenal source of regional marketing. In the early twenty-first century, Caribbean governments increasingly turned to tourism as a source of renewable economic activity and revenue. The region has, of course, always attracted the gaze of the wider world at various moments, for a number of reasons. Their exotic location and culture still remains a major sales pitch for the islands in the twenty-first century. The vestiges of a long history of conquest and exploitation, and the working out of imperialist politics, have added to the sense of mystique of these islands at the center of Western Atlantic history. In the twenty-first century, the region's position within the global tourism industry was still significant. But increasingly, there was threat of competition from other locations, as well as the falloff due to the new global foregrounding of "terror." These threatened the regional marketing potential. The region was also encumbered by the lurking censure of the OECD, which sought to monitor and control the functioning and processing of offshore companies and entities in the region. The region's iconographic trace and the increasingly troubled global climate made the Caribbean both a surrealistic object of desire and escape and a region in search of a role in an advanced technological world.

Caribbean presence and relevance was not only fought for in the realm of the arts, academic discourse, sports, and entertainment, but also in the real hard-sell world of direct cultural marketing. It is in the realm of tourism that the region has most stridently had to sell its image. As the arena of marketing has advanced, so Caribbean destinations have had to find ways of entering into the technological spaces that capture and project images and sounds to global audiences. Yes, Caribbean tourism organizations and entities continued to market through more traditional avenues of travel agencies, radio, television, word of mouth, and other low-tech cost-cutting promotions. But in the twenty-first century, the dynamic had changed, and Caribbean entities took to cyber marketing to help them in the quest to remain visible and viable. To achieve these aims, they also had to grapple with the challenges of "becoming virtual."

The reality of Caribbean marketing semiotics is that the region is regarded for its exotic, yet sensual themes. Traditional dedicated travel brochures from throughout the region have played out this theme for a very long time and even up to the present.[3] The Internet has already gained the reputation as a "sexy" medium. It is "sexy" and attractive in the sense that it appeals to a wide range of users, functions, tasks, and objectives. But it is also sexy in the sense that there is an active process at work within this technology that seeks to claim greater and greater space for sensual, sexual, and also near-pornographic material. It is indeed possible that among the wars being fought within the arena of the World Wide Web there is and will be an all-out confrontation between forces that are differently positioned with respect to their outlook on what is acceptable and what is not acceptable on public communications platforms like the Internet. The indices of sex, violence, and freedom are three categories that will preoccupy Web legislation and policy for a long time. The virtual culture wars are therefore destined to be fought on a number of different fronts. The region, partly because it is a hub for leisure and recreation, is destined to be a central site for the playing out of various confrontations.

In many instances the region has had to follow the major trends and practices that are first tested and instituted in metropolitan centers. Although some countries have attempted to remain rooted to aspects of their traditional beliefs and practices, there have been many challenges. Throughout the early years of the twenty-first century, the region was poised on the brink of an enforced regional union called the Caribbean Single Market and Economy (CSME). An even larger giant of unification and control called NAFTA loomed on the horizon. Inasmuch as these associations create larger economic blocks, they also serve to reinforce a set of stated and unstated cultural and legislative codes. Given the proliferation of interwoven and wired regional and extra-regional agreements, the Caribbean cannot for long hope to hold off the impending invasion of global norms, standards, and beliefs. All this is a prelude to the eventual outcome of a one-world government. Of course, the region's predicament has not been cast in these terms by its politicians, social commentators, and academics. This way of reading the contemporary and postcontemporary evolution of Caribbean culture is perhaps more clearly expressed by religious commentators. A reality of Caribbean cultural and social evolution and its critique in the new technological era is the effacement of core issues to do with essence, existence, identity, destiny, and truth. This calculated erasure has thrown into greater relief the need for emerging digital and cyber critics to work within, yet to work behind, the façade of the matrix of language, jargon, technology, and political correctness.

Tourism Marketing on the Web

Caribbean Web marketing politics cannot escape the already heavily sexually driven signature of Caribbean culture in export. The Internet's already sexually coated and undergirded pop-up construction makes it an almost ideal location for the playing out of the Caribbean iconographic symbols. Caribbean presence in the international world is therefore today constructed around an amalgam of its several global contributions in the realms of culture, sports, entertainment, politics, and economic activity. Its geographical proximity to the U.S. mainland also enhances its presence. A brief examination of tourism marketing practices on the Internet illustrates the extent to which Caribbean societies have begun to internalize their own image and how they regard their position in the world. This examination also considers the role that the Internet will play in the future simulation of Caribbean reality.

The region's umbrella tourist association, the Caribbean Tourist Organization (CTO), has since its forging in 1989 promoted itself as the unifying core of the region's several independent national tourism partners and associations. Its official Web site is called Onecaribbean.org. In keeping with its primary mandate to collect and disseminate research and data about the region's tourism, the official site dissuades casual surfers from browsing beyond its welcome page. This intranet therefore requires users of the site to become members and to have login IDs. The coldness of this all-embracing organization is in stark contrast to the much warmer and friendlier sites of individual tourist centers throughout the region.

It would be too great a task to discuss at length the range of sites devoted to tourism throughout the region. The reality is that tourism entities, ranging from small hotels to car rental companies have embarked on offering their services and facilities to tourists without much care for larger national imperatives. Conversely, some other entrepreneurs have sought to regularize and centralize their products and services by collaborating with other associations, sharing space on the Internet, or purchasing links on larger, more established Web sites.

Many national tourism boards have established their dedicated sites through which they have sought to control and shape the presence of their national product in cyberspace. Belize's Belizetourism.org is spare in its presentation, preferring only to give to inquirers some of the hard information and practical details about the organization and about Belize.[4] Its highlight therefore is the brightly written logo on the site's front page that says, "Catch the Adventure." Two backpackers sit atop a rocky hill overlooking a wooded plain. Its associated Web site,

Travelbelize.org, is much more colorful and provides greater insight into the world that the Internet opens up as Belize. Its highlight is a virtual tour that one hopes is true multimedia but that turns out to be text and still-image based. By undermining your expectations for a true virtual tour, the official site forces you to refocus on the hard data that it presents as scribal document within the otherwise trendy multimedia matrix called the Internet.

In contrast to the fact-based presentation of Belize's official site, there is the much more trendy, yet formulaic, presentation at Stkitts-tourism.com, which comes with an introductory slideshow that you have the option of skipping.[5] But you get to see it anyway. It is a fifteen-second juxtaposition of the hustle of the city against the packaged tranquility of an island. This contrast is also cleverly conveyed at the level of visual and aural experience. In the opening show, the noise of congested motorways gives way to what is intended to be melodic strains of the steel band. The steel band samples are weak and are much closer to bells, but you are meant to supplement these absences and to know that this Caribbean location will offer pan, real pan, among other stock items. Its virtual tours and slide shows distinguish this site from the previous one on Belize. Of course, whereas you have near seamless control of the several experiences, because you can navigate through or across pages of information, the promise of moving shows on the slick St. Kitts and Nevis site keeps you back as you have to wait on the technology to appropriate the graphic experience that will bring the Caribbean near-fully alive.

Most of the tourism Web sites affiliated with governmental agencies are formulaic. Or maybe put another way, they are aware of marketing imperatives and market expectation, and so they do not veer too far away from stereotypical or stock images and iconographies. For example, Svgtourism.com, Anguilla-vacation.com, and Stlucia.org all display the tranquil sea, lazy days of relaxation, coconut palms, and underwater splendor.[6] Dominica's Dominica.dm replaces these with an overpowering photo of its children wishing visitors to the site and the island a merry Christmas during Christmas season of 2004.[7] The children wear what appears to be national dress. A recurring item of focus on most regional Web sites is their foregrounding of festivities, such as Creole Festival in Dominica, Grenada's sailing and carnival festivals, St. Lucia's Jazz Festival, and "the Caribbean's only Blues Festival," in St. Vincent and the Grenadines, of course. Jamaica, Barbados, and the Bahamas also display their celebrations.

Over the Internet, it is not easy to differentiate the more-developed Caribbean tourism locations. Many of the sites make use of various technologies that can give the illusion of having the capacity to deliver the goods to all who visit from across the world. Most sites, government sanctioned and otherwise, still invest heavily in visual impact and imagery, with emphasis on stock photos and slide shows using dissolving frames. Text is crucial to Web marketing, because sound technology on the Internet is not always a stable medium for advertising. Like moving video, Internet sound is still heavily dependent on a range of factors. Among these factors are considerations of the various users and the range of computer or wireless systems they will use to access the World Wide Web. Text is therefore still a dependable medium within virtual transaction. Streaming audio and video are indeed trendy facilities that demonstrate the power of technology, and accordingly too the wizardry and near magic that should appeal to tourism interests, but these tools are at times too quirky to be invested in by marketing agencies within the business of tourism. Caribbean tourism–related pages are therefore safe sites of technological display. This mistrust of the Internet's imagined potential reflects a shrewd awareness of what is and isn't possible in the real, hard world of techno-marketing.

But that having been said, the point must also be made that there are relatively few sites in this arena that have consciously sought other ways of circumventing technology's limitation in order to present less formulaic marketing. For instance, few sites employ humor, irony, nontraditional images, or maybe even cartoon-type imagery within their marketing frontlines. They therefore do not aim to set themselves apart as much as they hope to remain the same within the perception of the potential tourist. Locked into this conventional marketing politics is the perception that potential visitors want direct messages; they do not want to be bogged down with difference, and they do not want to think of "natives" as anything more than stock figures with island personalities.

If I have cast the impression that Caribbean marketing aesthetics on the Internet is predictable, safe, and lacking in inspiration, then that is largely so, but another reality of Web marketing and tourism is the fact that virtual technologies and industries like tourism are excellent associates. The Net's potential for interactivity and dialog has created a more dynamic set of relations between potential land visitors and their eventual hosts. Most sites therefore offer facilities to book rooms, choose the type of vacation, flights, transportation—all online in a single domain. Caribbean interests have used these facilities to advance their position within the market.

If the Internet is a medium of illusion, then few entities have better exploited the mystique of the Caribbean within this technological matrix than has the cruise industry. Of course, the cruise industry is owned by large transnational corporations and players. In the first decade of the twenty-first century, Caribbean tourist destinations were locked in contentious debate with the cruise ship industry over the proposal by some islands in the region to increase the head tax on cruise ships. The cruise industry resisted and even threatened to boycott some islands of the region. The region could not unite on this matter. The large conglomerates had again won out. For, as they have proclaimed, no one knows the Caribbean as they do!

All of this confrontation took place in the traditional open domain of debate. In the new virtual arena, cruise conglomerates had for some time prior taken charge of projecting the region as though it were owned by them and constructed for the purpose of hosting their floating virtual hotels. Cruise lines like Royal Caribbean and Princess Cruises have marketed themselves as symbols of the region. This is done on a number of sites where, again, stock images and sounds of placid, complicit natives provide the backdrop for the moving adventures that only a cruise will provide. A recurring feature of many of the front pages of sites that exploit the region is their foregrounding of usually white travelers and of the impressive cruise ships. The destinations are usually covered beneath a layer or two of navigational space, hidden away, only to be uncovered as exotic ports and welcoming harbors. The effect of much of this marketing is that it inscribes fixed notions about who is a tourist and who is a native. But the control of the region's images and facilities through the virtual domain also explains why the cruise industry reacts disdainfully to any suggestion that the region should derive greater benefits from the tourism transaction. For, after all, in the virtual domain, the reality is that the cruise industry is preeminent. The owners of the cruise liners are foremost. The islands hardly have an existence without the presence of the cruise industry. It is instructive how the virtual arena can so starkly reflect the underlying tensions and power relations within the tourism industry.

Part 2: The Western Blockbuster and Caribbean Culture

Who Let In the Beltway Sniper?

Back in 2002, the international media seized upon the knowledge that the so-called Beltway snipers had a Caribbean connection. Reporters were sent to Antigua and Jamaica, and the press revealed a range of procedural breaches to do with national and travel documents. The Jamaica Tourist Board pulled a number of their ads in the United States for fear that these might remind the world of the Jamaica connection in the sniper saga. The need to pull those ads revealed the extent to which tourist-oriented international press advertising is dependent on other kinds of conditions for effectiveness. A significant emphasis in the international press had to do with loopholes in Caribbean systems of granting identification and other official documents. For some days, the press explored the route by which the horrifyingly mysterious events were brought upon citizens of the United States. This was not a U.S. root cause. The source of this tragedy and terror emanated from another global location. In a November 4, 2002 article, "Who Let in the Beltway Sniper," Patrick J. Buchanan expresses grave concerns about the tarnishing of the United States by "gatecrashers," especially those from the Caribbean.[8] In the Beltway sniper episode, emphasis was therefore deflected partially from the saga as a U.S. problem and recast as having its roots in other societies. The promulgation of the incident in these terms throughout the various technological media created negative buzz about the region. This was a direct attack on the capabilities of the region. It could have had negative consequences for immigration and tourism. Some regional governments performed a silent retreat from international attention until the negative reading of the region abated. But while stories about the Beltway sniper and the Caribbean connection died down, the region was hardly outside the gaze of the Western news and entertainment media. In the same way that the islands could do little to nothing about the publicizing of the Beltway incident, they were similarly challenged in the face of ongoing treatment of the region in the less directly offensive technological construction of the region through popular television and popular films.

Prior to the birth of the Internet, no other single medium had impacted Caribbean society while also shaping its perspective of technology more than the Western media, and in particular the big-budget film industry. I want to go on to examine aspects of referencing within the film industry. There are more references (direct and indirect) to the Caribbean in popular feature films than the average citizen might believe. The value of this exercise is that when they are mapped out, we begin to better understand the complex set of references that over time construct notions of the Caribbean and eventually threaten to stand in for the real Caribbean.

References, References, References

Some of the films, not major ones, that make some reference to the Caribbean over the past ten to fifteen years might include *Confined*, starring Michael Ironside, in which a minor character and his wife reveal that they are going to the Caribbean for vacation. In the movie *Thursday*, a black man with an exaggerated Jamaican accent pretends to be a pizza man but is really out to get drugs. When he gets to the door of a white man, this man asks of him a favor: "A little ganja?" In *Shattered Image*, the female protagonist with a split personality meets a man who befriends her, and they go on a vacation to the Caribbean, where much of the movie is set. They go away in order to get away from a mysterious caller who torments her psyche. In the Caribbean setting, some locals do speak, but they are peripheral. More substantial speakers are the stereotypical taxi driver and the all-knowing native witch. *Kidnapped in Paradise* explores the tensions between two estranged sisters who are reunited in the corrupted world of the Caribbean. In *Canadian Bacon*, the American strategists and advisors to the President inform him that Canada would prove an easy foe to overcome—almost as easy as Grenada. *Heartbreak Ridge* stars Clint Eastwood, who is the no-nonsense officer selected to train a bunch of soldiers for a final assault on the island of Grenada. Before he leaves in the noble service of his country he must visit an unsatisfied wife, possibly for the last time. In the ABC high-budget television movie *Future Sport*, it is Wesley Snipes who enters as a quasi-dreadlocked sport network business tycoon. He speaks in an African Caribbean accent. *Tracked* also tampers with identities. It has the plot of a white protagonist who is captured and imprisoned and charged with keeping dogs, which will later chase him as he is released in some sick game instituted by a deranged jailor. In prison, the protagonist is befriended by a black prisoner with a Caribbean accent. But the black man soon sheds his accent to reveal an American intonation and his special undercover agent status. Soon after the film establishes a more stable basis for the black man's development, he is taken out.

At the ending of the big release *Blade 2*, the protagonist (played by Wesley Snipes) returns to reap retribution on a black Caribbean voodoo priest. Of course, in the first film, *Blade*, Miracia, the priestess who lives in a landfill ghetto, has her cabin filled with, among other things, voodoo dolls. She requires "an offering for the orishas" for giving insight to the protagonist. He throws a handful of bills across the table. It is as much a commercial enterprise as it is a spiritual transaction. In the box office behemoth *Spider Man 2*, when Spidey gives up his power and is confronted with a burning house with people trapped inside, it is a black man who urges Spidey to save the day. The black man, placed in the same position of fear and helplessness, turns to Spidey, who must now do what the black race is not able to do, that is, overcome inner doubt and fear. *Open*

Water's soundtrack plays Krosfyah's song "Pump Me Up," and in the movie, a black man's negligence leads to the death of two white tourists. *Sharktale* has two jellyfish brothers in Rasta tams (hats). They are subservient hit men for the big, bad shark. Their alter egos are the blond dreadlocks in *The Matrix Reloaded*. In the 2005 movie *Hitch*, the female protagonist walks into the office and someone asks her "Barbados alone"? Rupee's hit single "Tempted to Touch" plays in the dance club. In the 2005 box office hit *The Wedding Crashers*, Shaggy and Rayvon's song "Summertime" plays when the party of family and friends vacation somewhere in the United States. There is an allusion to the Caribbean without even going there. In this same film, there is a minor black character with a contrived Caribbean accent. He is a servant: he waits on the table of the main protagonists, or otherwise one of his masters turns off the television in his face when he seeks a space of respite from the demands of servitude. *The Forty Year Old Virgin* casts a number of characters that persistently discourse on sex and more sex. Among these characters are two minor intrusive characters. One is of East Indian descent, and the other aspires to having a Caribbean accent and identity. Their role punctuates the excesses of the movie's fixation with sex. The Caribbean character is especially crazed and holds a fixation with goats. Another of the characters asks him why he continually refers to goats. Apart from this, there is also a young black brother who enters the electronics store wearing a shirt boldly declaring JAMAICA. At least he does not talk dirty about sex. He is more concerned about doing a clandestine, illegal transaction. At the end of the 2006 *Superman*, Lex Luthor is banished to the islands.

Needless to say, there are other films and television programs that do not give these (predominantly) Caribbean characters voice but that still inscribe their Caribbean identities through some semiotic indicators. The Rastafarian hairstyle is one such sign, though this is not absolutely foolproof, because all Rastafarians are not of Caribbean origin. But to the extent that Rastafarianism began as a popular religion and lifestyle and fashion motif in the Caribbean, there is still some measure of referencing to the Caribbean when dreadlocks are centered. In the same way, one supposes that certain fast food signs like KFC, in spite of its various local ownerships worldwide, are still always linked to the United States. Cultural signs are therefore interpreted in this way. Film writers, producers, and directors are aware of this system of interpretation and meaning.

This chapter is not so much concerned with overt referencing. It is more interested in strategic and covert referencing so that, for example, it does not concentrate on films like *How Stella Got Her Groove Back*, which is an obvious exercise in Caribbean re-creation. The history of Western cinema and big-budget industry is quite well known; the number of Hollywood and large-budget mainstream productions that have been shot on location in the Caribbean is also quite well publicized. This chapter's approach allows for a closer examination of the subtle and potentially insidious strategies that often define Western entertainment corporate philosophy. Technology is at its most potent and influential when its underlying politics and motives are concealed beneath the spectacle of technology's creative power. What is the nature of Caribbean references in selected big-budget films and Western media? Is there really, though, such a thing as a Caribbean reading of science fiction and technology-driven film? These are just a few of the questions that surface.

The apparent inconsequential function of a single frame within film has been challenged by developments in film techniques and technology during the 1990s. "Product placement" reinforced the value and power of fleeting references. This practice was first popular in film but spread to television where it was termed "product integration." It then also infiltrated video games in the 1990s. Product placement attracted revenue from companies that wanted to have their products appear, if only momentarily, during the normal course of a film. Products from sunglasses, to beverages, to vehicles paid for their fleeting moment of glory within the gaze of viewers. Companies dished out very substantial sums in actual cash, or even of the actual product, from the 1980s until the present. But product placement through its subliminal strategy is considered to have improved the profile and profitability of products over the decades. The appearance of Reese's Pieces in the 1982 blockbuster film *ET* is considered to have started the product placement movement, when Reese's sales apparently increased by 65 percent. When Hackman invited Cruise to a Red Stripe in the movie *The Firm* (1993), the Caribbean beer is said to have increased U.S. sales by more than 50 percent, and soon thereafter, the company sold majority stake in their company to Guinness Brewing for approximately $62 million U.S.[9] Video games and popular songs are also sites for the covert display of products. The sheer power of this kind of soft referencing brings home the reality of how audiences are impacted by subliminal references. This chapter therefore begins with this observation and in full sight of film and television's impact through subtle and indirect reference. Is it possible therefore that seemingly casual, inconsequential allusions or references to the Caribbean contain the seeds of ideological, cultural and (to a lesser extent) economic fortune or damnation?

Finding the Region in Science Fiction

Caribbean societies of the 1970 and 1980s were fed a heavy diet of Western cult and popular science fiction films. Books like *To Seek Out New Worlds: Science Fiction and World Politics* show how the science fiction genre reflects the global political climate and Western anxieties about the (usually threatening) non-Western world.[10] This is a valuable way of reading some genre films. But this approach hardly leaves substantial space for interpreting this genre from a regional perspective. A regional perspective would of course focus on the absences within dominant readings of the genre, but would also focus on absences within the very genre itself. These films can very well be interpreted as gesturing to the uncharted regions of Western society. The unknown, peoples of alien society are potential representations of non-Western but also regional cultures. Whereas in the 1970s and prior, the science fiction genre tended to reflect aliens as deserving of aggressive and violent treatment, by the 1990s, programs like *Star Trek: The Next Generation* were espousing a kind of political correctness. They advocated the inclusion and acceptance of all; but it was the carefully constructed Western heroes who condescended to make this so.

Caribbean viewers have reacted in different ways to this genre. They have been impressed by the technological wizardry on display in the creation of these films. This sense of awe and mistrust has carried through into contemporary Caribbean society. When the computer became a cultural symbol and purchasable item, Caribbean society was at the same time awestruck, as they were slightly suspicious of its motives. Kamau Brathwaite's 1987s collection *X/Self* explores the nervousness of the first contact in a poem like "X/Self xth letter from the thirteenth provinces."[11] Much of this (worldwide) skepticism is harnessed in late 1980s and 1990s big-budget films like the *Terminator* and carried on by the *Matrix* franchise. But some Caribbean viewers have questioned the failure to locate their intimate and peculiar circumstance reflected more overtly within a lot of 1970s and 1980s tech-driven films. If Caribbean critics do not readily see the region's discourse represented in contemporary science fiction and related genres, it might be because regional discourses hardly consider this genre and also because regional themes are hardly on the surface but are submerged and have to be retrieved.

Caribbean societies have always seen their heroes in the slightly odd, mysterious, and strong characters like Mr. Spock and Mr. Warf from *Star Trek*. These characters are aliens. They are, however, essential to the larger project of the Federation and the *Enterprise*. They are not the chief officer but have tactical and security functions. Mr. Warf is an odd Klingon. He gestures to be human but comes up short. In regions like the Caribbean, slaves were also once reminded that they were not humans. In spite of his every effort, the film reminds him and the viewer that he cannot enter into the mainstream of Federation cultural behaviors symbolized by Picard and Riker.

Where other viewers from the Caribbean have had difficulty locating their alter egos, they have tended to read characters like Billy Dee Williams of *Star Wars* the movie as North American alter egos, because there is little inherent in the casting of such characters that inscribes them as Caribbean or regional. The Caribbean cultural critic does have some reason for discussing the racial and cultural references to the region as presented by the portrayal of the loyal slave. In *Star Wars*, Chewbacca is Han Solo's loyal sidekick. He speaks a language that is incomprehensible to the human ear. He is ape. He is a primate species, hence he loyally aligns himself to master Han Solo, with whom he shares a relationship in the bowels of technology. The *Millennium Falcon* helps to circumscribe their actions. Their relationship resonates with that of Crusoe and Friday and also has implications for application to Shakespeare's *The Tempest*. Chewbacca was a slave until he was freed by Han Solo, to whom he swore his loyalty. Known for his particular knowledge of the *Millennium Falcon* and brutish strength, Chewbacca has stood loyal to his friend and master. The postcolonial possibilities are very present. Han and Chewbacca's unifying space is the *Millennium Falcon*. It is here that they beat out their frustrations through death defying maneuvers. Chewie's occasional unleashing of anger on the old freighter also reflects his anxieties about his relationship with Han and his voluntary confinement within the "fastest piece of junk in the galaxy."

It could be argued, as others have intimated, that a character like Jar Jar Binks references the baby talk once associated with Creole languages, as those of the Caribbean. In the movie, this character's function is primarily for comic relief. *The Phantom Menace* presented Jar Jar and his race the Gungans as living under water, whereas the much more advanced Naboo people live in the enlightened world. Reference has been made to Jar Jar's long ears as referencing Caribbean hairstyles of Rastafari and to his exaggerated black walk. Of course, all of this is compounded by the fact that the young actor Ahmed Best, who played Jar Jar (for some Jah Jah), was a black dancer from the Bronx, whose family is of Caribbean descent. George Lucas refuted any claims that Jar Jar's accent was Caribbean and blamed the Internet for starting and fueling this talk.

The name Jar Jar was a codename used for the character. It is interesting that the character on screen is a concoction of technology. He is computer generated. This has implications for the way we perceive of his being. On the one hand, there is the voice and its cultural markers. But the bodily presence of the actual actor (Ahmed Best) in the original shoot is edited out and replaced by Industrial Light and Magic's computer-generated surrogate. The computer-generated movements were based on the antics of the real actor captured via the computer and regenerated. In an interview, the actor reports that he did the actions that they required and perhaps even more.[12] The Lucas film diffuses the makeup of this composite being by altering its appearance and distancing the voice from its corporeal essence. Actors on the set were therefore interacting with an empty space, where the computer would later, after the action, interpose the technological image of Jar Jar. This manipulation of image and voice and sound and presence is a critical action. It points to the very intricate and political process that defines Hollywood's practice of dismantling, disembodying, reconstructing, and redeploying the symbols of nations and cultures for global consumption.[13]

The Phantom Menace's intrigue for many more viewers revolved around the film's show of technological wizardry. But although most Caribbean viewers missed these references, or cared really little about them, they stand as heavily encoded bits of knowledge. Caribbean viewers are more inclined to see their representation in someone like the Samuel L Jackson's character Mace Windu or even in the earlier Billy Dee Williams character of Lando Calrissian. Lando, after all, is the hustler. He is duplicitous. He is showman. But it is clear that films of this kind reference if only indirectly the kinds of social relations that define Western and non-Western industrial and nonindustrial peoples. In many of these films, the marginal characters mentioned above operate the technology at their disposal, but they are hardly its creator and shaper. Their relationship to the technology is manipulated by the deeper motivation to satisfy their superiors and by doing so to uphold the good of ship or colony or federation. It is indeed technology that diffuses the underlying tensions between the diverse subjects on these fictional arenas in space. Caribbean societies have therefore viewed many of these films nervously, and with some suspicion. They have often felt that the relationship between, say, Han Solo and Lando Calrissian ignores the underlying social, racial, and cultural tensions that the Lucas film does not explore. Hollywood has compensated for this failure by interposing the technology factor to occupy the space that once would have been devoted to ethnic and cultural debate. Star Wars therefore presents psychic power and its control over human action as a strategic distraction from debates about social, cultural, and racial power. The quest for control is fought in the technological realm. The light saber therefore represents a tool of mastery. Darth Vader is representative of the evil empire USSR and its subsidiary equals. But Darth Vader is also Caribbean creature. Like the primate rogue Smeagol from *The Lord of the Rings*, he is the antithesis of light. He has fallen from grace. He is an outcast. He is a rebel. He is enslaved in his dark outer coating. His visage is a mystery. He is too deformed to behold, much like the Orcs in *Lord of the Rings*. But as we come to learn, Darth Vader has aspired to master the technology; ultimately it is this same technology that dooms him to oblivion. Many of these films have therefore presented ambivalent perceptions of technology's role in shaping the relationship between Western heroes and their support cast of obscure subjects and objects.

In the 1990s and thereafter, many of the references to the Caribbean are more identifiably direct, though still covertly coded within the technological matrix of film production. As the entertainment industry embraces world music and exotic cultures, regional spaces like the Caribbean become more readily represented. Yes, Hollywood has shown some fascination with the Caribbean for a long time now. One can go back to a series of films that have used the region in some way over the decades. Many of these have exploited the background, some have exploited labor, others have promoted the region, its music, and its exotic lifestyles. Some of these films would be, *Water, Mosquito Coast, Romancing the Stone, The Deep, Illegal in Blue*, and *Into the Blue*.

The 2003 blockbuster *Pirates of the Caribbean*, based on the Disney flagship ride of the same name, raised a number of questions about the extent to which practices and relations and cultural politics have changed significantly over the years. The producers chose to shoot segments of the action on location in the Caribbean. The locations scout visited countries from as far north as the Bahamas to South America in the south. They wanted to recreate seventeenth-century Port Royal, Jamaica, so they chose the location of Wallilabou, St. Vincent. The extras were sought among locals. They required rusty people, befitting of the decayed moral standards of a buccaneer haven. The economic benefits were played up. Locals received temporary jobs and revenue through rentals by Disney, the production company. The film was a box office behemoth, starring everybody's favorite, Johnny Depp. The 2006 and 2007 sequels established the franchise and brought even greater popularity to Disney's theme park ride of the same name.

The post-2000 film *The Matrix Reloaded*, of course, cast two dreadlock villains. The dreadlock ghostlike albino "virus twins" are an enigma within the matrix. They represent two rogue viruses within the matrix's mainframe. They are not developed as characters. But they are inherently evil. In the movie, they are alternative programs that also hunt for Neo. In the industry literature, as well as on the Internet, they attracted much attention. Better known in the real world as the Rayment twins from England, their rasta hairstyle was a defining marker in the film, as well as the fact that they were white men wearing dreadlocks. Part of the insider interest with these two characters had to do with the carrying of their hairstyles and its impact on production. The styles were described as "hip Hollywood hairdos," and the brothers revealed the difficulties of working with this appendage in near-mocking terms: "You do a fantastic take and they yell 'Cut,' and then you realize that one of the dreads was caught in your sunglasses and is sticking out your ear."[14]

Predator stars Schwarzenegger in combat against an invisible foe. *Predator 2* casts the Predator as a half-dreadlock enigma. He or it wreaks havoc in a city terrorized by Colombian drug lords and the Caribbean posse. In the movie, drugs and marijuana are recurring tropes of Caribbean society. *Scary Movie 2* exploits this association, as does the less well known *Thursday*, which features some discussion about illegal money in the Caribbean and represents a rastaman as one of a number of characters who harass the main protagonist for hidden drugs. In the much more publicized *Predator 2*, the beast follows the scent of violence, which leads it to a modern metropolis gone haywire. In the 2004 *Alien vs. Predator*, the beast (preditor) sides with the black female protagonist. They share a symbolic and symbiotic relationship. She and her black race are not far removed from the primitive origin of the predator. He has roots in the cradle of civilization. She too is just one step away in the process of evolving from ape into human. The monster has, of course, been a recurring imaginary figure that has an association with the exotic culture of the region. It is therefore not surprising that in the 1998 movie *Godzilla*, the creature is purported to have landed on a small, unspoiled island within the Caribbean. The late-twentieth-century production was a reworking of one of the first major Japanese sci-fi blockbusters. The original 1950s film was very much a commentary on the nuclear arms race and on human action and technological aberration.

Computer Generated: Natural and Unnatural Disasters

Godzilla begins with a series of aberrations. It begins with a series of catastrophes. The reference to the Caribbean in Godzilla is punctuated, sharp, immediate, and part of that film's buildup to the audience's eventual beholding of the monster. The film therefore begins as other classic horror—or rather, monster—films do. There is a formulaic, systematic showing of the monster's genesis. Then there is a showing of its route to the film's center by way of other global outpost colonial regions in Asia and then in the Caribbean. On its way to the center, it leaves a trail of destruction, capsizing fishing vessels and crippling anything that stands in its path. By the time the monster reaches Jamaica in the Caribbean, it has already drawn the attention of the film's major players. The camera therefore fixes onto the house-size footprints of the monstrous beast. Movement is therefore suggested in one important opening scene by the camera zooming outward and upwards from ground level in order to reveal a trail leading into some other country. The film therefore establishes the process of movement as necessary for tracking and discovering the destructive creature. So the prints lead to the north Caribbean.

In the movie, the camera zooms in spiritedly on an open beach where a huge cargo ship has been laid waste with the print of the monster on its hard outer shell. The rising strains of music and the slower panning shot of natives in turbans and dreadlocks in the background makes the point that the action is indeed all on location. But the reality of production is that VisionArt Design and Animation prided itself in having fooled the world into thinking that the scene was shot in a way other than through computer-generated tracking technology.[15] The reliance on virtual creation and simulation technology draws attention to the intricate relationship between the real and its other manifestations. In the mid-to-late 1990s, the entertainment and research industry placed substantial investment into computer-generated imaging. The scene was therefore shot in Jamaica, but the film industry inserted tracks of computer-generated data. This blurring of reality marked the possibility of other kinds of ideological insertions.

(CG) Computer Generated

In 1995, Pixar released the first feature-length computer animated film, *Toy Story*. The film's use of computer animation marked it as different from more traditional productions. This trend was continued in post-2000 blockbusters like *Finding Nemo* and *Shrek 2*, whose characters were all computer generated. In the post-2000 years, the production industry experimented further with interlacing CGI and real actors and actions. Of course, earlier movies, like the 1988 *Who Framed Roger Rabbit*, superimposed drawn cartoon characters that appeared to interact with flesh-and-blood human characters. But the more recent flesh-and-blood films used real and computer-generated feats with seamless subtlety. The 1998 Dreamworks computer generated production *Antz* is fun. It is an entertaining movie with a cast of leading voices from Sylvester Stallone, Sharon Stone, Danny Glover, Gene Hackman and Christopher Walken. It is also a surprisingly mature story that explores issues such as class distinction, militarism, social responsibility and individual freedom. One of the soldier ants is interestingly named Barbados. He is a soldier ant and is voiced by the black actor Danny Glover. When Z the protagonist ant is mistakenly sent off to battle, he is given words of advice by Barbados before *he* dies. Z is told "Don't make my mistake, kid. Don't follow orders your whole life. Think for yourself." This message resonates throughout the film. The naming of this character after a Caribbean island might very well be an insignificant observation. Or maybe there are underlying political and cultural statements embedded.

The death of Barbados produces one of the more delicate moments in the film's sound score. The soundtrack has the tune "Death of Barbados" as the tenth track on the twenty-track album.[16] Of course, the original soundtrack also features the Caribbean-inspired "I Can See Clearly Now." The track "Death of Barbados" is a solemn hymn that contrasts to the generally upbeat mood of the soundtrack. The solemn hymn, while marking the death of a loyal soldier, also defines an important point of recognition on the part of the protagonist, although the name given to the character also appears as Barbatus and General Formica in versions of the screenplay. The termite battle scene presents Z as a fumbling misfit whose every statement punctuates the battle between ants and termites with biting wit that undermines human actions in the real world of war and global conflict. The black character that saves the protagonist's life and that of the other characters is a recurring trope in film. The irony of this sequence is that the brave hero in Barbados is suddenly transformed into a regretful, unfulfilled sage who warns viewers about the dangers of being typecast. The typecasting of Glover and his association to the nomenclature of a black Caribbean state opens up an interesting moment for debate about the place of insignificant people and states that undertake an audacious march into the arena of global domination. The montage shot of live ants marching across a bridge while they are getting stepped on is an apt depiction of the insignificance of micro-states in the world of global confrontation. Of significance also is the fact that all this action is meant to be taking place in the cosmopolitan city of New York, in its Central Park, this city that has been a real site of migration for many Caribbean workers.[17]

In the Guillermo del Toro-directed *Blade 2*, which set new standards for sustained adrenalin-driven special effects, there is substantial interlacing of real actors and their CGI counterparts. The seamless interplay is hardly recognizable in some sequences. The inconspicuous nature of this technological feat reflects the extent to which technology can fool the viewer. This visual wizardry is but part of the industry's deceptive pleasures. Its deceptive practices are in some cases, at face value, meant to dazzle audiences, gaining attention, increasing sales, and upping the standards of production. But these practices in another sense can also serve to promote the ambitions of a group or set of groups while wearing the guise of entertainment.

Because computer generated technology is able to measure the real, it also threatens to go one step better. Already it has replaced and set new standards for "the real," especially in its fashioning of futuristic films. My critique of the Caribbean setting for Godzilla is therefore a more complex issue than first appears. Not only should I interrogate the kind of representation given of Caribbean place, but I also have to consider the objective of approximating "the real" through simulation technology. An assessment of the Caribbean shot is therefore also an examination of how leading-edge technology samples the real while also recasting it as film, as text, as "the real."

The script to *Godzilla* by Dean Devlin and Roland Emmerich demands a camera cut to a "bumpy Jamaican highway."[18] On the screen, this highway is no more than a dust-covered track in the outback to nowhere. The script refers to three of the protagonists in a jeep. In the filmed sequence, there is a fourth, supposedly a local military chauffeur, who comes across more like a commandeered civilian security guard. He bumps around in the foreground while the other three main actors play out their dialog oblivious of his presence. But he is also incapable of communicating, because he is too busy bobbing around like a buffoon. The fourth character, the native, is therefore inserted as a necessity for the mobility of the real characters. He is there to drive the motor vehicle. Not to utter a word. The real characters must be given full freedom to verbalize.

The suppression of the minority is a recurring trope in countless other films. But there is nothing more unsettling than the execution of this feat at the level of production and action. The movie *The Perfect Storm* was aired in the middle of 2000. It was preceded by the usual hype given to major blockbuster films. It starred the former ER star George Clooney. He had come off a series of big-screen flicks. Prior to this film, he starred in an David O'Russell's ironic reading of the first Gulf War. *The Perfect Storm* begins with the caution: "This film is based on a true story." This is always a paradoxical sign, because it at once suggests that the events are real-life events, but that an interpretation is being given to these real-life events. It is ironic therefore that the relatives of the character TY, whom Clooney portrays, accused the producers and director of misrepresenting their relative in the film. He had been portrayed as a callous, death-defying maverick who continually placed the lives of his men in danger. There were threats of lawsuits against the producers. They had taken the privilege of poetic license too far, and in the process done harm to the name and reputation of an individual, the family felt.

The prerelease hype did not convey much about the individual members of the crew. But there was a black man among them. It is a crew of fishermen who would undertake this rite of passage with their captain. Their symbolic journey, of course, echoes that in *Moby Dick* and certainly that of Wilson Harris' *Palace of the Peacock*. The black man, though a part of the approximately six-man crew, is noticeably silent within the screenplay. When the men first turn up to sign on for the trip, other characters are open to the camera's focus. They are given words. The black character stands out of focus somewhere in the camera's blurred background. When he approaches to be interviewed, the camera turns away, and when we see him again, the camera shoots him from the back walking away. We are to assume that he has spoken and has been chosen to be a part of the crew. When next we see the men together, they are in a bar with drinks and some women moving around between clients and patrons. The black man is seen going upstairs with a woman under his hugging arm. We are to interpret that he has taken her to bed as a prelude to confronting the virility of nature itself. Finally, he is given words just before they leave land; he is singing a work song while on deck, and the camera swoops with a wide angle past him in search of the captain. Later on, he shouts while working to throw the buoys out. Still later on in the film, when the members of the crew speak in private, away from the captain and they question the captain's character and strength, it is the black man who comes to the captain's defense. Of course, he knows the captain better than all the rest, and so he loyally reminds them (as Chewbacca might say of Han Solo in *Star Wars*, if we could understand him): "Skippa don't get scared. He just disappointed."

Again, at another pivotal moment for the crew, when they must decide whether to turn back or go on to the Flemish Cap, the mood is to turn back. But the black man supports his leader; he feels they should continue. And so the captain tells his man to let the others know why they should go to the Cap. The black man begins to say, "Because . . . " But his words are taken away again, stolen by the camera and through the screenplay. The captain sounds the revelation: "Because that is where the fish are." Of course, this is obvious, given the focus of the crew's discussion. But the captain's right to control and seize the discourse at will reflects the deeper relational politics that grants near directorial rights to major white characters while depriving their support cast, in this case one who is noticeably black. The other significant point to be made about this black character is that his accent is different from that of the other characters. Hence his difference is established. While the others use the first person personal pronoun "I," he prefers to use "me." When the men plot what they will do with their money from the trip, one of them plans to buy a new car and take a trip with his girl. The black character has less lavish plans. His are simple and basic. His notion of self-gratification is founded on this principle: "Me wannah get drunk wid it, brother, eat like a pig, and sleep like a child. Fish and Fungi!!" he exclaims excitedly.[19]

While there has been a publicizing of the film's miscarriages, little to no mention, as far as I know, has been made of its subtle and not-so-subtle transgressions. After the film's showing, the wave of reviews ignored the film's most indictable offense. The portrayal of this African West Indian man was overshadowed by other controversies. The central issue of minority representation was washed out by a perfect storm.

The Caribbean as disaster zone is produced in the 2004 movie *The Day after Tomorrow*. This movie, written by Roland Emmerich, also makes passing reference to the Caribbean. In the movie, the rapid change in global climate is captured through on-screen and off-screen reference. A televised bulletin is heard in the background to say that a number of "hurricanes are affecting the Caribbean" region. Because the region is situated to the southeast and south of the United States and within path of some weather systems that approach the mainland, the short reference wants to take care of that meteorological reality. But the rest of the movie dispenses with the effects of the end-time catastrophe on other cultures to focus on its impact on the perceived center of human activity. This is the United States. It is ironic that the same week as the film's release, there were catastrophic floods in the northeastern Caribbean. Haiti was hardest hit. This event was relayed in the popular press around May 31, 2004, as in a Kelly Cobiella CBS video clip seen on the Internet called *Desperate Flood Relief*.[20]

When one goes to the CBS site, General Motors' summer drive promotion pops up before the video stream. It is a commercial for a range of classy vehicles. All this takes place before you recognize an on-screen option for skipping the commercial. In the Kelly Cobiella report, virtual real-life images of the devastation are captured. One sees the level of destruction a true natural disaster can inflict on real human beings. In a strange, surrealistic way, this flood appeared to be the untold story cleverly glossed over in the disaster blockbuster *Tomorrow*. The Web video, professionally produced, scripted, edited and platformed, transmitted the horrendous ramifications of natural, social, and political disaster. Missing from the CBS video stream was the buildup of character that can give a story depth and locate it in the realm of all human experience. The victims, the Haitian subjects, do not speak in the video clip. The only other voice heard apart from Cobiella's is that of another reporter, who reports on the phone about stories told to her by actual victims of the flood. Apart from this, there are no local speaking voices. The camera provides shots of a flooded landscape, destroyed houses, dead victims, rescue operations, and relief efforts at home in the United States. The Haitian subjects are helpless victims of the flood; they are also visual objects of the camera's montage. They therefore perform a series of actions, including draining water from their homes and sitting and staring blankly, and they search for dead or missing relatives while weeping uncontrollably. The report therefore has the effect of detaching itself from the personal experience and pain of the average victim. In this way, the viewer does not connect to the Haitian experience with a sense of intimate empathy. There is rather a sense of detached sympathy. In the movie, however, the Dennis Quaid character, climatologist Jack Hall, battles the elements to save his son, who is holed up in the New York Public Library. The movie attempts to elevate the story from mere catastrophic spectacle into a tale of human wrong, retribution, hope, salvation, and courage. It does so primarily through its characterization. The Haiti streaming video clip does not weave these human notions into production. There is therefore something of spectacle about the Web video. Not that it sets out to be cruel to the already unfortunate victims, but its treatment goes for video montage, overview, descriptive language, and third person reportage. This is not peculiar to a single network, because other major Western networks have also perfected this filmic method.

There are necessarily incoherencies that arise when you talk about big-budget movies and news clips within the same discussion. These movies tend to be fictitious, having their own conventions, while news reports are done with another set of imperatives in view. This is somewhat true.

But increasingly, there are many points of convergence between these traditionally different conventions. As the chapter on video games began, there is a thinning line between news and entertainment. Entertainment media and news media are increasingly sharing the same space in terms of technological use. It is significant that entertainment divisions and subdivisions also partner many news networks. Movie studios and news studios are often indistinguishable. Given the interconnectivity of technologies, where soft and hardware platforms are used quite widely across corporations, it seems inevitable that different users will come under the influence of the technology, whose functionality often tends to help shape the end product outcome. Given the culture of shared technology use, the world, apart from expressing divergent opinions, is also becoming increasingly streamlined. The proximity of technology makes it even more plausible to perceive *The Day After Tomorrow* and the CBS story "Desperate Flood Relief" as related, as reflections of Western entertainment and mass media culture. Because technological tools are at the heart of the systems by which we experience, process, and disseminate information, truths, realities, and ambitions, we increasingly have got to struggle to separate the range of media and genre experiences that bombard our societies.

Leisure, Fantasy: "Change of Plans. Let's Go to Barbados"

But Caribbean referencing is not only restricted to films that want to gesture to the Caribbean as specific location and culture. Indeed, by the early twenty-first century, references to the Caribbean were even more entrenched and cast in symbology. In Western film language, there are specific real and imagined attitudes, experiences that are the stuff of the Caribbean. The Caribbean is clearly a symbol of the ultimate tourist leisure haven for shipwreck, exile, retreat, sex, decadence, and exoticism. The extent to which these states have become entrenched features of the Caribbean is well depicted in very recent big-budget films.

50 First Dates, starring Adam Sandler and Drew Barrymore, was set in Hawaii. But the music used to create the tropics was predominantly the musical references of the Caribbean. This is acknowledgement of the way in which iconography, musicscape, and cultural reference have crystallized through Hollywood and popular culture. Because of the system of meaning that has evolved to stand in for the Caribbean in film language, viewers are often being asked to substitute the system of meaning every time a Caribbean reference (for example, a soca or reggae song) is produced in film. In the Martin Lawrence–starred *Black Knight*, reggae strains drive the early part of the soundtrack. This is a complex foreshadowing of his eventual transportation to a mythical paradise, where he will become a hero, as he stands outside the real everyday world of experience. In *Shattered Image*, the Anne Parillaud lead character is a schizophrenic avenger of men; in another life she is the new wife traveling to the Caribbean with her husband. In the Forrest Whitaker-starred *Ghost Dog*, the lead character's philosophical predilection and his race endear him to experimental strains originating from somewhere off the radar, the Caribbean.

Unlike the movie *Godzilla*, which concocted Caribbean place through a montage of computer-generated images and dreadlocked, blank-faced natives, there were other movies that gestured to the region through sound and song. The 2005 *In Her Shoes* comes to mind, and certainly the much more popular *50 First Dates*. *In Her Shoes* inserts a flurry of reggae songs at the ending, for feel-good effect, while the Jewish wedding ceremony is played out. But the Caribbean songs protrude like an afterthought. There is no sign that the characters have an inkling of awareness of events beyond their closed world. *50 First Dates*'s soundtrack made generous use of Bob Marley and Caribbean reggae and for more obvious reasons. Of course the use of Marley love songs was in keeping with the movie's love theme. But their use also played on the awareness of Marley's sexual appetite, in order to dramatize the movie's concern with sexual promiscuity at the end of the road. The playing of island music also seems to be used strategically (and too evidently) to suggest tropical life. In the film, the Caribbean musical reference therefore serves as a stock motif to suggest a range of other tropically rooted tendencies, like uncontrolled passion. The reference also conjures up earlier films located in the region, such as the 1957 *Island in the Sun*.

Caribbean reference has therefore served as a sign to viewers, who affix a set of meanings to a mere on-screen reference. Many films have therefore made passing reference, while going on to deal with more substantive matters. In *13 Going on 30*, the Jennifer Garner character plays a game on her thirteenth birthday and wakes up as a thirty-year-old. She no longer lives with her parents. She scrambles and calls their number, only to get the answering machine, which tells her that they are in the Caribbean. She winces something to the effect of "How could they go there without me?" In her moment of total loss she chooses their shipwreck over her own. In the Ben Stiller-starred comedy *Along Came Polly*, the character played by Alec Baldwin says he is going to Barbados with his mistress and wants the whole mess in the company cleared up by the time he returns. Implicit in this reference is the suggestion that the region is a place of planned escape and shipwreck. Cameras do not have to go there. Yet viewers are able to supplement meaning, even if the meaning they insert is inspired by that same entertainment industry. All the references to the region are not alike. They do not all necessarily produce a straight-up response. Indeed, an overall assessment of these references might very well show some various meanings and have several implications. A dominant attitude evoked by some references is that of derision. Satire often accompanies reference to the Caribbean in Hollywood and large, independent productions. For instance, in the movie *Soul Plane* (dubbed a *Barbershop* clone), political, social, and cultural satire rule. The Caribbean is not spared ridicule. When the airplane is about to crash and the crew scrambles to make contact with the tower by radio, it is difficult to raise a response, so the plane's owner takes to the radio and recites the words, "Booyaka, booyaka, wheel and come again." These are familiar dancehall shout-outs and hollas. Their use here is out of context with the action in the plot. This serves to highlight the desperation of the crew. It also shows up the ignorance of people, even black Americans, about the significance of other black cultures. The treatment of dancehall slang as "baby talk" therefore brings an indictment against African American and black culture as a whole. The movie's satire highlights the distance between black American and other black cultures. Implicit in the shout-out is the suggestion that dancehall subjects are limited in linguistic performance.

Harrison Ford, near the beginning of the action packed movie *Air Force One*, makes an ironic comment to the ship's pilot: "Change of plans. Let's go to Barbados." The reference to the Caribbean here is without full effect and meaning unless one understands the oppositional symbolism of Ford and of the Caribbean reference. In the first place, Ford had set the standard for action film throughout the 1980s and early 1990s. Films like his *Indiana Jones* trilogy set the benchmark for action in big-budget films. His later *The Fugitive* along with Tommy Lee Jones took the adrenalin meter to new sustained levels in Hollywood action flicks. Other stars like Sylvester Stallone and Arnold Schwarzenegger often played the role of pumped-up, larger-than-human personas. Stallone was the heavily decorated war vet in *First Blood* and *Cobra*. Schwarzenegger was part machine, part human in *The Terminator*. But Ford's leading characters tended to be the average man in terms of physical build and strength. He was man under pressure. His characters therefore tended to rely on guile, thrift, and determination. There is also an underlying streak of satire and irony that has been worked through a number of scenarios featuring his character. In *The Temple of Doom*, therefore, when confronted by a martial arts swordsman who parades his skill before the camera and Ford for about ten seconds of spectacle, Ford does not play by those rules of engagement (as other heroes might have), but rather pulls a gun to dispatch his foe.

By the time of *Air Force One*, therefore, audiences and Hollywood had internalized the Ford iconography. They knew not to take his demeanor lightly; they were well aware of his ironic disposition. His every action was a reference to its very opposite. When, therefore, in the early sequences of *Air Force One*, Ford enters his private jumbo jet and says to his pilot, "Change of plans," it is said in an ironic tone on film. But it is also a larger ironic pronouncement on the distance between high-energy world of political confrontation and global engagement and the obscure dream paradise at the periphery of peril and political meaning. Barbados is a marker of difference. The Barbados reference is therefore a promise that what is to come in the film exists outside the tranquility of paradise. But read another way, the Barbados reference also suggests that exotic paradises are just that. They hardly have an impact of significance outside of the stereotype. Any suggestion of their active role in high-powered games can only be treated as ironic statement, as jest. They do not figure as participants in the global domain of power and in the arenas that stage human qualities such as bravery, courage, or grace under pressure.

Caribbean on the Networks. Caribbean on Digitized Satellite Maps

The major powers of the twenty-first century, apart from their military fleet and nuclear might, also harness a great deal of power from their control of information and communication networks—such networks as produce and project culture. In fact, the outward show of military might really masks the more dangerous and insidious processes that control people indirectly.

American satellite television and other communication initiatives support a regime of control by larger countries over smaller nations. Although there are a few regionally placed people in the industry, like Tanya York, president of York Entertainment (founded in 1990), a leading independent financier, producer, and distributor of testosterone-driven urban films, the region has resigned itself to impotence. The beaming of Western culture to the region is but part of the entire process of cultural subordination. It is not often considered how Caribbean culture is affected by the constant flow of information from without. It is even less considered how Caribbean culture is taken up by similar interests, shaped, and then disseminated worldwide and back to the Caribbean to complete the cycle of perpetual manipulation.

A clear example (although I suspect it would not be considered a major happening) is a December 1999 televised performance on TNT's *Hard Rock Live* featuring Third Eye Blind. In their performance of the alternative chart-topper "Semi Charmed Life," the rockers gave the song a blatant Caribbeanized treatment. This was met with raucous response from the audience. In the performance, the lead vocalist chanted in the style of dancehall. But the dominant musical reference was to soca. The bassist played a soca bass, and the drum pattern and the guitar strum were all soca in style. The performers performed this segment of the song with playful delight. Their attitude was one of almost mocking gestures. It is these kinds of moments that often go unnoticed, especially by Caribbean interests. But it is clear that these moments are marked and inscribed deliberately. In the Third Eye Blind performance, the live audience reacted to the variation in rhythm. It was their reaction at the moment of difference that opens up the performance to further scrutiny.

At the 2000 U.S. Grammy Awards, Roseanne, the host, in Oscar tradition, took a jab at many artists. She brought up the subject of strange accents. She proceeded to accuse Tina Turner and others as having started the trend of importing and assuming new accents. She mentioned Tina's accent when receiving recent acclaim at the World Music Awards, alluding to Tina's new British West Indian accent. She feigned an American Britishized West Indian register and said, "Firstufall Iwant totank theacademy." This was greeted with uproarious laughter.

E! the Entertainment Channel makes regular trips to the Caribbean and other destinations in search of hot entertainment. Spring break segments have regularly featured Caribbean destinations. The style of E! during its featured programs of this kind is to use its anchors to both pose questions to locals and to feign the antics of the people being visited. The Caribbean's exotic appeal has been featured quite often throughout the years. Sea, sand, and sex have gone together on that network. E! has sacrificed depth for quick pace and hyperbole. The fast-paced, offbeat presentation of the network has tended to skirt the surface of what the featured societies are really about. In the process, Caribbean and other destinations visited have continued to wear the stigma attached to them for years. But this is not a concern for E! After all, they are about entertainment and little else. They can therefore claim innocence in the face of charges of playing out stereotypes, industry desires, and senseless gratification. But networks like *E!* are especially powerful agents of "education," information, and misinformation.

Around mid-1997, St. Vincent and the Grenadines was the center of international media attention. In the trial of an American couple, James and Penny Fletcher, the American press cast doubts on the ability of the Caribbean nation to carry on a fair and just judicial inquiry and trial. The American president Bill Clinton was also caught in the act of seeming to undermine the credibility of the nation state to uphold justice when he urged the Vincentian Prime Minister to insure "due process" and hand down the right verdict. At the end of the eighteenth Caricom Heads of Government meeting, a press release was issued supporting the judicial system of the Eastern Caribbean and deploring any form of interference in the process of justice. Then-Prime Minister James Mitchell saw it necessary to make a U.S. tour in order to do damage control in light of the negative press received by the tourist destination. His appearance on CNN did little to rectify the situation. He is reported to have said afterwards, "If I were to die tonight, I would not make the CNN news . . . They are not interested in our opinion."[21] Almost a decade later, in 2005, the disappearance of an American teen, Natalee Holloway, in Aruba produced a replication of the St. Vincent version.

If large movie production houses and enterprises gave cursory, yet revealing, reference to Caribbean society, then large news agencies also reinforced the notion that the new formulation of world nationalities was inclusive of more people than before. But these corporations also revealed an inevitable truth about the biases, inequalities, and inherent inconsistency of new global doctrines. In the same way that more traditional representations of the countries of the world tended to position Europe and other Western nations at the center of the world, many large corporations with international reach also reflected this kind of semiotic arrangement in some of their productions. One representative example of this tendency is located at CNN's satellite image for Central America/Caribbean. The image is clearly skewed towards Central America, with very little focus given to the archipelago. Arguably such a focus might also be said to reflect on the term "Caribbean" itself, which for some users, especially in the United States of America, connotes images of larger land masses, and so parts of Latin American. The Caribbean archipelago is therefore for some people but a small part of the wider Caribbean space. Even with this perception in mind, it is unjustifiable that a satellite image that purports to cover the Caribbean should center the states of central and southern United States and Mexico, and central America, while almost placing the nations of the archipelago off the very map that is set up to locate them.[22] This experience, however, does not represent the only site source for information on the Caribbean and its weather. Because new technologies are defined by some degree of divergent perspective, it is possible to locate other images of the entire Caribbean region and with better focus than that given by the CNN page. Many news corporations provide truer images, as does Yahoo.[23] Others even give individual maps and forecasts for individual islands. But the fact of skewed representation, even in the apolitical arena of weather forecasting, reveals the all-pervasive reach of the culture wars paradigm.

Caribbean Film and "Filming" Caribbean Popular Culture

By 1914, countries like France, Australia, Russia, the United States, the United Kingdom, India, Argentina, and Brazil, among others, had produced feature films. In the wider Caribbean context, Cuba had produced its first filmed production, *El Brujo Desapareciendo*, directed by Romulo Bertoni, in 1898; their first dramatized film, *El Cabildo de na Romualda*, by 1908; and their first feature film by 1913, *El Rey de Los Campos de Cuba*, directed by Enrique Diaz Quesada. Their first talkie came in 1930, *El Caballero de Max*, directed by Jaime San-Andrews and starring Nancy Norton and Wilfredo Genier.

Other nations of the Anglophone Caribbean ventured into these areas some time later. Guyana's first feature film came in 1975, *Aggro Seizeman*, directed by James Mannas and Brian Stuart-Young, starring Gordon Case and Martha Gonsalves. Trinidad's first dramatized film was produced in 1937, *Callaloo*, starring Ursula Johnson. Their first talkie/feature film was the 1970, *The Right and Wrong*, directed by Harbrace Kumar and starring Ralph MarMaharaj and Jesse McDonald. Jamaica's first feature/talkie was the popular *The Harder They Come*, directed by Perry Henzell and starring Jimmy Cliff and Janet Bartley. Its gangster theme borrowed from mainstream Western films. Its success spawned a number of other productions like *Third World Cop*. *Third World Cop* presents the events experienced by a young, tough Jamaican detective who is restationed in his old hometown. When he returns there, he reestablishes contacts with old hometown yardies. But he soon realizes that things are not the same as they used to be. His close friend is now linked up with the new town drug dealer and Kingston mobster. This is therefore a re-creation of the familiar plot about the tough cop who must battle crime and corruption. But the movie also wants to dramatize the inner turmoil that he confronts, torn between filial and legal and moral duty. The film *Dancehall Queen* is arguably one of the most popular Anglophone Caribbean films of the late 1990s. Its popularity in the Caribbean had to do not only with the marketing thrust that gave the impression that Jamaican cinema was making bold claims to achieving great recognition as its music had done, but also due to the word that was getting around concerning the film's submersion in the music and music culture that has attracted the attention of many people within and outside of the region. *Dancehall Queen* is, of course, the story of a Kingston mother who defies inhibitions and social censure to go on stage and take part in a Jamaican dancehall competition. The sub-plot also centers the troubles of the society relating particularly to crime and seduction and sexual abuse. A major drawing card for the film is, of course, the appearance of a number of actual DJs who play themselves in the film. The dancehall scenes are therefore some of the more gratifyingly centered episodes in the film. The method employed here of centering the dancehall bears some reference to the methods of filmic discourse that impacted and controlled images of Jamaica and the Caribbean when Dancehall music was making a significant impact in the early-to-mid 1990s. What salvages the film from degenerating into a glamorized conundrum of stereotypes is, of course, its employment of the national language and its use of dancehall culture to explore a number of challenges facing Caribbean society, including the injustices perpetrated on citizens by a repressive social order. *Dancehall Queen* has therefore attempted to go beyond the discourses of most videos of leading dancehall acts of the earlier period of the 1990s. Some will argue, and with merit, that the longer version of the feature film allows for all types of lateral explorations of characters and sub-plots. But there are also other ways of suggesting depth of character and society, even in the shorter video clip format.

But while Caribbean film was discoursing upon the mainstream gangsta tradition and using Caribbean popular culture as a foundation for establishing its film industry, there were other cinemas and producers who were discoursing upon Caribbean popular culture. The film *Ali G in the House: The Movie* can be considered just harmless fun. It can also be interpreted as a crude slapstick that parodies contemporary British culture. It has been read as a snubbing of the very foundations that uphold British authority and power in the modern world. In the movie, for example, Ali G is elected to the House of Commons. The film turns upon a series of absurdities. It is absurd that political bureaucrats, technocrats, and strategists would choose an ill equipped loser like Ali G. It is absurd that he would accept. It is absurd that he would win. It is poetic justice that he should play upon their personal desires and disrupt the conventions and procedures that define British political culture. But, read another way, Ali G's antics in parliament are no less absurd than those of real politicians.

Some critics might also read the film as a caricature of white British wannabe ragamuffins. Ali G's assuming of a black West Indian-British persona reflects a reality of British society, of cultural transformation and the export of Caribbean culture. The film is therefore an exploration of this complex process. On another level, it celebrates the pleasures and absurdities of cultural and identity politics. The film is, however, retrograde in its banal fascination with a fossilized set of stereotypes about the Caribbean and Jamaican and black British culture. It exploits and promotes many of the worse features of black roots and popular culture. When read against other regional films that treat popular culture, it appears to be a spoof of some of their serious themes. If there is a subsidiary message that this movie leaves with viewers, it is that black British culture and its Caribbean originary are base, crude, pretentious, and most of all primitively idiotic. Ali G therefore in the end of the movie heads the British mission to Jamaica, and his home is surrounded with countless shrubs and plants, all of the marijuana family. His sexual prowess and show is also undermined. All these suggest the fickle nature of the character himself and of the culture that his behavior approximates. *Ali G* the movie, though meant to be a social commentary on the foibles of social ordering, ultimately reinforces the age-old human belief that Caribbean and black culture are not far from the potential of animals that live in trees and procreate and depend on the favors of nature and luck and others to shape their futures.

Movie Industry, Internet, Video Stores, and Distribution

With the advances in new technology, these filmed productions were being made more widely available. They were available at video stores in several formats, as well as in other retail stores. Increasingly, these products were sold in dedicated virtual domains. They were advertised and promoted through Internet sites. The movie industry and the Internet worked hand in hand in some respects to further the vision of leading corporations and export their intentions across the world. Movies, like music videos, found an outlet via video stream and video on demand sites. But while some videos and movies were legally available online, others were illegally posted. The wider distribution networks afforded these films greater coverage and arguably increased currency, as audiences more and more gave in to the power of technology and tech-culture.

The impact of tech-culture on society was forcefully reflected through the ways in which Caribbean and other societies sheepishly followed the trends being forged through the profit-driven practices of the Western entertainment industry. So, apart from the Western entertainment industry misrepresenting and deploying Caribbean culture, Caribbean culture also circulated the myths perpetuated by the Western media about Western civilization and about the region itself. The gravest irony, though, was that the images of Caribbean society reexported to the region were in many instances imbibed by the region, so that some of the traits and aberrations projected about the Caribbean were actually accepted as accurate by segments of Caribbean society. Popular youth culture, for instance, preferred Hollywoodized versions of themselves to those versions being reasserted by more traditional agents, like their parents, the church, and the school. In many cases, youth culture seemed oblivious to the insidious lure of technology. Given the nearly seamless relationship between their real and virtual (technologized) lives, it was difficult for many to see that new virtual media technology represented a contemporary extension to their real experiences; it could be connected and disconnected. Instead, to many youths, the extension of experience was difficult to work through. They preferred therefore to treat their new environment as a homogenous space. In this regard, they were thinking into the future.

Enter the Machines

Whereas Caribbean governments were urging citizens to embrace new technologies, in many respects Caribbean youths were several stages ahead of most other segments of society in terms of tech savvy. Caribbean youths were already wired for the future. They were not only being connected through actual hardware and software gadgets, but they were (in many cases) psychologically connected. Their psychological connectivity had been wired throughout the decades by way of a careful, though innocent, set of communications transactions. But this rewiring of minds was also a political, economic, and cultural transaction that took place under the close, blind watch of major institutions within the region.

The age of the machines was ushered in.

Notes

Introduction

1. There are a number of texts that sought to give closer consideration to the contemporary dynamics of Caribbean society while also calling attention to its global interconnection: Hopeton Dunn, ed., *Globalization, Communications and Caribbean Identity* (London: Macmillan, 1995); Humphrey Regis, ed., *Culture and Mass Communications in the Caribbean* (Gainesville: University Press of Florida, 2001).
2. Throughout this book, the term *2000s* in the phrases "early 2000s," "mid-2000s," and "late 2000s" will refer to the first decade of the twenty-first century, analogous to "2010s" or "2020s," not to "1900s." While "mid-2000s" could reasonably refer to the years around 2050 and "late 2000s" to years after 2070, because this book is being published in 2007 and I refer to these time periods using past tense, the reader should not be confused.

Chapter 1

1. Robert J. Samuelson, "Debunking the Digital Divide," *Newsweek*, March 1, 2002, 25.
2. Ricardo Gomez, "The Internet Why and What For," *Fundación Acceso or Access Foundation*, February-March 2001, http://www.acceso.or.cr/PPPP/conectividad/index_en.shtml (accessed March 16, 2006).
3. Lester Henry, "Digital Divide, Economic Growth and Poverty Reduction," *Journal of Eastern Caribbean Studies* 29, no. 1 (March 2004): 1–22.
4. Alan Aycock, "Technologies of the Self: Foucault and Internet Discourse," *Journal of Computer-Mediated Communication* 1, no. 2 (1995), http://jcmc.indiana.edu/vol1/issue2/aycock.html (accessed March 16, 2006).
5. Aston Cooke, "Caribbean Cultural Identity on the Internet," *The House of YAD*, July 2002, http://www.dwightday.com/yardculture0702.html (accessed March 16, 2006).
6. Morris Rosenthal, "What Amazon Sales Ranks Mean," Foner Books, 2007, http://www.fonerbooks.com/surfing.htm (accessed April 20, 2007).

7. Danny Sullivan, ed. "How Search Engines Work," *Search Engine Watch*, October 2002, http://searchenginewatch.com/webmasters/article.php/2168031 (accessed March 16, 2006).

8. Online writing lab at Purdue University, "Evaluating Internet Sources," n.d., http://owl.english.purdue.edu/handouts/research/r_evalsource4.html. Also see the British Council's article on the "Rise of the Internet," *Electronic Magazine*, 17, 2001, http://www.britishcouncil.org/eteg/eemag/iss17/webrec.htm (both accessed March 16, 2006).

9. Caribbean Single Market and Economy.

Chapter 2

1. Louis James, ed., *The Islands in Between* (Oxford: Oxford University Press, 1968); Kenneth Ramchand, *The West Indian Novel and Its Background* (London: Faber and Faber, 1970).

2. Dr. Dirk Sinnewe, "The Derek Walcott Site," *Dirk's Home Page*, n.d., http://www.geocities.com/SoHo/Exhibit/6107/ (accessed April 20, 2006).

3. Any major search engine will provide reference sites for well-known writers, and even lesser-known writers.

4. At Northwest Passages's site, it is hard to ignore the presence of the Canadian maple leaf. "Austin Clarke, Book Profile," Fiction, n.d., http://www.nwpassages.com/profile_book.asp?ISBN=0771021305 (accessed April 25, 2007).

5. In April 2007, Caryl Phillips's site gave a full listing of his major readings for the year, ending on Nov. 3 at University of Dundee. "2007 Scheduled Appearances," http://carylphillips.com/content.php?page=readings&n=3&f=2 (accessed April 25, 2007).

6. Philip W. Scher, *Carnival and the Formation of a Caribbean Transnation* (Gainesville: University of Florida Press, 2003); Curdella Forbes, *From Nation to Diaspora: Samuel Selvon, George Lamming, and the Cultural Performance of Gender* (Kingston: UWI Press, 2005).

7. Colin Channer, "Question and Answer," *Passing Through*, Interviewer unknown, n.d., http://colinchanner.com/books/passing_through/index.html (accessed March 16, 2006).

8. British Broadcasting System.

9. Pin-chia Feng and Kate Liu, "Jean Rhys's *Wide Sargasso Sea*," *World Literature in English*, Fu Jen University, n.d., http://www.eng.fju.edu.tw/worldlit/caribbean/rhys.htm (accessed April 25, 2007).

10. Tiffany Cohill, "About Zee Edgell," *The Compendium of Electronic Resources*, English Scholar, n.d., http://englishscholar.com (accessed April 25, 2007).

11. See for instance, at TomFolio.com, "The Antilles. Fragments of Epic Memory," n.d.; the following link records a sample of the Nobel Speech,

but really offers a pathway to sale: http://www.tomfolio.com/ SearchAuthorTitle.asp?Aut=Derek_Walcott (accessed April 30, 2007).

12. This page, titled "Merle Collins," has links to "Gallery, News and Events, Contact . . . " modified April 25. http://:geocities.com/merlecollins (accessed April 25, 2007).

13. Merle Collins reading at University of Maryland, "Digital Dialogue," April 11, 2007, http://www.mith2.umd.edu/hughes/quicktime/mcollins .html (accessed April 25, 2007).

14. Research Channel, a consortium of research universities and corporate research divisions features Collins on video stream. "Merle Collins Talks about her Work" Feb. 2002, http://www.researchchannel.org (accessed March 16, 2006).

15. "Welcome to 57 Productions," "Artists, Events . . . Links," *57productions.com* (accessed April 25, 2007).

16. See Ingrid Kerhoff, "Dub Poetry," Bremen's site map *Dub Poetry*, April 2002, http://www.fb10.uni-bremen.de/anglistik/kerkhoff/DubPoetry/ index.html (accessed April 25, 2007).

17. Benjamin Zephaniah, "A Poet Called Benjamin Zephaniah," "words, Rhymin . . . Frienz," n.d., http://benjaminzephaniah.com (accessed April 25, 2007).

18. Mervyn Morris, "Biography," Mutabaruka, n.d., http://www .Mutabaruka.com (accessed April 25, 2007).

19. Adisasaf.com was spare in its material when accessed September 2005. By 2007, he had changed his name fully to Aja, and his Web site reflected a much richer presentation in terms of his poetry, music, and humanitarian work. "Aja Poet Musician Humanitarian," n.d., http://www .ajapoet.com (accessed April 25, 2007).

20. "About Brother Resistance," n.d., http://brotherresistance.com/biography .htm (accessed April 25, 2007).

21. 3canal.com could only be accessed with a user name and password back in 2004 (accessed January 15, 2004).

22. Macmillan Caribbean, "Welcome to Macmillan Caribbean," n.d., http://www.macmillan-caribbean.com/ (accessed April 25, 2007).

23. Jeremy Poynting, "The Best in Caribbean Writing," n.d., http://www .peepaltreepress.com (accessed April 25, 2007).

24. Faber and Faber, http://www.faber.co.uk/ (originally accessed March 12, 2005). It was still near impossible to identify their Caribbean affiliation on their Web site by April 25, 2007.

25. Taylor and Francis, "Annual Report," 2004, http://www.taylorand francisgroup.com/pdf/reports/TF_annual_03_FINAL.pdf (accessed April 25, 2007).

26. A reviewer's opinion concerning *The Post Colonial Studies Reader*. "Jargon-Ridden and Boring," 20th Century History Books, n.d., http://20th-century-history-books.com/0415096227.html?readReview= true#readReview (accessed April 25, 2007).

27. "Caribbean Integration Studies," Ian Randle Publishers, n.d., http://www.ianrandlepublishers.com/carint.html (accessed April 25, 2007).

28. University of the West Indies Press's "Caribbean Cultural Studies" is an area in which the University itself has invested substantial energies, http://www.uwipress.com/cgilocal/shop.pl/SID=1177549711.63910/page=culturalstudies.html (accessed April 25, 2007).

29. University of Miami, "Caribbean Writers Summer Institute Digital Archives," n.d., http://scholar.library.miami.edu/cls/speakersDisplay.php (accessed March 16, 2006).

30. See Skidmore College's, University Without Walls, "UWW Advantage," n.d., http://www.skidmore.edu/administration/uww/prospects/distance_ed_advantage.htm (accessed April 25, 2007).

31. Stanford University, "Copyright and Fair Use," Learning and Academic Information Resources Document, Chapter 9, n.d., http://fairuse.stanford.edu/Copyright_and_Fair_Use_Overview/chapter9/index.html (accessed April 25, 2007).

32. Coshe.com site offers access to "Essay and Term Paper Database," "Features," n.d., http://www.Coshe.com (accessed April 25, 2007).

33. See Arthur Kroker, *The Will to Technology and the Culture of Nihilism: Heidegger, Nietzsche and Marx* (Toronto: Univ. of Toronto Press, 2003). Seen at Digital Futures Series, n.d., http://www.ctheory.net/will/codes.html (accessed April 25, 2007).

34. Maurice A Lee, "Introduction," *Journal of Caribbean Literatures*, n.d., http://www.jcls.net/intro.html (accessed April 25, 2007).

35. See "Journal Details, *Latin American and Caribbean Ethnic Studies*," n.d., *Taylor & Francis*, http://www.tandf.co.uk/journals/boards/rlac-edbrd.asp (accessed April 25, 2007).

36. See *The Caribbean Writer*, updated March 28, 2007, http://www.the caribbeanwriter.org/about.html (accessed April 28, 2007).

37. Routledge's "Journal Details, *Postcolonial Studies*" *Taylor & Francis*, n.d., http://www.tandf.co.uk/journals/titles/13688790.asp (accessed April 25, 2007).

38. Deborah Wyrick and Jonathan Beasley, "Editors' Introduction," *Jouvert* 1, no.1 (1997), http://social.chass.ncsu.edu/jouvert/v1i1/int11.htm (accessed April 25, 2007).

39. University of Miami, See the editorial comments to the online free access journal *Anthurium* 1, no. 1 (Fall 2003), http://scholar.library.miami.edu/anthurium/volume_1/issue_1/editorsnote.htm (accessed April 25, 2007).

Chapter 3

1. See the chapter on gospel in Curwen Best, *Culture @ the Cutting Edge: Tracking Caribbean Popular Music* (Kingston: UWI Press, 2005), 54–90.

2. See "Company History," Integrity Music, n.d., http://www.integritymusic .com/company/company.php?target=history/body.html (accessed April 25, 2007).

3. See further, fuller discussion of the music video genre in the following chapters of this book.

4. From *Fastforward*, introduction to the airing of DC Talk, "My Friend (So Long)," *Supernatural*, dir. Tryan George, ForeFront/Virgin, 1998, videocassette.

5. Newsboys, "Everybody Gets a Shot," video, *Step up to the Microphone*, dir. Michael Ashcraft. Virgin/StarSong/Sparrow, 1999, videocassette.

6. See my discussion of this process in *Culture @ the Cutting Edge*, 165–66.

7. Simon Frith, Andrew Goodwin, and Lawrence Grossberg, ed., *Sound and Vision: The Music Video Reader* (London: Routledge, 1993), also bears this out with reference to secular music videos.

8. Kirk Franklin, "You are the Only One," *God's Property*, dir. Christopher Erskin, Gospocentric, 1997, videocassette.

9. Grace Thrillers, "Make Us One," *Make Us One* (Showers of Blessing, 2000), videocassette.

10. From the video "Make Us One."

11. Curwen Best, *Roots to Popular Culture* (London: Macmillan Education, 2001). See the final chapter, titled "Routes to Gospel and Popular Culture," in particular the pages 172–188.

12. Promise, "It's Not Raining," video. It was not commercially produced for distribution, but it did air on television stations throughout the region during the middle and late 1990s.

13. This video, "Love Letters," was also not commercially available but aired on television stations in the region during the middle and late 1990s.

14. Caribbean Gospel Network, caribbeangospel.com (accessed February 10, 2006).

15. Pope John Paul II, "Internet: A New Forum for Proclaiming the Gospel," Good News Web Designers Association, May 2002, http://gnwda.org/ tutorials/evangelize/Pope-May2002.htm (accessed April 25, 2007).

16. See the Web article by Thomas Wagner, "Church of England creates virtual parish. Applicants sought for position of 'Web pastor,'" March 2004, http://www.msnbc.msn.com/id/4458082/ (accessed February 10, 2006).

17. Box office figures *The Passion of the Christ* in selected Caribbean territories from Kenan Bresnan, "Around the World Round Up," March 19–21, 2004, http://www.boxofficemojo.com/intl/weekend/2004/12 .htm (accessed February 10, 2006).

18. This gross relates to the United States and was measured some twelve weeks after the release in October 1999. "*The Omega Code*," Box Office Mojo, January 2000, http://www.boxofficemojo.com/movies/?id= omegacode.htm (accessed February 10, 2006).

19. See Barry Bowen, "A History of Christian Films," Christian Headlines, n.d., http://www.christianheadlines.com/filmhistory.html (accessed February 15, 2006).

20. The Crosswalk staff "About us," n.d., Crosswalk, http://www.Crosswalk .com/aboutus.asp (accessed February 15, 2006).

21. See, for example, a list of their best sellers, which reflects the emphasis of the site. "Best sellers," April 2007, http://www.christianbook.com/ html/specialty/81468.html/476991500 (accessed April 25, 2007).

22. See the Caribbean Christian Publications company Web site, "Beaming the Light of God's word to Caribbean People," "About us, Publications and Resources, Partner with Us," April 2007, http://www.ccpcbf.org/ index.html (accessed April 25, 2007).

23. Caribbean Christian Publications, "Publications and Resources," n.d., http://www.caribbeanchristianpublications.org/index.php (accessed April 25, 2007).

24. In Caribbean national language usage, the term "true-true" means "real, authentic." See Richard Allsopp, *Dictionary of Caribbean English Usage* (Oxford: Oxford University Press, 1996), 568.

25. Nigel Best, "Bringing the Message of Prayer to the People of the World," n.d., http://www.Prayline.com (accessed August 1, 2005).

26. See information, for instance, on "Churches in Dominica," among others in the Eastern Caribbean, n.d., http://eastcarib.org/Churches.php? Island=Dominica&PID=23 (accessed April 25, 2007).

27. See this link via "Nazarene Missions International," n.d., http://www .nazarenemissions.org/education/gin/caribbean/ (accessed March 16, 2006).

28. New Testament Church of God "Caribbean" simply lists a mailing address for each Administrative Bishop in each island. New Testament Church of God, n.d., http://www.cogmd.org/mrc/wmno/wmo_menu .htm (accessed April 26, 2007).

29. See the *Holy Bible*, Numbers 13: 30: "And Caleb stilled the people before Moses, and said, Let us go up at once, and possess it; for we are *well able* to overcome it."

30. Donna Pierre, "Sean Daniel Reaps Gospelypso Success," Trinidad Guardian, http://www.guardian.co.tt/mambeta/index.php?option= content&ask=view&id=108&Itemid=288 (accessed February 9, 2006).

31. See list of additional artists. "Lion of Zion Artists," n.d., http://www .lionofzion.com/artists/all/list.html (accessed March 16, 2006).

32. See a short review of his life and music. "Joe Country," "Brooklyn country," n.d., http://www.brooklyncountry.com/performers/joe_country .htm (accessed March 16, 2006).

33. See one of the several well set out links, e.g., Neil Burke, "Biography," n.d. http://www.georgebanton.com/biography.html (accessed April 36, 2007).

34. See Gospocentric's uninspiring "Artist Page: Papa San," *Gospocentric*, n.d., http://gospocentric.com/artist.php?artistID=11&pop=vid (accessed March 16, 2006). By April 2007 Papa San seemed to see the wisdom of doing better justice to his calling by placing a link to his own Web site, "Welcome to Papa San Online," n.d., http://www.papasanministries .com/ (accessed April 26, 2007).

Chapter 4

1. Caribbean Broadcasting Corporation (CBC), *Annual Report* (St Michael: GIS, 1993).

2. Lynette Lashley, "Television and the Americanization of the Trinbagonian Youth: A Study of Six Secondary Schools," in *Globalization, Communications and Cultural Identity*, ed. H. S. Dunn (Kingston: Ian Randle, 1995).

3. "The Blair Witch Project," Answers.com, http://www.answers.com/topic/ the-blair-witch-project (accessed April 28, 2007).

4. Embert Charles, "Low Level of Support for Regional Initiatives May Lie Behind CMC's Closure," Government of St. Lucia, January 2002, http://www.stlucia.gov.lc/pr2002/low_level_of_support_for_regional_ initiatives_may_lie_behind_cmc's_closure.htm (accessed March 16, 2006).

5. David Gauntlett et al, ed., Introduction to *Web.Studies*, 2nd ed. (London: Edward Arnold, 2004). Also see Michael Goldhaber's talk on the "Attention economy," *First Monday*, April 1997, http://www.first monday.org/issues/issue2_4/goldhaber/ (accessed March 16, 2006).

6. Unity Marketing, "Why People Buy Entertainment and Recreation," *Research and Markets*, December 2003, http://www.researchandmarkets .com/reports/42740/ (accessed March 16, 2006).

7. For an overview of some challenges faced by Caribbean designers who hope to break into the International scene, see Tanya Jensen, "First Annual Caribbean Fashion Week: Fashion Goes South," November 2001, http://www.fashionwindows.com/fashion_review/carribean/ default .asp (accessed April 26, 2007).

8. Information on MTV is now widely published. MTV's history is widely known. But see a text like Alan Light, ed., *Vibe History of Hip Hop* (New York: Three Rivers Press, 1999).

9. See the even more trendy MySpace site, where he promotes, for instance, his CD *Global*, n.d., http://www.myspace.com/bunjigarlin (accessed April 26, 2007). Original site http://www.Bunjigarlin.com (accessed March 16, 2006).

10. See a range of artists bundled on the site Queenofsoca.com (accessed March 16, 2006).
11. In 2007 the site was still up, though it did not list any of his coming appearances. Its news items all related to 2006 gigs. "News, Rupee's Coming to You," September 2006, http://thisisrupee.com/site/main.htm (accessed April 26, 2007).
12. David Jeffreys, "Elephant Man," *All Music Guide*, n.d., http://www.vh1.com/artists/az/elephant_man/bio.jhtml (accessed April 26, 2007).
13. Elephant Man, "Elephant Man Interview," Rudegal.com, 2003, http://www.rudegal.com/interviews/int.elephantman03.htm (accessed April 26, 2007).
14. See, for instance, Tom McCourt and Nabeel Zuberi, "Music on Television," *Museum of Broadcast Communication*, April 2, 2005, http://www.museum.tv/archives/etv/M/htmlM/musicontele/musicontele.htm (accessed March 16, 2006). Also see Tom McGrath, *Video Killed the Radio Star: How MTV Rocked the World* (New York: Random House, 1996).
15. See Track One of *Culture @ the Cutting Edge*, titled "Reading Culture as Multi-Tracked," 1–9.
16. Paul Eng, "Wi-Fi Companies Help—and Hurt—Efforts to Build Metro Networks," *ABC News*, August 22, 2005, http://abcnews.go.com/Technology/story?id=1048622&page=1 (accessed March 16, 2006).
17. Chamanade Information Systems, "Streaming Video Primer," January 2005, http://www.chaminade.org/MIS/Articles/StreamingVideo.htm (accessed March 16, 2006).
18. Regarding Web construction and costing, see http://www.seeitfirst.com (accessed March 16, 2006). Or see "Streaming Video Hosting Costs," CyberTech Media Group, n.d., http://www.cybertechmedia.com/charges.html (accessed April 29, 2007).
19. David Kleiler Jr, and Robert Moses, *You Stand There: Making Music Video* (New York: Three Rivers Press, 1997).
20. See, for example, Steve Waksman, *Instruments of Desire: The Electric Guitar and the Shaping of Musical Experience* (Massachusetts: Harvard University Press, 2000).
21. Xtatik, "Media," http://www.xtatik.com/xtatik_media.htm (accessed March 16, 2006).
22. Accessed March 16, 2006. In 2007 the link redirected you to a newer high definition site still devoted to Machel Montano, http://www.machelmontanohd.com/ (accessed April 26, 2007).
23. See the ambitions of this site: http://www.realvibez.net (accessed April 29, 2007).
24. See these two leading sites http://www.carnivalpower.com and http://www.calypsoarchives.co.uk (accessed April 29, 2006).
25. See "Kingdom of soca," http://www.kos.com (accessed April 28, 2007).

26. Browse for Caribbean artists on the multiple-artists sites like http://www.artistsonly.com (accessed April 29, 2007).

27. See the real Morgan Heritage Web site, http://www.morganheritage music.com (accessed April 27, 2007).

28. See http://music.realbuy.ws/B00004UAJ7.html (accessed March 16, 2006).

29. See http://www.afiwi.com (accessed April 29, 2007).

30. In Umberto Eco, *Travels in Hyperreality* (Florida: Harcourt Brace, 1986).

31. By 2007 Capleton was no longer featured on VP Record's site, but he breathed fire under his own steam at http://www.capletonmusic.com (accessed April 29, 2007).

32. The site Davidkirton.com (accessed September 3, 2005). But by 2007 his 2006 album is listed on the site, which has been given new life, and you are warned at "Tour Dates" to watch out for David Kirton in 2007 http://davidkirton.com/tourdates.html (accesssed April 28, 2007).

33. The site Arawakindian.com was up and down at various points subsequent to March 2006 (accessed March 16, 2006).

34. The link to http://www.belgrafix.com/entertainment/joecountry/ ajamu/ajamu.htm has been quirky over the years, but also see the range of artists and media at "Culture and Entertainment," http://www. belgrafix.com/culture/Made-in-Grenada-30/made%20in%20Grenada %2030th%20anniversary.htm (accessed April 28, 2007).

35. The site Apachewaria.com has also been up and down over the years, but some of his performances moved to the now more trendy YouTube, http://youtube.com/watch?v=Dv-6L5kaZkk (accessed April 28, 2007).

36. See the roster of artists from all over the world at http://www.IUMA.com (accessed April 29, 2007).

37. Welcome to the Official Gregory's Dream website," http://members. fortunecity.com/gregorysdreamonline/id46.htm (accessed April 27, 2007).

38. Paul du Gay et al, *Doing Cultural Studies: The Story of the Sony Walkman* (London: Sage, 1997).

39. John Urry, "Mobile Cultures," Dept. of Sociology, Lancaster Univ. December 6, 2003, http://www.comp.lancs.ac.uk/sociology/papers/ urry-mobile-cultures.pdf (accessed March 16, 2006).

40. For further information on Cable and Wireless in the Caribbean, see Bill Maurer, "Islands in the Net," *Comparative Studies in Society and History* 43, no.3 (July 2001): 467–501.

41. Helen Fallon, *WOW—Women on the Web: A Guide to Gender-Related Resources on the Internet* (New York: Women Ink, 1997), 10.

Chapter 5

1. In 2006, this link provided valuable information on world cricket. The base site was still operational in 2007, but the specific link could not

always be accessed. http://www.indiantelevision.com/headlines/y2k3/
july/july14.htm. (accessed March 16, 2006).

2. See Chris Dehring's comments in "West Indies Cricket," *Barbados Advocate* December 17, 1999, 32.

3. Ellis Cashmore, *Sports Culture* (London: Routledge, 2000). 199.

4. WindiesCricket.com still holds the same basic structure that defined it when it was originally launched (accessed April 29, 2006).

5. See further specifics on player salaries at "Team and League History," *Birmingham Thunderbolts*, May 2000, http://www.birminghamprosports .com/birminghamthunderboltshistory.htm (accessed March 16, 2006). Also see http://www.XFLboard.com for other links to articles and press releases about the league.

6. For this and other comments on the XFL's production aesthetics, see "Jump the Shark," http://www.jumptheshark.com/x/xfl.htm (accessed March 16, 2006).

7. A commentary at the Hole City Web site. "Lights! Camera! Smashmouth!" February 5–11, 2001, http://www.holecity.com/asp/tvhole.asp?issue= 76&sec=2&hole=2accuses (accessed March 16, 2006).

8. Sky Sports, "Another First for SKY Sports Cricket," press release, April 19, 2001, http://nocache.corporateir.net/ireye/ir_site.zhtml?ticker=BSY .UK&script=411&layout=0&item_id=167844 (accessed March 16, 2006).

9. Tony Cozier, "Umpires getting it wrong," *Nation* (Barbados), December 19, 1999.

10. "CBU's Release Re: Cancellation of Regional Cricket Broadcasts due to 'Financial Difficulty,'" *Nation* (Barbados), December 16, 1999, 6.

11. See "Survey of Popular Sports in the Caribbean," *Advocate* (Barbados), December 17, 1999, 6.

12. See David Morley, *Family Television: Cultural Power and Domestic Leisure* (London: Comedia, 1987).

13. Jack Steehler, "Sports on the Internet," Sports *Technology and the AthletesSports*, n.d., http://www.roanoke.edu/Chemistry/JSteehler/ HNRS301/Sports/(accessed September 15, 2006). Steehler is a professor at Roanoke College. Also see the site for a listing of Web presence of major Western sports franchises.

14. "Internet Gambling Booms in Caribbean," *Associated Press*, December 17, 1997, http://www.cnn.com/TECH/9712/17/internet.gambling/ (accessed March 16, 2006).

15. Caribbean teams can be accessed through the Internet. For Trinidad and Tobago's "Soca Boyz," see http://www.socawarriors.net/; for Jamaica's "Reggae Boyz," see http://www.thereggaeboyz.com/ (both accessed April 28, 2007).

16. See Gordon Rohlehr, "Music, Literature, and West Indian Cricket Values." *In an Area of Conquest: Popular Democracy and West Indies*

Cricket Supremacy, ed. Hilary McD. Beckles (Kingston, Jamaica: Ian Randle, 1994), 55–102.

17. Icc-cricket.com is a hub of information about what is taking place in international cricket, but the site is more concerned with giving information about ICC matters.

18. See the International Cricket Council's (ICC) first three issues of their online newsletter called "ICC Cricket Quarterly Newsletter," n.d., http://www.icc-cricket.com/print/news/quarterly.html (accessed March 16, 2006).

19. See the centrally located cricket site http://www.cricinfo.com and its array of services, including the offering of live video feed from the 2007 World Cup via Willow TV; http://content-usa.cricinfo.com/wc2007/engine/current/match/247506.html (accessed April 28, 2007).

20. The site itself continues to be uninspiring, but its promise is much more captivating; http://www.setanta.tv/faq.asp (accessed March 16, 2006).

21. K. R. Nayar, "Indian Cricket Board to launch Official Website," *Gulf News*, April 21 2004, http://www.gulfnews.com/Articles/Sport2.asp?ArticleID=118681 (accessed March 16, 2006).

22. B. V. Swagath, "Brian Lara:The Prince of Cricket," May 2004, http://banglacricket.com/alochona/viewthread.php?tid=5483 (accessed March 16, 2006).

23. See "ECB Mistreatment of Windies," CaribbeanCricket.com, June 24 2004, http://www.caribbeancricket.com/modules.php?name=News& file=article &sid=1441 (accessed March 16, 2006).

24. Brian Lara's comments, "Lara Deflects Sir Viv Issue Ahead of Nat West Assignment," *CMC*, June 25, 2004, http://www.windiescricket.com/article.asp?id=210687&Title=LARA+DEFLECTS+SIR+VIV+ISSUE+AHEAD+OF+NAT+WEST+ASSIGNMENT+%281st+ODI+Preview%29 (accessed March 16, 2006).

25. See Amit Phansalkar, "Technology in Cricket—More or Less?" March 9, 2004, http://www.buzzle.com/editorials/3-9-2004-51460.asp (accessed March 16, 2006).

26. This segment, as most others, was written before the actual tournament of the ICC Cricket World Cup in the Caribbean.

27. See Minale Bryce Design Strategy, "Scribble Newspaper," July 2005, http://www.minalebryce.com.au/thescribble/index.php (accessed February 16, 2005).

28. See Dictionary.com word search "Mellow," http://dictionary.reference .com/browse/mellow (accessed February 16, 2007).

Chapter 6

1. Jean Baudrillard, *The Gulf War Did Not Take Place* (Bloomington: Indiana University Press, 1995).

2. See such sources as William Hunter, "The Dot Eaters: Video Game History 101," n.d, http://www.emuunlim.com/doteaters/; Leonard Herman, Jer Horwitz, Steve Kent, and Skyler Miller, "The History of Video Games," CNet Network International Media, http://www.gamespot.com/gamespot/features/video/hov/Spot, Feb. 2002 http://www.gamespot.com/gamespot/features/video/hov/index.html (accessed March 16, 2006).

3. See Karen Collins, "Grand Theft Audio? Popular Music and the Video Games Industry," January 2005, http://www.dullien-inc.com/collins/texts/grandtheftaudio.pdf (accessed March 16, 2006).

4. Rich Hingston, "Cricket 2005—The Review," July 14 2005, http://www.cricketweb.net/article.php?CategoryIDAuto=23&NewsIDAuto=5 32 (accessed March 16, 2006).

5. Andrew Harvey, "BBC uses 3G phones for news report," November 4 2003, http://www.cyberjournalist.net/news/000793.php (accessed March 16, 2006).

6. Gonzalo Frasca, "Videogames of the Oppressed," *The Electronic Book Review*, June 2004, http://www.electronicbookreview.com/v3/ (accessed April 29, 2007).

7. See more on Frasca at Ludology.org "About Gonzalo Frasca," September 2006, http://ludology.org/staticpages/index.php?page=200301290041 46960 (accessed April 29, 2007).

8. Grand Theft Auto: Vice City, Rockstar Games, New York, USA.

9. See critics like Lev Manovich, Jay David Bolter, and Richard Grusin for further writings on narratology.

10. See some works that have helped to flesh out ludology. Gonzalo Frasca, "Simulation Versus Narrative: Introduction to Ludology," *Video/Game/Theory*, ed, Mark J. P. Wolf and Bernard Perron (London: Routledge, 2003). Aarseth Espen. *Cybertext: Perspectives on Ergodic Literature* (Baltimore: Johns Hopkins University Press, 1997).

11. Julian Kucklich "Literary Theory and Computer games," (paper at the Cosign Conference Amsterdam Netherlands September, 2001), 10-12, http://www.cosignconference.org/cosign2001/papers/Kucklich.pdf (accessed March 16, 2006).

12. Marie-Laure Ryan "Immersion versus Interactivity: Virtual reality and Literary Theory," *Postmodern Culture* 5, no.1, September 1994, http://www3.iath.virginia.edu/pmc/text-only/issue.994/ryan.994 (accessed March 16, 2006).

13. See Brian Lara, "Connected," *The Telegraph*, October 1, 1998, http://blc.sports-gaming.com/review.html (accessed March 16, 2006).

14. *Brian Lara International Cricket 2007*, 2007, Codemasters "Genius at Play," Warwickshire, UK.

15. *Cricket World Cup '99*, 1999, EA Sports "It's in the Game,"Surrey, UK.

16. See EA Sports' overview of *Cricket 2004*, n.d, http://www.gamearena
.com.au/pc/games/title/cricket-2004/index.php n.d, http:// www.elec-
tronic-arts.com.au/easports/product_description.php?product _id=234
(accessed April 29, 2007).

17. Kevin Parker, "Free Play: The Politics of the Video Game," April 2004.
http://reason.com/0404/fe.kp.free.shtml (accessed April 26, 2007).

Chapter 7

1. *Shall We Dance*, (Miramax, 2004).

2. See Royal Caribbean, Inc., "Our Company, Our Leadership,"
http://www.royalcaribbean.com/ourCompany/ourLeadership.do; Royal
Caribbean, Inc., "The Caribbean, You'll find water in every shade of
Blue," http://www.royalcaribbean.com/findacruise/destinations/home
.do;jsessionid=00000-WmXID-tFX172nDCYlxwcQ:vnkcfls6?
dest=CARIB (both accessed April 26, 2007).

3. See, for example selected tourist brochures from the region. *Truly
Discover Grenada Carriacou and Petit Martinique* (St George's: Concepts
Marketing Inc., 2003/2004); *Vacances/Holidays Saint Martin/Sint
Maarten no.11* (no publisher, but circulated in St Martin around
October 2005); Alfredo Weatherhead, editor-in-chief, *Great Escapes*
Issue 4, (2005/6).

4. See "Belize Tourism. Welcome to the Belize tourism website," http://
belizetourism.org (accessed April 29, 2007).

5. See "Explore St Kitts: An Experience like No Other," http://www.stkitts
tourism.kn/ (accessed April 29, 2007).

6. See St Vincent and the Grenadines (www.svgtourism), The Anguilla
Experience (www.anguilla-vacation.com), St Lucia Simply Beautiful
(www.stlucia.org), Grenada The Spice of the Caribbean (www.grenada-
grenadines/cal.html) (accessed March 16, 2006).

7. In 2007, there is more variety and intrigue on the site: "Defy the everyday. The Nature isle of Dominica," http://dominica.dm/site/index.cfm
(accessed April 29, 2007).

8. Patrick J Buchanan, "Who Let In the Beltway Sniper?" *World Net Daily*,
November 4 2002, http://www.worldnetdaily.com/news/article.asp?
ARTICLE_ID=29531 (accessed March 16, 2006).

9. Dale Buss, "A Product Placement Hall of Fame," *Business Week*, June 22,
1998, http://www.businessweek.com/1998/25/b3583062.htm (accessed
March 16, 2006).

10. Jutta Weldes, ed, *To Seek Out New Worlds: Science Fiction and World
Politics* (New York: Palgrave Macmillan, 2003).

11. See Kamau Brathwaite's poem "X/Self's xth Letter From The Thirteenth
Provinces" in the more recent and more easily obtained trilogy titled
Ancestors (New York: New Directions Books, 2001), 444–456.

12. Ahmed Best, "Ahmed Best Captures Jar Jar Binks," interview by Melissa Perenson, *Science Fiction Weekly*, April 3, 2000, issue 154, vol. 6, no. 14 http://www.scifi.com/sfw/issue154/interview.html (accessed March 16, 2006).

13. Also see Perenson's interview of Best for a discussion of actors interacting with empty space.

14. Chris Gardner "Rayment Twins Aim for Stardom in *Matrix Reloaded*," *Hollywood Reporter*, May 12, 2003, http://www.rayment-twins.com/hollywoodarticle.html (accessed March 16, 2006).

15. See more information concerning computer-generated technology at Side Effects Software, http://www.sidefx.com/products/profiles/godzilla/ (accessed March 16, 2006).

16. John Powell and Harry Gregson-Williams [composers], "Death of Barbados," *Antz*, [orchestral performance by Bruce L. Fowler, Yvonne S. Moriarty and others] Angel [72435567822].

17. See a draft of the screenplay of *Antz* at http://myhome.naver.com/leghorn/script/antz.htm (accessed March 16, 2006).

18. See a version of the screenplay for *Godzilla* at http://leonscripts.tripod.com/scripts/GODZILLAfirst.htm (accessed March 16, 2006).

19. *A Perfect Storm*, 2000. Dir. Wolfgang Petersen. Warner Bros. Pictures.

20. Kelly Cobiella, "Desperate Flood Relief," *CBS* video clip 620274, May 31 2004, http://www.cbsnews.com/htdocs/videoplayer/newVid/video_display_new.html?/media/2004/05/28/video620274.wmv&vidId=201&title=Desperate$@$Flood$@$Relief&hitboxMLC=national, (accessed March 16, 2006).

21. The appearance of then Prime Minister of St Vincent, James Mitchell, on CNN. Rick Alperin, "Threats to Jurors in Murder Trial of White Couple," Hartford Web Publishing, August 2, 1997, http://www.hartford-hwp.com/archives/43/044.html (accessed March 16, 2006).

22. See CNN's hatchet job of locating the Caribbean at http://www.cnn.com/WEATHER/CAmerica/satellite_image.html (accessed March 16, 2006).

23. See Yahoo's map of the Caribbean at http://weather.yahoo.com/img/carib_outlookf_en_GB_440_mdy_y.html (accessed March 16, 2006).

Bibliography

Allsopp, Richard. *Dictionary of Caribbean English Usage*. Oxford: Oxford University Press, 1996.

Aycock, Alan. "Technologies of the Self: Foucault and Internet Discourse." *Journal of Computer-Mediated Communication* 1, no. 2 (1995), http://jcmc.indiana.edu/vol1/issue2/aycock.html (accessed March 16, 2006).

Baudrillard, Jean. *The Gulf War Did Not Take Place*. Bloomington: Indiana University Press, 1995.

Best, Curwen. *Culture @ the Cutting Edge: Tracking Caribbean Popular Music*. Kingston: University of the West Indies Press, 2005.

———. *Roots to Popular Culture*. London: Macmillan Education Ltd., 2001.

Bowen, Barry. "A History of Christian Films." Christian Headlines. http://www.christianheadlines.com/filmhistory.html (accessed February 15, 2006).

Brathwaite, Kamau. *Ancestors*. New York: New Directions Books, 2001.

Bresnan, Kenan. "Around the World Round Up: Box office figures for *The Passion of the Christ*." Box Office Mojo. http://www.boxofficemojo.com/intl/weekend/2004/12.htm (accessed September 15, 2007).

Buchanan, Patrick, J. "Who Let In the Beltway Sniper." *World Net Daily*. http://www.worldnetdaily.com/news/article.asp?ARTICLE_ID=29531 (accessed March 16, 2006).

Buss, Dale. "A Product Placement Hall of Fame." *BusinessWeek*, June 22, 1998. http://www.businessweek.com/1998/25/b3583062.htm (accessed March 16, 2006).

Caribbean Broadcasting Corporation. *Annual Report*. St. Michael: GIS, 1993.

Cashmore, Ellis. *Sports Culture*. London: Routledge, 2000.

Charles, Embert. "Low Level of Support for Regional Initiatives May Lie Behind CMC's Closure." Government of St. Lucia. http://www.stlucia.gov.lc/pr2002/low_level_of_support_for_regional_initiatives_may_lie_behind_cmc's_closure.htm (accessed March 16, 2006).

Cobiella, Kelly. "Desperate Flood Relief." CBS News video clip 620274. http://www.cbsnews.com/htdocs/videoplayer/newVid/video_display_new.html?/media/2004/05/28/video620274.wmv&vidId=201&title=Desperate$@$Flood$@$Relief&hitboxMLC=national (accessed March 16, 2006).

Collins, Karen. "Grand Theft Audio? Popular Music and the Video Games Industry." http://www.dullien-inc.com/collins/texts/grandtheftaudio .pdf (accessed March 16, 2006).

Cooke, Aston. "Caribbean Cultural Identity on the Internet." In *The House of YAD*. http://www.dwightday.com/yardculture0702.html (accessed March 16, 2006).

Cozier, Tony. "Umpires Getting It Wrong," *Nation* (Barbados), December 19, 1999, 15B.

du Gay, Paul, et al. *Doing Cultural Studies: The Story of the Sony Walkman.* London: Sage, 1997.

Dunn, Hopeton, ed. *Globalization, Communications and Caribbean Identity.* London: Macmillan, 1995.

Eco, Umberto. *Travels in Hyperreality.* Florida: Harcourt Brace, 1986.

Frith, Simon, Andrew Goodwin, and Lawrence Grossberg, eds. *Sound and Vision: The Music Video Reader.* London: Routledge, 1993.

Eng, Paul. "Wi-Fi Companies Help—and Hurt—Efforts to Build Metro Networks." ABC News. http://abcnews.go.com/Technology/story?id= 1048622&page=1 (accessed March 16, 2006).

Espen, Aarseth. *Cybertext: Perspectives on Ergodic Literature.* Baltimore: Johns Hopkins University Press, 1997.

Fallon, Helen. *WOW—Women on the Web: A Guide to Gender Related Resources on the Internet.* New York: Women Ink, 1997.

Forbes, Curdella. *From Nation to Diaspora: Samuel Selvon, George Lamming and the Cultural Performance of Gender.* Kingston: UWI Press, 2005.

Frasca, Gonzalo. "Videogames of the Oppressed." *The Electronic Book Review.* http://www.electronicbookreview.com/v3/ (accessed March 16, 2006).

———. "Simulation Versus Narrative: Introduction to Ludology." In *Video/Game/Theory*, edited by Mark J. P. Wolf and Bernard Perron, 221–36. London:Routledge, 2003.

Gardner, Chris. "Rayment Twins Aim for Stardom in *Matrix Reloaded.*" *Hollywood Reporter.* http://www.rayment-twins.com/hollywoodarticle .html (accessed March 16, 2006).

Gauntlett, David. Introduction to *Web.Studies*, 2nd ed. London: Edward Arnold, 2004.

Goldhaber, Michael. "Attention Economy." *First Monday.* http://www.first-monday.org/issues/issue2_4/goldhaber/ (accessed March 16, 2006).

Gomez, Ricardo. "The Internet Why and What For?" Access Foundation. http://www.acceso.or.cr/PPPP/conectividad/index_en.shtml (accessed March 16, 2006).

Harvey, Andrew. "BBC Uses 3G Phones for News Report." Cyberjournalist .net. http://www.cyberjournalist.net/news/000793.php (accessed March 16, 2006).

Henry, Lester. "Digital Divide, Economic Growth and Poverty Reduction." in *Journal of Eastern Caribbean Studies* 29, no. 1 (March 2004): 1–22.

Herman, Leonard, Jer Horwitz, Steve Kent, and Skyler Miller. "The History of Video Games." CNet Network InternationalMedia. http://www .gamespot.com/gamespot/features/video/hov/index.html (accessed September 15, 2007).

Hingston, Rich. "Cricket 2005—The Review." Cricket Web. http:// www.cricketweb.net/article.php?CategoryIDAuto=23&NewsIDAuto=5 32 (accessed March 16, 2006).

Hunter, William. "Video Game History 101." The Dot Eaters. http:// www.emuunlim.com/doteaters/ (accessed March 16, 2006).

James, Louis, ed. *The Islands in Between*. Oxford: Oxford University Press, 1968.

Jensen, Tanya. "First Annual Caribbean Fashion Week: Fashion Goes South." Fashion Windows. http://www.fashionwindows.com/fashion_review/ carribean/default.asp (accessed April 26, 2007).

Kerhoff, Ingrid. "Dub Poetry." University of Bremen. http://www.fb10 .uni-bremen.de/anglistik/kerkhoff/DubPoetry/index.html (accessed April 25, 2007).

Kleiler, David, Jr., and Moses Robert. *You Stand There: Making Music Video*. New York: Three Rivers Press, 1997.

Kroker, Arthur. *The Will to Technology and the Culture of Nihilism: Heidegger,Nietzscheand Marx*. Toronto: University of Toronto Press, 2004.

Kucklich, Julian. "Literary Theory and Computer Games." Paper at the Cosign Conference Amsterdam Netherlands September 10–12, 2001. http://www.cosignconference.org/cosign2001/papers/Kucklich.pdf (accessed March 16, 2006).

Lashley, Lynette. "Television and the Americanization of the Trinibagonian Youth: A Study of Six Secondary Schools." In *Globalization, Communications and Cultural Identity*, edited by H. S. Dunn, 83–97. Kingston: Ian Randle, 1995.

Lee, Maurice A., "Introduction." *Journal of Caribbean Literatures*. http:// www.jcls.net/intro.html (accessed April 25, 2007).

Light, Alan, ed. *Vibe History of Hip Hop*. New York: Three Rivers Press, 1999.

Maurer, Bill. "Islands in the Net." *Comparative Studies in Society and History*. 43, no.3 (July 2001):467–501.

McCourt, Tom, and Nabeel Zuberi. "Music on Television." *Museum of Broadcast Communication*. http://www.museum.tv/archives/etv/M/ htmlM/musicontele/musicontele.htm (accessed March 16, 2006).

McGrath, Tom. *Video Killed the Radio Star: How MTV Rocked the World*. New York: Random House Inc., 1996.

Morley, David. *Family Television: Cultural Power and Domestic Leisure*. London: Comedia, 1987.

Nayar, R. K "Indian Cricket Board to launch Official Web site." *Gulf News.* http://www.gulfnews.com/Articles/Sport2.asp?ArticleID=118681 (accessed March 16, 2006).

Parker, Kevin. "Free Play: The Politics of the Video Game." *Reason Online.* http://reason.com/0404/fe.kp.free.shtml (accessed April 26, 2007).

Perenson, Melissa. Interview "Ahmed Best." *Science Fiction Weekly.* http://www.scifi.com/sfw/issue154/interview.html (accessed March 16, 2006).

Phansalkar, Amit. "Technology in Cricket-More or Less?" Buzzle. http://www.buzzle.com/editorials/3-9-2004-51460.asp (accessed March 16, 2006).

Pierre, Donna. "Sean Daniel Reaps Gospelypso Success." TrinidadGuardian. http://www.guardian.co.tt/mambeta/index.php?option=content&task=view&id=108&Itemid=28 (accessed February 9, 2006).

Pope John Paul II. "Internet: A New Forum for Proclaiming the Gospel." Good News Web Designers Association. http://gnwda.org/tutorials/evangelize/Pope-May2002.htm (accessed April 25, 2007).

Ramchand, Kenneth. *The West Indian Novel and its Background.* London: Faber and Faber, 1970.

Regis, Humphrey, ed. *Culture and Mass Communications in the Caribbean.* Gainesville: University Press of Florida, 2001.

Rohlehr, Gordon. "Music, Literature, and West Indian Cricket Values." In *An Area of Conquest: Popular Democracy and West Indies Cricket Supremacy,* edited by Hilary McD. Beckles, 55–102. Kingston: Ian Randle, 1994.

Rosenthal, Morris. "What Amazon Sales Ranks Mean." Foner Books, 2007. http://www.fonerbooks.com/surfing.htm (accessed April 20, 2007).

Ryan, Marie-Laure. "Immersion versus Interactivity: Virtual Reality and Literary Theory." *Postmodern Culture* 5, no.1 Sept 1994. http://www3.iath.virginia.edu/pmc/text-only/issue.994/ryan.994 (accessed March 16, 2006).

Samuelson, Robert, J. "Debunking The Digital Divide." *Newsweek,* U.S. Edition, March 1, 2002. 25

Scher, Philip. W. *Carnival and the Formation of a Caribbean Transnation.* Gainesville: University of Florida Press, 2003.

Sky Sports. "Another First for SKY Sports Cricket." Corporateir. http://nocache.corporateir.net/ireye/ir_site.zhtml?ticker=BSY.UK&script=411&layout=0&item_id=167844 (accessed March 16, 2006).

Stanford University, "Copyright and Fair Use." Learning and Academic Information Resources Document. http://fairuse.stanford.edu/Copyright_and_Fair_Use_Overview/chapter9/index.html (accessed April 25, 2007).

Steehler, Jack. "Sports Technology and the Athletes." Roanoke College. http://www.roanoke.edu/Chemistry/JSteehler/HNRS301/Sports/ (accessed March 16, 2006).

Sullivan, Danny. ed. "How Search Engines Work." *Search Engine Watch*. http://searchenginewatch.com/webmasters/article.php/2168031 (accessed March 16, 2006).

Swagath, B. V. "Brian Lara—The Prince of Cricket." Bangladash Cricket. http://banglacricket.com/alochona/viewthread.php?tid=5483 (accessed March 16, 2006).

Taylor and Francis. "Annual Report for 2003." Taylor and Francis Group. http://www.taylorandfrancisgroup.com/pdf/reports/TF_annual_03_FI NAL.pdf (accessed April 25, 2007).

Urry, John. "Mobile Cultures" Dept. of Sociology, Lancaster University. http://www.comp.lancs.ac.uk/sociology/papers/urry-mobile -cultures.pdf (accessed March 16, 2006).

Wagner, Thomas. "Church of England Creates Virtual Parish. Applicants Sought for Position of 'Web pastor.'MSNBC. http://www.msnbc .msn.com/id/4458082/ (accessed February 10, 2006).

Waksman, Steve. *Instruments of Desire: The Electric Guitar and the Shaping of Musical Experience*. Massachusetts: Harvard University Press, 2000.

Weldes, Jutta, ed. *To Seek Out New Worlds: Science Fiction and World Politics* New York: Palgrave Macmillan, 2003.

Wyrick, Deborah, and Jonathan Beasley. "Editors' Introduction." *Jouvert* 1, no.1. 1997. http://social.chass.ncsu.edu/jouvert/v1i1/int11.htm (accessed April 25, 2007).

Selected Web Sites

Chapter 1

http://www.caribe.com/
http://www.caribbeanmusic.co/
http://www.Afromix.com/
http://www.cme.com.jm/
http://www.rhyners.com/
http://www.niceup.com/
http://www.reggaeweb.com/
http://www.amazon.com/
http://www.reggaesource.com/

Chapter 2

http://www.geocities.com/
http://www.contemporarywriters.com/
http://www.postcolonialweb.org/

Chapter 3

http://www.jahpickney.com/
http://www.aquannette.com/
http://www.silvertones.net/

Chapter 4

http://www.caribbeannewspapers.com/
http://www.cananews.com/
http://www.carnivalpower.com/
http://www.timeplusbeats.tv/
http://www.toronto-lime.com/
http://www.islandmix.com/
http://www.bashmentradio.net/
http://www.calypsoarchives.co.uk/
http://www.artistsonly.com/
http://www.geocities.com/
http://www.bashmentringtones.com/
http://www.mvpvideos.com/

Chapter 5

http://www.cricket365.com/
http://www.cricketfundas.com/

Index